MW01036384

Advance Praise for "Journalistic Writing: Building the Skills, Honing the Craft"

"A much-prized desk companion ..."
— Kenneth D. Ackerman, author of *J. Edgar: Hoover, The Red Scare, and the Assault on Civil Liberties*

"A helpful primer and reference work ..."
— Claude G. Berube, co-author of *Congress: Games and Strategies*

"Not just for journalists, but for everyone who wants to write clearly, concisely and with a certain amount of wit."
— Fred Brown, semi-retired political columnist for The Denver Post, adjunct instructor of journalism ethics at the University of Denver and former national president of the Society of Professional Journalists

"This book will help anyone, beginner or veteran, craft stories on deadline that will hook readers and keep them reading until the last graf."
— Joseph B. Cahill, managing editor, Crain's Chicago Business

"A veteran journalist's careful take on the craft and art of writing."
— John C. Curry, literature and writing professor, University of Maryland, author of the novella *The Medina Wall*

"A well-packaged guide to better and more successful writing methods."
— Donald O. Graul Jr., executive director, American Independent Writers, Washington, D.C.

"A semester's worth of J-school crammed into one invaluable volume."
— Kelly James-Enger, author of *Six-Figure Freelancing* and *Ready, Aim, Specialize!*

"Refocuses soon-to-be journalists on the fundamentals of good writing."
— Kirsten A. Johnson, Ph.D., assistant professor, Dept. of Communications, Elizabethtown College

"An essential guide for journalists or for anyone interested in a journalism career."
— Paul LaRocque, author and editor of *The Concise Guide to Copy Editing: Preparing Written Work for Readers*

"A terrific primer ..."
— Darnell Little, associate professor, Northwestern University's Medill School of Journalism

"Illuminates the craft and the art of writing ..."
— Don Parker, a Huffington Post Blogger

"A solid book ..."
— Susan S. Stevens, president-elect of the Chicago Headline Club chapter of the Society of Professional Journalists.

"As comprehensive and useful a handbook on the craft of journalism as you are likely ever to see ... an absolutely excellent guide for writing anything well, from a sound bite to a news story to a magazine article to a book."
— John C. Waugh, author of *One Man Great Enough: Abraham Lincoln's Road to Civil War*

"A well-written book about how to write well ..."
— Oliver Witte, journalism professor, Southern Illinois University

Journalistic Writing

Building the Skills, Honing the Craft

Third Edition

Journalistic Writing

Building the Skills, Honing the Craft

Robert M. Knight

 **Marion Street Press**

Portland, Oregon

Published by Marion Street Press,
an imprint of Acorn Guild Press, LLC
4207 S.E. Woodstock Blvd. # 168
Portland, Ore. 97206-6267
USA
http://www.marionstreetpress.com

Orders and desk copies: 800-888-4741

Copyright © 2010 by Robert M. Knight
All rights reserved. First edition 1998
Second edition 2003. Third edition 2010

Printed in the United States of America

ISBN 978-1-933338-38-5

"Africa's Last and Least: Cultural Expectations Ensure Women are Hit Hardest by Burgeoning Food Crisis." From The Washington Post, © July 20, 2009 The Washington Post All rights reserved. Used by permission and protected by the Copyright Laws of the United States. The printing, copying, redistribution, or retransmission of the Material without express written permission is prohibited.

Perry, Tony. "Ancient Greek plays resonate with Marines" Los Angeles Times, © 2008. Reprinted with Permission.

Fox, Ben. "Alleged shooter made reference to Columbine," March 24, 2001. Used with permission of the Associated Press Copyright 2009 All rights reserved.

Klaus, Mary. March 21, 2001. "W. Hanover Twp. Feline Hospice Overrun with Rabbits." The Patriot-News, Harrisburg, Pennsylvania. P. B1. Used with permission.

Reprinted courtesy of Sports Illustrated: "Faster than Fast", Tim Layden August 25, 2008, copyright © 2008 Time Inc. All rights reserved.

Roberts, David. "Romancing the Stone," © David Roberts. Originally appeared in SMITHSONIAN (July 2002). Used with permission of the author.

Dunn, Marcia. "Spacewalkers pull off toughest Hubble repairs yet," May 16, 2009. Used with permission of The Associated Press Copyright© 2009. All rights reserved.

©2002, NPR®, News report by NPR's Renee Montagne and Mary Luoise Kelly was originally broadcast on NPR's Morning Edition® on August 9, 2002, and is used with the permission of NPR. Any unauthorized duplication is strictly prohibited.

Cover Art Direction by Nicky Ip
Back cover photo by Donnie Thompson

Library of Congress Cataloging-in-Publication Data

Knight, Robert M.
  Journalistic writing : building the skills, honing the craft / Robert M. Knight.
     p. cm.
  Includes bibliographical references and index.
  ISBN 978-1-933338-38-5
  1. Journalism--Authorship. I. Title.
  PN4783.K558 2010
  808'.06607--dc22

                                        2010012080

To the dozens of students who contributed to this book, and the hundreds whose attempts to put up with its author didn't make it into these pages. Without them and their efforts, I would not have been able to reflect on what — at least I think — I needed to shoehorn into a manual on journalism and journalistic writing for people willing to face the real world of writing for the public. Many of you remain friends.

Contents

Journalistic Writing in the 21st Century

Anyone who claims to know what journalism is or where it's going in the early 21st century is either lying or delusional. That doesn't mean, however, that we can't address what journalistic writing will look like as we progress. I'm voting for the accepted journalistic style to revert to what is today's lowest common denominator of journalistic writing as elucidated in The Associated Press Stylebook.

Are blogs or tweets going to replace the newspaper as that other lowest common denominator, the medium from which all other forms of journalism derive? If so, we face a huge ethical challenge, one that parts of this book allude to but don't actually address. My guess is, though, that once the blogosphere settles down, it will have little choice but to accept the AP style as a base. (But Twitter could destroy punctuation and spelling as we know it.)

As we witness, condemn, celebrate and endlessly discuss the convergence of the news media and the new forms they are taking, we need to again concentrate on the skills of journalistic writing, editing and reporting.

Of course, reporting comes first. Solid, balanced reporting is and must be the number one goal of any responsible news organization. But if it doesn't communicate with its audience, good reporting doesn't do much good.

As one who edited, reported and wrote news and features for decades before I taught it, I've watched what appears to be a steady decline in writing skills among those in the news media. We've seen it in newspapers, we've seen it in magazines and we've seen it on radio and television. Now we see ample evidence of it in the blogosphere, which displays some of the worst examples of writing ever to emerge in public prose. Hence this book.

A Beginning

This book is designed to be a compact, all-in-one-source antidote to bad, even mediocre, journalistic writing. It borrows from experts on reporting, writing and editing. It borrows from my experience. It borrows from my students. Many of their writing stumbles are chronicled in this book.

It isn't fair, but that's how news people like me learned. First, as a wire service "deskman," I learned to do it not only right, but fast; then as a newspaper reporter, then as a TV and radio reporter and editor, then as a full-time freelancer and, finally, as an editor at the late, great reporter training ground known as the City News Bureau of Chicago. Nearly everyone I know in the business went through a similar boot-camp experience, learning the skills not only of reporting, but writing and editing. And in journalism, at least, writing is a skill, not an art form.

My tendency to be a curmudgeon has been tempered by years of teaching, mainly adults at Northwestern University and undergraduates at Gettysburg College. I thought, and still think, that the journalistic style of writing has much to offer the greater world of writing, especially nonfiction.

In 1997, I wrote a book for another publisher. Its purpose was to expose journalistic writing to a wider audience. This edition is better focused. It is a distillation of the skills imparted from that first edition, but aimed at people in the business or in school who need to learn journalistic writing or need more practice at it.

Acknowledgments

I couldn't have written this book by myself. (I know that's a cliché for authors who want to appear modest and publicly thank others, but I can't be accused of false modesty. It's true. I couldn't have done it by myself.) For one thing, I have become insulated from the brave new world that has developed around the Internet. I am grateful to one professor in particular for showing me around, Kirsten Johnson of Elizabethtown College in Pennsylvania.

By the time this snapshot of current trends in electronic journalism gets printed, it will no doubt be out of date, but that won't be Kirsten's fault. She remains on top of the phenomenon called digital media convergence. And she did her best with someone who must have reminded her of a few of her slow students.

There simply is not a greater resource for a writer than a good editor, and I was blessed with several. The two men who now own Marion Street Press in Portland, Ore., Kel Winter and Jim Schuette, showed me what truly thorough editing can do. With the help of Mel Wells, they fussed over every sentence to make sure it conformed to AP style and obeyed all the journalistic writing rules that I spent a whole book writing about.

My great old friend from undergraduate days at the University of Colorado, John P. McLaughlin, donated hours and effort to make sure this book accomplished what I set out to do with it. So did my wife, Susan. She helped me from the perspective of someone who majored in English and proved we journalists have no monopoly on writing and editing skills.

Chapter 10, which is about writing for broadcast, would not be nearly as compact if Susan Stevens hadn't codified the rules at the City News Bureau during the 1980s. Sue has been a friend, co-worker and occasional boss for decades. We both have roots at United Press International. She also had a number of editing suggestions in other chapters, most of which we accepted gladly.

I can't ignore the great people in several writing and journalistic groups whose support has been critical to getting a decent how-to-write book out. These include the Society of Professional Journalists – especially its Chicago chapter – the Independent Writers of Chicago and especially American Independent Writers who, along with the National Press Club in Washington, D.C., provided a kickoff and a venue for this edition.

Twenty-six years ago, the founder of Marion Street Press, Ed Avis, began to grow his enterprise on Marion Street in the Chicago suburb of Oak Park, Ill. Ed built a small publishing house that today has to be considered one of America's top purveyors of books on journalism and communication. Ed turned over to Kel and Jim a high quality, highly respected operation. They continue to nurture that level of quality.

For me, it was enough that Ed accepted my proposal and made sure the upcoming book stayed in view for the new publishers. It's a plus that he left journalistic publishing significantly better than he found it.

I thank those students who contributed writing examples and learned from them. They helped me be a better teacher and helped me build better teaching tools. Most stuck it out and became good writers, and I remain friends with many of them. I commend them for putting up with the abuse, and dedicate this book to them.

Why and How Good Writing Counts

The Deadline Dilemma

You're fighting a deadline. Why add the story itself to your list of enemies?

Take a deep breath. (Not a figure of speech. Literally, take a deep breath.) Now, do what your gut tells you not to do: Let the story come to you.

No time for that? You have little choice. By taking the time to craft an introduction, or "lede," you're saving time. (Many journalists intentionally misspell "lead" to distinguish it from a police clue or graphite.) Note that verb: craft. This is precisely what you must do. A well-crafted lede will help you organize the rest of the story, and this organization will help you make your deadlines.

You can apply a formula to ease this process, but start by refusing to make a big psychological deal of your apparent dilemma. As with most formulas, this one is deceptively simple.

Craft a lede that feels good. This is not necessarily an intellectual process; it involves the heart and gut more than the brain.

Establish a dialogue with the audience.

Let that dialogue organize the story for you.

Unless you're working on a story of 3,000 or more words, don't outline. Outlines usually waste time and disturb the flow of the story.

More on this formula later, but first let's talk about what you're actually doing when you apply fingers to keyboard.

Getting the Subject from One Mind to Another

Maybe you're a reporter, editor or news director. Maybe you're none of these. Good journalistic writing can appeal to anyone who wants to write well in every situation. As a writer, it's your job to take a slew of facts, descriptions, ideas, concepts and quotes that are already blended together in your head and transfer the most important parts of that mixture to the mind of the reader, viewer or listener.

This mixture, this story, should reach your audience exactly as it was before you applied fingers to keyboard. It should look, feel, sound, smell and taste just as it did when it lay unexpressed in your mind and your notes. It should have the same heft, the same mass.

It's tempting to call the writer a conduit, but you're more than that. You're a reporter, not a recorder. As a professional journalist, you decide what to leave out of a story because it is not newsworthy, accurate or does not contribute to fairness, balance or perspective. Selecting what to take out might be more important than what you leave in the story. Everything you do keep in should come across clear, crisp and concise.

Your writing should follow the KISS principle: Keep It Simple, Stupid. The KISS principle has become a journalistic cliché, but it's as appropriate as clichés get. Keeping your writing simple without insulting your readers is one of the biggest challenges of journalistic writing — a challenge not often well met.

The adjective in the KISS principle is "simple," not "simplistic." In The American Heritage Dictionary of the English Language, one definition of "simple" is "Without embellishment; not ornate or adorned." This dictionary has no definition of "simplistic," but it does offer one for simple's root noun, "simplism." This is the "tendency to oversimplify an issue or problem by ignoring complexities or complications."

The best journalistic writing can address a complicated subject and convey it to the reader in easily digested components. The writer does not accomplish this by leaving out important components, but by using plain English dominated by the language's Anglo-Saxon roots. (See Appendix B, "The Beautiful Mongrel.") The writer should reduce the components to bite-size, but in no way write down to the reader. To do that would be simplistic and insult the audience.

This is not a new concept. A Cornell University professor, William Strunk, and a student of his, E.B. White, articulated the concept more than a century ago. In The Elements of Style, Strunk and White say:

> A sentence should contain no unnecessary words, a paragraph no unnecessary sentences, for the same reason that a drawing should have no unnecessary lines and a machine no unnecessary parts. This requires not that the writer make all sentences short, or avoid all detail and treat subjects only in outline, but that every word tell.

The Jargon Trap

Sometimes a jargon test helps writers keep it simple. If you use the term "writ of summons" for an audience other than the legal profession, you most likely are going to have to explain what you mean. You can expect attorneys to know that a writ of summons is a legal tool that usually begins a civil action. But you wouldn't expect most readers of a daily newspaper to know the term — not because they lack intelligence, but because they don't deal with legal writs every day.

If you're writing for a group of corporate software managers, you can get away with using acronyms such as MIS or IT without explaining that they stand for management information systems and information technology. To talk about diastrophism without explaining that it is a force that deforms the earth's crust and helps create mountains would be inexcusable unless you're addressing an audience of geologists or geophysicists.

Jargon isn't always bad. It provides special meanings that are appropriate for people who belong to the same profession. "Expenses" and "expenditures" might sound the same to a reporter. But to a certified public accountant, getting them confused can guarantee a visit by someone from the Internal Revenue Service.

Jargon becomes a problem when the writer uses it for a general audience. In this situation, jargon sounds unclear at best and pompous at worst. When you use it, the reader is likely to receive messages you might not have meant to send:

"I think you'll be impressed with my use of pompous-sounding words that you probably don't understand."

"I am too lazy to take the time to find words that say specifically what I mean and that make sense to you. (Is it possible that I don't know what I mean?)"

"I don't know what I'm writing about, but I can fool you into thinking I do."

"I am conning you."

All of this may appear to have little to do with the formula that gets you out of deadline trouble, but it does. Clear, crisp, concise writing begins with a clear, crisp, concise lede, and that lede is critical to shaping the rest of the story — and doing it quickly.

The Blessings of a Well-Crafted Lede for the Reporter and Reader

For the writer, the lede helps shape the rest of the story. It accomplishes the same task as an outline, without the bother. For the reader, though, the lede sets up the story. It tells the reader what the story will cover, summarizes the entire story or entices the reader to read on. Or it can do all three.

Getting the audience's attention is always a good thing. For a newspaper, magazine or Web journalist, it's imperative — especially if the audience includes an editor. A reporter rarely gets a better compliment than, "You got the lede right." Experienced journalists might argue about what makes a good lede, but they know a good lede when they see one. (See Chapter 3.)

Lead with what is interesting; lead with what is newsworthy; lead with what is dramatic and captivating. Inform the reader; tease the reader; anger, challenge, tickle or prepare the reader for what is coming next. But don't bore the reader.

Readers are picky. If your lede bores them, they retaliate — they refuse to read the rest of what you've written.

The most commonly stated excuse for writing boring ledes is that the writer didn't have time to fashion an interesting one. But you don't really have a choice; you must take the time to craft an excellent lede. Ironically, if you take time, you save time.

The Time-Saving, On-Deadline Formula

Remember that formula? (Keeping in mind that writing is not an exact science.) Here's how it works: You spend half your time crafting the lede so it feels just right. When it does, the lede repays you by setting up the rest of the story's organization. This means you can write it twice as quickly. How? The lede sets up a dialogue with the reader — for comfort's sake, an imaginary reader. It could be mom, who's standing over your computer as you write.

So you've crafted a good, strong lede — one that feels right. This is your first paragraph (or "graf," as it's often written in newsrooms). Next, if possible, insert a direct quotation from someone in the story. Find an engaging quote that will grab the readers. Let this quotation continue the dialogue. Then look up and ask mom what she needs to know next. Imagine she tells you. Answer that question, and your response becomes the next paragraph. Ask again, "OK, Mom, what do you need to know next?" Imagine she tells you, and your answer becomes the next paragraph. This dialogue continues until the story is exhausted or you have reached the editor's word or space limit.

The Reporter Writes:	The Reader Responds:
Paragraph 1	The lede
Graf 2	A direct quote, and then ask, "What does the reader need to know next?"
Graf 3	The answer to the reader's response. You again ask, "What do you need to know next?"
Graf 4	The answer to the reader's response. You again ask, "What do you need to know next?"

And so it goes.

That's it. That is how you organize a story, even under deadline pressure — especially under extreme deadline pressure. No outlining (unless the story is about 3,000 words or longer); just a simple dialogue with mom.

Obviously there's more to good journalistic writing than this; otherwise, what you're reading right now would be a magazine article, not a book. But if you absorbed nothing more than this formula, you could go out and use it tomorrow.

The Style Trap

Let's talk about the elusive thing called "style" and why you shouldn't have to worry about it. We're addressing literary style, as opposed to newspaper or broadcast style, which is rule-based and defined by long lists of dos and don'ts — mainly don'ts — that make up volumes such as The Associated Press Stylebook. Here we're addressing the type of style that your high school or college literature professor made you study by reading and comparing authors. The goal was to make you a better writer by absorbing and imitating their styles.

How many students have come away from such a class thinking they must have style because they have exposed themselves to so much of it?

Style, in the literary sense, can be as elusive as a poltergeist. This doesn't mean style doesn't exist. It's just that when the aspiring writer tries to meet it head-on, it can destroy the message and then flutter away. Instead of toiling away to develop a style, beginning journalistic writers (and most other writers) should develop true writing skills. "Skills" is the key word. These come with practice.

Good journalists concentrate on writing simply, honestly and directly to the reader. Your style will develop on its own, organically.

Some Basic Guidelines for Developing Writing Skills

We'll take a look at developing style in more detail in later chapters. But for now, here are some basic guidelines for developing your writing skills:

- Know who your audience is and write directly to it.

- Use strong nouns and verbs.

- Cut down on your use of modifiers (adjectives and adverbs).

- Avoid clichés.

- Be specific. Use color when you can — color illuminates — but illuminate with detail. Color can provide the reader "the feeling of truth to life, or of the reality of a particular setting," according to the New Webster's Dictionary and Thesaurus. It can also provide depth and background, as does the "color announcer" covering a sporting event.

In other words, don't just say a dress is pretty; describe its material, how it fits, its length, any embellishments such as lace or embroidery and, of course, its actual color.

• Beware of the murkiness of passive voice. Active voice sounds more honest and usually is. Active voice also cuts down on wordiness and accepts responsibility.

• Make every word count. If a word doesn't carry its own weight, get rid of it.

• When all else fails, write with energy. Convince the reader that you're convinced.

That last point is especially important. You can commit a slew of writing sins in a story or report, but if you've managed to keep your energy level up, you've succeeded. The reader — the only person who should count — will forgive you. Maybe even the editor will forgive you.

All these criteria add up to the journalist's dictum: Show, don't tell. But you need to add three ingredients before crafting your story with good journalistic writing.

First, force yourself to fall in love with your subject. This eliminates much frustration for the reporter who didn't want to cover it to begin with.

Next, write for the ear, even in print. Doing this will help you join the rhythm and flow of English.

Finally, fall in love with the language. English deserves to be loved, and your writing will be better for it.

A Word about the English Language

Few who know and love the English language would ever confuse its beauty with the smooth, sophisticated sound of French, the music of Spanish or Italian, or the seductive sibilance of the Slavic languages. English is a Germanic language, as are Dutch, Swedish, Danish, Norwegian and Flemish. English shares much of German's reliance on athletic diphthongs — abrupt changes in vowel sounds in the same syllable — that create harsh consonants and guttural utterances.

Don't, however, make the mistake of assuming that because English carries occasional dissonance it is without rhythm, music or grace. To write or edit English well, the writer must listen to its "tumble of words," as Robert MacNeil calls it. MacNeil, who for years co-anchored "The MacNeil/Lehrer NewsHour" on PBS, put it this way in his book "Wordstruck":

> We forget perhaps that human language is primarily speech. It has always been and it remains so. The very word "language" means tongue. The ability to read and write is, at the most, five thousand years old, while speech goes back hundreds of thousands, perhaps a million years, to the remotest origins of our species. So the aural pathways to the mind — to say nothing of the heart — must be wondrously extensive. Like the streets of a big city, you have many ways to get there. By contrast, the neural pathways developed by reading are arguably less well established, like scarce roads in uninhabitable country.

Four qualities set English apart — even from other Germanic languages. Three of them are positive.

First, the structure of English is simpler and more direct than that of other Western languages. English provides more emphasis on active voice (the agent of the sentence performs the action instead of receiving it). English spends less time bothering with reflexive verbs. ("He shaved himself" becomes a simple "He shaved.") And English uses fewer verb tenses.

Second, English has dispensed with the need to match nouns and verbs by gender, so you don't have to know what sex a table is before you can correctly talk about a table.

Third, the vocabulary of English is greater, far greater, than that of any other Indo-European language — a group that involves about one-third of the world's population. The biggest reason is that English has found room for the equivalent of two whole languages — Anglo-Saxon and Norman French — and large chunks of several others, especially Latin.

These three positive qualities derive from the fact that English is a mongrel language. But the fourth quality of English, namely its variety of pedigree (or lack thereof) is responsible for its maddening inconsistency in spelling and verb forms. Keep in mind, though, that this inconsistency also contributes to the richness of English. Its richness is the prime source of the beauty of the language.

Bigger Does Not Always Mean Better

Each new influence on English has added richness to the language, a fact that is both a curse and a boon. About half a million new scientific, medical and technological terms lend themselves to bad writing by swamping the language. But not counting these terms, English comprises more than 600,000 words — three or four times that of any other Western language.

Not that we use them all. William Shakespeare got by with only about 34,000 words, and that's several thousand more than most modern writers use. The vocabulary of the King James Version of the Bible totals only about 8,000 words.

Being heir to a huge vocabulary is akin to being heir to a great fortune. It is most tempting to squander it, abuse it and create a feeling of artificial status with it.

You can easily do that with English. It's a language that can help you sound artificially important as few other languages can. The rules for such deception are simple: Never use one syllable when two or more will do; never use a simple sentence when a compound or complex one will do; never use a sentence when a paragraph will do — you get the idea.

This progression into verbal oblivion begins by using a greater choice of words than most people can handle. Writers or teachers who are inclined to enhance their self-importance will go for the big words first. They have traded the advantage of a large vocabulary — the ability to find the exact word that conveys the precise meaning and nuance they intended — for the pomposity that big words often carry.

The Beauty — and the Bane — of a Big Vocabulary

The true beauty of English is its ability to make the writer or speaker sound honest. The way this works is to use short, Anglo-Saxon words and usages that form the core of the language.

English is fraught with latinizations — words that usually end in -ate, -ance, -ant, -ence, -ent, -ity, -ly, -ous, -sion and -tion. Latinizations are not necessarily bad. They come in handy for journalists who strive for word precision. But latinizations should serve as accessories to the core language, not replacements for it.

This brings up another aspect of English; it gives the reporter the ability to find the precise word or phrase that expresses the exact idea, concept or fact with just the right nuance.

For example, when the owners of Ollie's Discount Outlets in Dauphin County, Pennsylvania, needed a motto, they most likely asked themselves who their customers were. Perhaps they tried "Quality Merchandise at Reasonable Prices," and rejected it. In the end, they adopted "Good Stuff Cheap." By choosing words with Anglo-Saxon roots over words with Latin roots, they replaced 13 syllables with three.

In languages that lack the massive vocabulary of English, the reader is usually forced to extract precise meaning from the context or where the word falls in a sentence. In English, the task becomes a simple matter of selecting the exact color you want from the riotous palette available.

To accomplish this, you need to first master the vocabulary and then refrain from abusing it. You must also love the language enough to enjoy playing with each usage until the message — or maybe the lede — comes out precisely right.

It is the humble Germanic idiom of the Anglo-Saxon peasant that gives the English language its force and its inherent power to communicate. Nowhere is that fact better illustrated than in an excerpt from one of the language's great wordsmiths, who happened to be prime minister of the United Kingdom at the time. Winston Churchill's radio speech in June of 1940 came after the British had salvaged most of its army, and some of the French army, from the Nazi invasion of northwestern Europe that ended in the French village of Dunkirk. Churchill threw Adolf Hitler what might be the most elegant verbal gauntlet in the history of English:

>We shall fight on the beaches; we shall fight on the landing grounds; we shall fight in the fields and in the streets; we shall fight in the hills; we shall never surrender.

As Robert McCrum, William Cran and Robert MacNeil point out in "The Story of English," of all the words in that celebrated excerpt, "only 'surrender' is foreign — Norman French." Each of the other 32 words displays Anglo-Saxon (what we now call Old English) roots. The majestic structure that is the English language is built with small bricks.

Chapter 1 Exercises

If all published writers followed the simple rule "Make every word count," whole forests might be saved. One simple way to get rid of words that don't carry their weight is to train yourself to look for *that's*. Chances are eight of 10 are added baggage. Another is to delete wherever possible *there is*'s, *there are*'s, *there was*'s and *there were*'s.

Eliminate the unneeded *thats*, *there is*'s, *there are*'s, *there was*'s and *there were*'s from the following sentences, and rewrite if you have to:

1. There were half a dozen vintage airplanes standing in the foreground of the museum.

2. He said that there was a 13 percent decrease in drunk-driving citations on the state's highways, roads and streets last year, but there was a substantial increase in the number of accidents blamed on drivers' cell phone usage.

3. There was a surgeon working intently on a prone figure.

4. The president said that making the country greener is part of his plan to increase jobs.

5. Around the world there are millions of children that are starving.

6. There are three things that can happen when you drive through a yellow light, and two of them are bad.

7. The police officers said that they had a warrant and they wanted to inspect the house for weapons and drugs, but there was a pit bull preventing them from entering the front door.

8. There was Yogi Berra who said that "it ain't over 'til it's over."

9. She quoted her grandfather, who said that "many a damned fool went to college."

10. The ambassador said that she wanted to know why there were not enough limousines waiting for members of her delegation.

Is It Newsworthy?

The Lede, the Story, the Medium

The lede performs two critical functions: one for the writer and one for the reader. In newspaper and magazine copy, and in some writing for the Internet, the lede helps the writer organize the story and introduce the story to the reader. One way or another, the lede must persuade the reader to continue reading. (In broadcast news or any audio medium, the "intro" performs a similar task, but it rarely makes or breaks the story.)

Chapter 3 is devoted entirely to print ledes — they're that important. But first we need to look at newsworthiness among all the media, including those introduced by the Internet.

We can't talk about ledes without addressing newsworthiness, the collection of criteria that determines what stays in and what gets excised from the news. But the topic doesn't end with the newsworthiness of ledes. This profession, or craft, is laced with references to newsworthiness — it defines journalism.

How do we determine newsworthiness? By using a process called news judgment.

News judgment comprises the skills and instincts that reporters and editors develop to guide them through the labyrinth of criteria that make up newsworthiness. In our minds, news judgment often is unconscious and comes out in a form of mental shorthand that ignores all the complexity that the concept of newsworthiness brings with it.

Here, we are talking about the traditional news media: newspapers, magazines, radio and television. We'll stick with this limited list first and then take a look at how the general rules of newsworthiness percolate — or don't — through a range of new media. We'll examine everything from newspapers' Web sites to the blogosphere to citizen reporting to YouTube, and even e-mail and Facebook.

In the traditional media, and most of the new electronic media as well, news judgment first considers the audience. For the general news media, the audience is anyone over the age of eight who is likely to read, see or view a news medium's offerings. But differences do exist, even among those in a general audience in the same metro or rural area. It's worth noting that within the same general audience, a television station and a newspaper might appeal to different people, but these two different media still share the same audience.

For example, KSTP-TV in Minneapolis and the Star Tribune of Minneapolis-St.Paul share roughly the same local audience. That audience includes nearly anyone in the Twin Cities, many other Minnesotans and some Wisconsinites who live just across the Mississippi River from Minnesota. USA Today and CNN have a similar relationship, but across a broader geographic market. Their prime audience is most Americans, including those who read the newspaper or watch the network in other parts of the world. (Note the use of the word "market" as a synonym for audience. Journalism is a profession and a craft, but it is also a business.)

Audience and Audiences

Many news outlets are national and international, but they are not aimed at everyone, everywhere. Travel+Leisure magazine has a relatively narrow audience, consisting of people who are financially comfortable and interested in travel. A syndicated AM radio talk show might aim itself at a general audience, but specifically appeal to one that agrees with the conservative, re-actionary or right-wing (depending on interpretation) views of Rush Limbaugh. A blog such as Moveon.org appeals to another relatively narrow audience comprised of people identified as liberals, progressives or left-wingers.

Even narrower national or international audiences pay sub-scription fees, which are often costly, to a newsletter. Print newsletters and their electronic equivalents provide detailed coverage of everything from suburban politics to pork-belly fu-tures to horse breeding. The Internet has proved to be fertile soil for newsletters, with many print newsletters converting to an electronic format and being distributed as e-mails or on Web sites with password-protected access.

Professional magazines abound, even within a single profes-sion. For example, American physicians might read the Journal of the American Medical Association, the New England Journal of Medicine and one or two publications aimed solely at their specialties. British physicians usually read Lancet along with their specialty journals.

News judgment must consider audience when deciding what pieces of information are newsworthy. They must determine not only what gets into the story, but what makes it into the lede.

The Prime Criteria of Newsworthiness

Generally speaking, news judgment decides what is new enough, interesting enough or important enough to warrant coverage. (It is tempting to add what is glitzy enough, but we will talk about "celebritism" and its hold on media later.) Newsworthiness de-termines which stories make it into a publication, newscast or Web site. It further determines which among the survivors ends up on the front page of a newspaper, the cover of a magazine, the top of a newscast or the home page. (Again, we're talking about the traditional media. A Web site can modify the rules. The top of YouTube's list of stories are those that have attracted the biggest number of hits from readers and viewers. Those hits might reflect traditional newsworthiness criteria or they might not.)

It is helpful to think of new, interesting and important as the primary "colors" of newsworthiness. Add audience as a base, and you get a kaleidoscope of criteria depending on how you mix those colors and that base.

Let's begin with prominence as one of the colors that can accompany new, interesting and important criteria to help determine if a fact, quotation, description or a whole story is newsworthy. But it is only one criteria, and some editors or instructors wouldn't even call it "prominence." They would use words such as "celebrity," "visibility" or even "power."

The process of determining newsworthiness can be rootbound. Each of the newsworthiness criteria sends out tendrils of its own, and each gets its tendrils ensnarled with those of the others. Yet the process is supposed to be efficient and quick. To meet deadlines, it must be. Many working professionals might not take the time to name all the criteria of newsworthiness — their attitude is likely to be, "Why bother?" But the good writers have adapted the process to work for them.

Note that the newsworthiness process might help to define journalism, but it also destroys the concept of "objective journalism." The moment reporters leave facts or quotes out of a story because they exceed the space or time limit issued by an editor, they have ceased to be objective. Deciding what to leave in is a subjective task, but it still is based on newsworthiness. When reporters determine what is newsworthy, they distinguish themselves from recorders. Recorders are indeed objective; they record everything, newsworthy or not. Many of the new electronic media do the same thing. Even some of the older ones, such as C-SPAN, simply report without comment, editing or explanation.

Because reporters abandon objectivity to create a story, does that mean they are biased? Not necessarily. The reporter can still be fair and balanced, but it takes effort. (And one must be careful — a news outlet might promote itself as "fair and balanced" to mask the fact that it often is neither.)

Let's take another look at prominence, in the sense that it means celebrity. If someone catches a head cold but doesn't die from it, you don't have much of a story. If the president of the United States catches a head cold, however light the cold is, it's newsworthy, and so are the president's bronchial tubes, temperature, voice quality, achiness, rheumy eyes and what the president's doctor has to say about all of them. (If Paris Hilton has a head cold, some general news outlets might replace the rest of a newspaper's front page, a magazine's cover story or a newscast's top three stories.)

What are some other newsworthiness criteria? In a large country such as the United States, news stories are often judged on how close they are to the particular broadcast or newspaper audience. Journalism professors tend to call this "proximity." Editors and reporters usually refer to it as "local angle."

Sometimes the local angle isn't clear-cut, though. The following lede in a Denver Post story is certainly of interest to local taxpayers. But since it refers to one of one of the nation's busiest airports, the story is of some newsworthiness to any airline passenger flying to or through Denver:

> Denver International Airport has struck a three-year deal with airlines to direct its share of state aviation fuel-tax revenues collected from carriers — approximately $7 million annually — toward the airport's $31 million snow plan.

Like most other criteria, local angle is being redefined by new electronic media, and the world of communication has taken notice. Kirsten Johnson is a former television news producer and professor at Pennsylvania's Elizabethtown College. Her doctoral dissertation at Philadelphia's Drexel University addressed the overlap occurring between different news media, also known as "digital media convergence." Johnson has developed a reputation for being able to ask the right questions about this new media universe, even as the answers are still being formed.

"I would say that the new media have really blurred the lines in terms of proximity, because we're now connected to the world, not just the person down the street," Johnson said in an interview. "You're connected to a wider community. There will always be a place for local news angle but, as people reach beyond their own community, they want to know more about the world. It will be interesting to see where we go with it."

Let's recap. Under the umbrella of "audience," so far we have featured prominence and local angle (proximity). What else determines newsworthiness? Timeliness certainly plays a role. If a television anchor is interrupted with a breaking story that says two passenger jets have struck New York's World Trade Center and a third has crashed into the Pentagon in Washington, viewers are obviously witnessing a story of great newsworthiness. And so it was newsworthy — in September 2001. The subsequent updates and how September 11 has affected the country and the world continues to make news, but the event itself no longer does.

But even prominence, proximity and timeliness wouldn't make a story newsworthy if the story lacked something special. In a state capital, for instance, the fact that the governor's mansion didn't burn down today is not news. But if it did burn down today, it is indeed newsworthy. The fire is even likely to make headlines — print and otherwise — across the country, partly because it's bad news. Critics of the news media often accuse us of emphasizing negativity, and they are mostly right. Negative events often make news.

Positive stories, often called "feel-good stories," can make it into print or on the air. But even a cheerful story about a child who is rescued from a well unharmed contains an embedded negative — the fact that the child fell in the well to begin with. Positivity might also find its way into stories about charity benefits, windfall tax revenues or a new office building. These types of stories might include the arrest of a serial felony suspect. They often include news medium specialties: sports, art, music, gourmet cooking, architecture or high-exposure gossip (remember celebrity). There are also any of a number of personal news segments: personal health, personal finance, romantic match-making, fashion or social skills development. Some media gather these personal news stories under the heading of "helpfulness." Some put them in the category of "entertainment."

A positive story could be something as lightweight as the one introduced here in The Commercial Appeal of Memphis:

> When Joe Gomez popped a pepperoni pizza in the oven Oct. 15, he had no idea the pie was for President Bush. ...
>
> "'This military guy came in and ordered three large pepperoni pizzas and told me to make them good for his boss,' said Gomez, manager of Milano's New York Pizza in Southaven. 'I thought his boss was some colonel, not President Bush.'"

Of course, conflict — the news equivalent of a school playground fight — is bound to attract attention. Especially if the conflict involves someone prominent, such as Donald Trump versus Oprah Winfrey, or something prominent, such as the debate on whether or how quickly U.S. forces should withdraw from Iraq, or the question of who was most responsible for the slow reaction to Hurricane Katrina: the federal, state or city government.

One reason negative stories make news is because they are (we hope) rare. According to a newsroom cliché, "'Dog bites man' is not news. 'Man bites dog' is news." If someone wins millions of dollars in a lottery, it is news for the inside pages of a publication or further down in a newscast. If someone wins millions of dollars two years in a row, it is astounding and therefore newsworthy. So we add rarity to our list of criterion of newsworthiness.

If rarity results in something funny, it becomes even more newsworthy. One wire service, United Press International, strings a group of unusual stories under the heading of "quirks." Here are the ledes to three quirks that appeared on one recent day.

SYRACUSE, N.Y., Nov. 5 (UPI) — A dentist in Syracuse, N.Y., faces a lawsuit from a patient for injuries she suffered when he allegedly began dancing during a tooth extraction.

BEIJING, Nov. 5 (UPI) — Female professionals in China are increasingly embracing culinary dishes featuring a variety of insects from worms to grasshoppers, a report says.

NEW YORK, Nov. 5 (UPI) — Students at the University of New York's Hostos Community College in the Bronx can enroll in a 19-week class on the street art of graffiti.

Human Interest: The Grab-Bag Criterion

Some of the criteria of newsworthiness might be well-defined, but at least one, "human interest," is not. Human interest can lead to the fluffiest of feature stories, such as an in-depth interview of a high school cheerleader. It can describe someone's successful struggle against a disease or the loss of a child. It might provide a nutshell case study of someone who overcame a sense of inadequacy. Or it can simply describe an event involving children; children and pets make ideal ingredients in a human-interest story. For example, here are the intro paragraphs to a recent human-interest feature from The Miami Herald:

FORT PIERCE — The kids grabbed their paintbrushes to join famed marine wildlife artist Wyland in creating a mural of undersea life on the side of a building at Harbor Branch Oceanographic Institution.

From whales and dolphins to starfish and jellyfish, the mural grew.

But the 200 youngsters are also something of a canvas on which the renowned artist is painting a message he hopes will become a rallying cry for a new generation: "Every drop counts."

This brings us to one criterion of newsworthiness that inevitably sparks a debate between those who would give the readers, viewers and listeners whatever they want to read, see or hear, and those who would argue that audiences should get what is good for them, whether or not it tastes good.

We'll call this category "impact," or the need to know. Case in point: a story about the average tax legislation that is difficult for most people to get through. Let's say it is as dry as the legislators who passed the bill, and the report seems to reflect just how dull the hearing was that the reporter covered. Yet every American is supposed to pay taxes, and for many the process is painful. Everyone stands to benefit or lose something from the way tax revenues are spent.

Although most tax stories are dull, the impact of taxes is not. Let's look at an effort by a reporter in Wisconsin:

> School property taxes will rise in Waukesha County by as much as 14 percent for the residents of one district and as little as 1 percent for those in another, under levies approved by school boards over the last two weeks.
>
> Although the Richmond School District is expected to have the highest percent tax increase in the county, at 14.4 percent, three other local school districts also anticipate double-digit percent spikes in their levies. The levy for the Arrowhead School District is scheduled to rise 12.2 percent, while residents in the Mukwonago and Muskego-Norway school districts can expect to pay 11 percent more for their public schools.

Just because the numbers don't exactly charm the reader doesn't mean the story need be dull. Beginning a story on taxes with two paragraphs laden with statistics is probably not the best choice. Instead, ask questions such as, "What is the impact of this story?" and "Who does this impact?" Answering those kinds of questions typically leads to good journalistic writing.

A more readable lede might go something like this:

Taxpayers in Richmond School District might feel a little disgruntled today when they learn their taxes increased 14.4 percent this year — the highest in Waukesha County. Those in the county's Lake Country School District might have a very different reaction than their Richmond neighbors. Lake Country's taxes rose only 1 percent.

Many reporters' inability to make an impact story interesting to a general audience — without writing down to that audience — might be one reason that a glitzy story about a celebrity seems to be more newsworthy than a tax story. "Celeb" stories are easier to write. And they are much easier to report for a radio or television newscast or as an item on YouTube, a blog or a podcast. In addition, since many Web-based media measure a story's importance by the number of hits it gets, the celeb story is going to appear more important, even if it's about Prince Andrew scratching his nose. We'll talk more about hit-inspired newsworthiness later in this chapter.

Newsworthiness for the Eye and Ear

News media can change newsworthiness depending on which human senses they touch. A case in point: Many people consider "The Lehrer Report" on PBS to represent the finest television journalism in the United States. It is among the most thoughtful newscasts, and examines stories and issues in depth and without obvious bias. But critics of the program say it fails to take advantage of its visual medium, that is, television. The show is heavy on "talking heads" and light on dramatic footage of events. But it is specifically the appeal of the visual element that has made TV by far the preferred news medium for more than 50 years.

In the average commercial television newsroom, the visual elements often take precedence over the story's content. For the staffs of newspapers and most magazines, words are more important than photographs. Not on television. The number of words in a 30-minute newscast, minus commercials, typically would fill less than half a newspaper page.

Suppose a spectacular fire breaks out in an empty warehouse. No one is hurt. A good color newspaper picture of the fire might make Page 1, but the story itself, if one is written, will appear pretty deep into the pages of the newspaper. On a normal TV news day, however, the fire will be at or near the top of the newscast, even though it hurt no one and damaged nothing except the warehouse.

The dominance of the visual is not unheard of in the print world, however. Many tabloid newspapers combine lurid headlines with over-the-top photographs that may or may not have been altered.

There is nothing intrinsically unjournalistic about a print medium dominated by pictures. Photojournalism is a highly respected branch of the business. When Life was a popular weekly magazine, it routinely supplied outstanding examples of photojournalism. Today, the availability of pictures often dictates what gets used and what doesn't in magazines. Photojournalism remains the focus of a quality sports medium such as ESPN The Magazine, and high photojournalistic standards have been set for years in high quality magazines such as National Geographic. The less journalistically appealing publications are those that take advantage of freedom of the press and make their living on what they purchase from paparazzi.

Radio and other audio news media have an obvious bias toward sound, but their sound doesn't often compete with the radio content. Just as with television news, radio news tends to use fewer words per story, but radio does use something called "natural sound" under the spoken word. (Actually, so does television, but it is overwhelmed by the visual elements.) In the warehouse fire story, for example, the radio's natural sound might take the form of the crackling and popping created by the fire.

Television and radio depend heavily on another form of audio news: the sound bite. In a newspaper or magazine, quotes are useful because they tell readers much more about the interview subject than they would otherwise know. A direct quotation reveals something about how the subject thinks and puts words together. Radio news adds another dimension — we know what the interview subject sounds like. Television news adds one more dimension: how the subject looks, and how he or she uses gestures and body language.

What don't the traditional electronic media, especially television, do well? They usually do a less-than-adequate job of covering complex news. Tax stories that newspapers often find difficult to make interesting are twice as difficult for the audio and visual media. Even though virtually all employed adults pay taxes, and tax stories are important, many electronic news media try their best to ignore them. We might say the same about multifaceted stories such as a war in the Middle East or the issues of a political campaign.

Some electronic media do a good job of covering complex news. In the United States, these are usually the stations and networks with the lowest viewer or listener ratings — public broadcast news operations paid for by individual donors, foundations and the U.S. taxpayer. On PBS ("The Lehrer Report"), NPR ("All Things Considered" and "Morning Edition") and their local affiliates, complex stories are often thoroughly conveyed to viewers and listeners by the talking heads that commercial broadcasters tend to shun.

However, the commercial electronic media are not always shallow. One network news show, "CBS Sunday Morning," manages to present the news thoughtfully and still use the medium each week as it should be used — with a great deal of relevant visual footage and a number of tantalizing feature stories. Perhaps the best example of in-depth television reporting continues to be the longest-running national program of any kind on the airwaves: "60 Minutes." The evening newscasts of all three of the traditional commercial networks — ABC, CBS and NBC — also continue to provide examples of responsible journalism.

It's apparent that we cannot make categorical statements about different types of media. The introduction of electronic media, including newspaper Web sites, has become a great equalizer of news distribution. And just as television dominated the news media for decades, now the electronic media (not counting broadcast) will most likely comprise the news media that future generations absorb.

What muddles the electronic-versus-print analysis of newsworthiness is the probability that both media have Web sites. Even though newspaper stories usually are longer than broadcast stories, the latter can be translated into Web stories that actually give the broadcast outlet the more in-depth coverage. Compare the two versions of a story covered first by The Seattle Times, then by a local TV station, KING-TV.

The Seattle Times version, updated on the newspaper's Web site, is 317 words. It begins like this:

> A wanted felon arrested in Pierce County on Wednesday may be responsible for stealing nearly 20,000 gallons of gasoline at fueling stations from Bellingham to Oregon, police said today.
>
> The man, identified as David Torres, 36, is believed to have tampered with at least 15 gas pumps along the Interstate 5 corridor — allowing him to fill several 55-gallon drums for free, said King County sheriff's Sgt. John Urquhart. Torres then resold the fuel for about half of what gas stations were charging.

The Seattle Times Web site version (still written in AP style) occupies 333 words. It starts like this:

> SEATTLE – The man suspected of stealing large quantities of gasoline in West Seattle, SeaTac and Gig Harbor may have stolen up to 20,000 gallons up and down the Interstate 5 corridor, King County sheriff's deputies say.
>
> The 36-year-old convicted felon was arrested forcibly Wednesday in Lakewood, Wash., after a Pierce County sheriff's detective spotted his truck. The driver had to be Tased after resisting arrest.

The TV news script is not available, but it was most likely written like this, in 56 words:

> King County sheriff's deputies say they have arrested a man suspected of stealing 20-thousand gallons of gasoline along the Interstate 5 corridor. Authorities say 36-year-old David Torres resisted arrest in Lakewood, Washington, and had to be Tased. Sheriff's Sergeant John Urquhart (UR'-keht) said Torres re-sold the fuel for about half of what gas stations were charging.

Designer Newsworthiness: Creating "News" for Ratings and Profit

Any discussion of newsworthiness must address the fact that things make it into newscasts that, by all journalistic standards, should not. Political bias does appear occasionally. In a few cases it is pervasive and by design.

More often, though, the bias is not political. The real journalistic crime that many local broadcast stations commit occurs when station managers, in an effort to boost ratings, order their newsrooms to run stories about celebrities who will appear later in feature programs on the same network. Such "pull-through" tactics make great marketing, but bad journalism.

Some station managers and news publishers go so far as to demand feature stories about their biggest advertisers, or suppress bad news about those same advertisers. A car dealer might be featured for sponsoring a picnic for underprivileged children, or the news of a fatal construction accident on the premises of a large retailer might not make it on the air or into print.

Under the normal rules of good journalism, advertiser bias and network promotion should not be included in the list of what makes a story newsworthy.

Taking the Electronic Hits

Some thoughtful journalistic pros have expressed annoyance at what they consider "junk news" filling paper, computer screens and time slots solely because the First Amendment allows it to exist. The freedom of the press was shoehorned into the U.S. Constitution precisely because the founders wanted to ensure an informed electorate. They therefore banned prior-to-publication censorship, so facts, quotes and opinions could flow freely to and between voters.

The United States has seen junk news before, even when print was the only news medium. There was the toxic bickering that characterized the highly partisan newspapers of the Jefferson, Madison, Monroe, Jackson and both Adams administrations; the yellow journalism that flourished in the late 19th and early 20th centuries; and the jazz journalism of the Roaring '20s. Those were all examples of newspapers pandering to the public's apparently insatiable demand for entertainment over substance.

The Internet appears to be bringing all that back. Professional journalists wail and gnash our teeth at the prospect of another form of media that bases newsworthiness not on the traditional criteria, but on the number of hits competing stories attract. Part of our angst comes from the question, "Who are the gatekeepers now?" To many, this question means, "Are we still going to have jobs?"

Elizabethtown College's Kirsten Johnson points out that YouTube, for one, is simply putting democracy back into the process. "It's putting control in the hands of the readers, viewers and listeners instead of the pros," she says.

When we judge newsworthiness by the number of hits, the most prominent story might turn out to be a cat in a tree, or an audience member might decide to construct a "personal newscast" covering only what he or she is interested in, sports maybe, or just football.

This could mean that no one is challenged to look outside their personal cocoon, and therefore whatever educational value the news has is lost on much of the audience. This conclusion is what many already suspect, that the so-called dumbing down of America would have grave consequences in the form of elected officials who prove to be corrupt, spotlight-seeking, shallow, obtuse or ignorant.

It might not matter that some people who contribute to group decisions — like elections — make bad individual decisions, according to New Yorker magazine columnist James Surowiecki. In his book, "The Wisdom of Crowds," Surowiecki maintains that as long as a large group of people have three characteristics — diversity, independence and decentralization — the chances are very good that the people in the group (in this case, the voters) will make reasonable collective decisions.

- Diversity: In Surowiecki's view, this means diverse in every way, including ignorant people as well as experts, with most people "not talking to each other or working on a problem together."

- Independence: This means people are "independent of each other." Independence "keeps the mistakes that people make from becoming correlated. Errors in individual judgment won't wreck the group's collective judgment as long as those errors aren't systematically pointing in the same direction." In addition, "independent individuals are more likely to have new information rather than the same old data everyone is already familiar with."

- Decentralization. For Surowiecki, this "implies that if you set a crowd of self-interested, independent people to work in a decentralized way on the same problem, instead of trying to direct their efforts from the top down, their collective solution is likely to be better than any other solutions you can come up with."

The fact that some group decisions go bad, and that election results turn sour, is why theorists such as Surowiecki use qualifying terms such as "systematically" and "likely."

But Does It Matter?

Regardless of how well the writer understands the newsworthiness process, the rules that govern the writing of a journalistic story, defined by The Associated Press Stylebook, remain the same. Also known as AP style, these rules are becoming the default writing style for serious Internet journalism. (See Appendix A.)

Memorizing each and every quirky journalistic writing rule sounds like a lot of work until you capture the logic behind them. When you understand how journalists really work and how they employ the practical criteria of newsworthiness — even if they aren't consciously aware of it — you grasp the framework that makes learning all those nitpicky rules easier. If you can display a comfortable understanding of newsworthiness, most of the style rules start to make sense.

A solid, working knowledge of the newsworthiness process makes it easier to develop the skill and the craft a journalist of any kind needs to begin a story. In broadcast writing, such a beginning is called the intro, and we will cover it more thoroughly in Chapter 8. In print journalism, the beginning (or lede) is the single most important element in the story. Let's talk about ledes and how to write them in the next chapter.

Chapter 2 Exercises: An Improbable News Day

On a normal news day, Most of the stories below would rate a banner headline above the fold on the first page, but this is no normal news day. Pick a newspaper from the list and determine which three stories should go on the front page:

- The Arizona Republic
- The Atlanta Journal-Constitution
- The Boston Globe
- Chicago Tribune
- The Dallas Morning News
- The Denver Post
- The Detroit News
- Los Angeles Times
- The Miami Herald
- The National Enquirer
- The New York Times
- The Seattle Times
- Star Tribune of Minneapolis-St.Paul
- USA Today
- The Wall Street Journal
- The Washington Post

1. 7 Teens killed in Oregon Interstate crash

2. Alien princess marries Dalai Lama

3. Chinese mine explosion toll reaches 120

4. Senate mulls increasing maximum tax percentage 2 points

5. J.K. Rowling to write 8th Harry Potter book

6. Israelis, Palestinians meet again to discuss 2-state policy

7. Texas legislators consider resolution to secede from union

8. Stock exchanges welcome uptick in housing market

9. 12 passengers survive crash in central Indiana, pilot killed

10. Reality show to take place in actual war zone

11. NCAA votes to provide major football playoffs

12. Colorado avalanche barely misses ski lodge, 2 rescued

13. Hurricane Zola takes aim at eastern Gulf of Mexico

14. 2-headed cow missing from Alabama farm

15. President ponders 'short list' of Supreme Court justice picks

Leading the Reader On

The Lede: The Critical Element

Writing a lede is simple. Or so it seems.

In newspapers or magazines, the first few words or sentences of a story dramatize the cliché, "Well-begun, half-done."

For members of a profession that prides itself on its clarity, print journalists can be pretty ambiguous about a story's single most important element. When we talk about the lede, we most often refer to the first paragraph of a story. But the lede can also easily refer to the conceptual beginning of the story — the first three or four paragraphs.

Technical or conceptual, the lede provides a basic direction for the reader and the writer. For the reader, it sets up the story. It might introduce the subject, entice the reader to read on, or both.

If the lede is important to the reader, it is critical for the writer. A well-crafted lede can help the reporter organize the story quickly and effortlessly. Well, almost effortlessly. It does so by creating the dialogue with the reader that we talked about in the first chapter — the one sparked by the implicit question, "What do you need to know next?"

If the lede is written well, there aren't many communication sins that cannot be forgiven. Mechanical problems, overblown sentences, too many modifiers, passive voice, dead-on-arrival (linking or being) verbs, too many complex and compound sentences, monotonous rhythms, clichés — if the lede is right, the story lives. If the lede is right, it creates an environment; it successfully launches a set of facts, quotes and concepts. A good lede communicates to readers who are going to care.

If, however, the reporter does everything else right — if the words roll out as Shakespeare's did; if the sentences are lean; if the copy speaks in active voice, strong nouns and action verbs; if compound and complex sentences are used sparingly to provide rhythmic counterpoints to basic, simple declarative sentences — if all that is in place and the lede is flat, the reporter might as well have taken an early lunch.

Notice how the following lede helps set a mood for a newspaper travel story about the pirate Edward Teach — the infamous Blackbeard — and the North Carolina coast.

> Here he was known as Mr. Thatch, a merchant from England by way of Jamaica and the Bahamas, a good friend of the colonial governor. Aye, a good friend indeed.

Some editors and teachers demand that the lede always be short — no more than 25 words. Such a demand is arbitrary and reflects the cynical assumption that the reader lacks the intellectual power to handle anything greater. But the dictum does have some value; it makes the point that shorter ledes usually have more impact.

For the reader, the lede can provide a fact; it can summarize; it can tease; it can entice; it can evoke. But the lede must set up the rest of the story. For the writer, the lede helps organize the story and, thus, save time. It's worth repeating: even if you are writing under deadline, a good lede will save time.

Historically, the most common lede in newspaper reporting is the summary lede, which shoehorns who, what, where and when into the first two or three paragraphs, with how (the four Ws and H) and why being picked up in the rest of the story, if at all. Breaking news stories lend themselves to summary ledes.

The first paragraph (or graf, as reporters and editors call it in shorthand) of a breaking story almost always tells what happened and, if possible, its effect on the reader. For example:

> A barge on the Monongahela River near Pittsburgh ran into a bridge piling Monday, collapsing the bridge and stranding motorists. No one was reported hurt, but drivers are likely to be forced to rely on alternative routes for weeks or even months.

In one paragraph, we have what (the collision), where (near Pittsburgh) and when (Monday). But the writer has waited until another paragraph to provide who, how and why — some of which might be covered with a good quote in the second graf. Not too many years ago, the reporter might have tried to stuff the answers to all these questions in the first graf, which would become the lede in an inverted-pyramid story.

Why all that in the first graf? The biggest reason was that when copy editors prepared stories for typesetting, the lazier ones saved time and effort by cutting the story — literally, with scissors from pages that had been pasted together — from the bottom. If the story had to be cut drastically, even to a one-paragraph news brief, the reader would still get the gist of the story. The problem was that inverted-pyramid ledes can be cluttered and nearly unreadable. They are responsible for more than a few reader naps. Inverted-pyramid ledes might even have contributed to the fact that, until the Internet began to take over, most people got all their news from television.

Here's an example of an inverted-pyramid lede that crams everything into one sentence:

> A 39-year-old man, identified as John Graham, was killed Wednesday morning when his car was struck by a van in the 600 block of Muriel Street NE in Albuquerque, according to police.

Although this type of lede is usually adequate, it displays a mass-produced quality that tends to sap the reader's energy. Spreading this information over two or three paragraphs would make it more comprehensible and allow the reporter to add some interesting information, including the how, an apparent why, and a good quote. In addition, it never hurts to use active voice:

A 39-year-old man is dead today, the victim of a two-vehicle crash on the 600 block of Muriel Street NE in Albuquerque, according to authorities.

The Bernalillo County medical examiner's office identified the victim as John Graham of the 300 block of Eubanks Avenue SE.

Police said the driver of the other vehicle, a van, was being held on charges of vehicular homicide. He was identified as Carlos Williams of Tucumcari, N.M.

"We have evidence that Mr. Williams was talking on his cell phone when he ran a stop sign and rammed the driver's side of the car Mr. Graham was driving," said Albuquerque police officer Julia Garcia.

A lede with a mass-produced quality invites the writer to become a worker on the assembly line — to fill in the blanks. The story has the look and feel of a template. In one two-day stretch, a local news service offered these ledes:

An 18-year-old Lockport woman died late Sunday of injuries suffered hours earlier when her car struck a car-hauling semitrailer truck head-on in the far southwest suburb.

A 50-year-old South Side man was killed when his car ran into the back of a semitrailer tractor truck in Elk Grove Village early Monday morning.

A 15-year-old boy died early Wednesday after being critically wounded in a gang-related shooting on the West Side.

A 35-year-old man was charged with sexually assaulting an 8-year-old girl in Englewood who had been left home alone in squalid conditions by her mother.

Such ledes not only wear out the reader, they foster sloppy thinking on the part of the reporter. Look at the last two ledes. One says the shooting was gang-related, the other says the girl's mother left her alone, but neither answers the question, "Who says so?" The shooting might have been gang-related, but that determination is not the reporter's to make. Only a quote, direct or indirect, of a law enforcement officer or attorney should reveal that.

The mother might well have abandoned her daughter in what the reporter can justifiably report are squalid conditions — if the reporter actually saw them. But the "left home alone" part must have come from a police officer or a prosecuting attorney, and it must be included as a quote with an attribution.

Unlike most inverted-pyramid ledes, summary ledes need not be tired, cluttered or unreadable, and they are usually spread over two or three paragraphs. This type of lede can invite the reader's attention as it summarizes a couple of pertinent points, leaving other points to later paragraphs. Let's look at an example from a feature story in a museum magazine about a survey of Nobel Prize winners:

DNA charms them. The human brain challenges them. The bomb frightens them. And they expect to be profoundly influenced by computers and robots.

At this point, readers have no idea who "they" are, but that's all right. The readers are sufficiently enticed to read on. ("They" turned out to be the Nobel laureates.)

Here is another summary lede applied to a news feature, this one capturing a little irony. (Irony usually makes a good lede better.)

Atlantans will mark the Christian celebration of Easter today in various parts of the city by dressing up as rabbits, rolling Easter eggs with their noses — and turning in illegal guns.

Another type of lede, which editors and reporters are inclined to call a "creative lede" or a "coming-out-of-left-field lede," provides the exact opposite of a summary lede — it informs the reader of almost nothing. But this doesn't mean it isn't effective.

"He did not know that the moment he stepped off the curb, his whole life would change."

Who? What? Where? When? How? Why? This lede answers none of these questions. But just because the readers haven't learned anything yet doesn't mean they should feel cheated. They will learn, and they know this. In the meantime, they're eager to read on.

Let's go back to irony. Few techniques work as well as its skillful application. Using irony can be a great way to make instant friends with your readers. You're sharing a subtle joke with them, and you're putting a fine point on what actually happened. For example:

The mayor of one of China's most exotic cities today visited the fertile flatlands of northwest Ohio to sample some products of a Chinese-American food factory. He pronounced the fare good — for American tastes.

Sometimes you can set a tone or mood by manipulating time. The most common way to do this is to use the "today angle" in a breaking news story for a newspaper audience. Recall the references to timeliness in the last chapter. In its simplest form, the today angle inserts the word "today" in the lede. Or, if the newspaper uses weekday designations for yesterday, today and tomorrow, it means inserting the specific day, such as Thursday, into the lede (if indeed the "today" will be Thursday).

The use of time in a lede need not be restricted to breaking stories. Witness this wire service story that appeared on an anniversary of the plane crash that killed three popular rock 'n' roll stars — Buddy Holly, Richie Valens and J.D. Richardson (the Big Bopper):

> Twenty-five years ago on a wintry February morning, a search party found the wreckage of a single-engine plane on a farm nine miles northwest of the Mason City Municipal Airport.

Despite the lede's importance, however, it need not be embellished. Another form — the anecdotal lede — simply tells a story and, without using any kind of setup, brings the reader into it. A good example is this business magazine article on product tampering:

> The phone rang at Robert Walker's suburban Denver home one Saturday in October. At the other end of the line was John White, the company's South Carolina broker.

There's not much information so far; we don't even know which company it is. But chances are the reader will read on to find out that information.

For the reader, if the lede hasn't done its job, the rest of the story represents wasted time and effort. If the lede has not convinced readers that the rest of the story will merit their continued time and effort, they will simply and deftly move on to another story, another publication or another medium. Or they will find something else to do.

For the writer, if the lede hasn't done its part, the rest of the story will be difficult to organize. It will suffer from a lack of focus — factual or emotional — and will provide no starting point to develop a dialogue with the reader. We'll talk more about building the story in the next chapter.

As we noted in Chapter 1, the imagined dialogue between the writer and the reader can set up the organization of the story. After each paragraph, the reporter asks, "OK, what do you need to know next?" The imaginary reader answers and the writer responds with a new paragraph, after which the writer again asks what the reader needs to know next. The dialogue continues until the story plays out or the writer has reached the space maximum dictated by the editor or instructor.

Without a good lede as an anchor, however, such a dialogue is difficult, if not impossible.

Avoiding Dull or Generic Ledes

If a story is worth telling, it is worth the reporter's effort to make the story interesting. This is next to impossible if the lede is dull. Even if the readers are generous enough to provide the extra effort they need to keep reading through the rest of the story, their perceptions of its subject will be skewed. They will have been robbed of the focus a good lede provides. Readers greet ledes such as this next one with a resounding "Yes, that's nice" or "Who cares?"

> SACRAMENTO — An assistant in the California secretary of state's office made a statement at a news conference today.

"But, but, but," the reader sputters. "What did the assistant say? About what issue? And what does the statement mean to me?" Readers aren't looking for a direct quote here (and I'll explain why shortly), but they need a reference to the story's impact. Let's try this:

SACRAMENTO — California drivers will now be able to register to vote when they renew their drivers' licenses, according to an assistant secretary of state.

Leaving out the possible impact from the lede often sounds ludicrous:

MIAMI — Mechanical difficulties with some punch-card voting systems were reported Tuesday by Miami-Dade County election officials.

Those punch-card problems led to the controversial decision to give the Florida vote to Texas Gov. George W. Bush and sealed the 2000 presidential election for him. Writing a lede without including the impact is like writing, "As its band played on deck, the S.S. Titanic nudged an iceberg."

Here are some other ledes that the reader is liable to greet saying, "So what?"

"Education is an important issue. Local, state and federal taxes are used to support our education system."

It is almost certain that the reader knew that already.

Prof. Lani Guinier, the assistant attorney general for civil rights-designate in 1993, gave a lecture at Gettysburg College last Monday. The Office of Intercultural Advancement in celebration of Black History Month invited Guinier, who usually teaches at the University of Pennsylvania Law School.

But what did she say? And why was Guinier newsworthy? (The U.S. Senate had failed to confirm the Clinton appointee to the Supreme Court because most senators considered her views to be too radical.) Her sponsorship by the Office of Intercultural

Advancement does not belong in the lede. It might be appropriate for the last paragraph.

"Jack Gonzales studies journalism at Highlands University to expand his communication skills."

"George Anderson teaches a journalism course on Tuesdays and Thursdays."

"Since 1999, Ron Jackson has been a student at the University of Wyoming. He is seeking a bachelor's degree in anthropology."

Some ledes are dull because they are hackneyed. The following lede might also fit in Chapter 8 under the heading "Avoid Empty and Trite Statements."

"Fall is a wonderful time of year. It indicates the end of summer and the beginning of a new season. Seasons are part of city living."

Many ledes look as if all they require is that the writer fill in the blanks — pick a person, pick an issue, and the rest of the lede will apply.

Ardith Johnson daily struggles between her concerns for financial and career security and her grander commitments to make significant contributions to the community.

There's nothing particularly wrong with that lede. It speaks of the human condition. But to make it effective, the writer should deal with Johnson's specific condition.

"The moral issue of abortion is being argued everywhere."

Yes. So? (It's worth noting that the use of "everywhere" is inaccurate. See "Red-Flag Words" in Chapter 9.)

"It can be said that a name suggests just as much about a person as does one's mannerisms and appearance."

"Obstacles are what you see when you take your eye off the goal."

"A little sincere praise is often all people need to discover a new direction to take with their lives."

Philosophical commentaries on the travails of life usually make bad ledes. Be more specific. A word of caution: As they try to avoid generic ledes, many journalists find themselves reaching. They try too hard, as did the writer of this next lede when, as he introduced a police story, he referred to the men who broke into Democratic headquarters at the Watergate complex.

> Burglary and plumbers have not been commonly associated since President Richard Nixon's henchmen coined that nickname for themselves — and those guys weren't even real plumbers.
> But police say they believe the burglars who stole nearly three tons of copper tubing this week from a suburban company really are in the plumbing business.

The lede is hiding somewhere in the second paragraph. It could be this simple and straightforward:

> Police believe that the burglars who stole nearly three tons of copper tubing this week from a suburban company are in the plumbing business.

Leading with a Question

Many editors are adamantly opposed to leading with a question. Others say the practice is all right, but only if used sparingly.

Those who do not like the practice offer this explanation: Leading with a question demands an answer that the reader probably cannot yet provide or might not want to spend energy finding. Readers might feel they are being interrogated or even forced by guilt into providing an answer. If the readers don't want to respond, the writer has made them feel as if they are being impolite. No writer with scruples wants readers to feel that way. Notice how these ledes make you feel as a reader:

"Who among us would deny that life is fraught with problems — with missed opportunities, missteps, bad decisions and bad luck?"

"How would you like to do your own job and almost half of someone else's work every day?"

"Have you ever looked into the starry sky and wondered about life?"

Paula LaRocque, an author of books about writing and a seminar star, put it this way in an article in Quill magazine:

Among the questions to avoid are those that evoke a "no," a "who cares?" or a "beats the hell outta me":

- Want to be a midwife?
- Ever wonder how Fortune 500 company execs start their day?
- How many times do you suppose Rob Willis has remembered the crazy 60s?

LaRocque does not, however, place a blanket prohibition on question ledes. She cites a story by Neil Strauss in The New York Times as an example of a good question lede:

> How many people have you killed in your lifetime? Have you shot them with a cap gun or a cocked forefinger in a game of cops and robbers? Have you blown them up with a laser or torn their heads off in a video game?
> Simulated murder has become an acceptable form of play in American culture. Such games are the only way we're allowed to live out our destructive impulses without crossing moral or legal boundaries.

"Strauss' lead shows us that in certain hands, almost anything can work — even devices that in uncertain hands have become trite or worn," LaRocque writes.

Leading with a Direct Quote

As much as editors and journalism instructors like a story packed with direct quotes, a quotation makes an awkward lede. Generally speaking, the lede is too important a responsibility to leave to the subject of the story. A quote in the lede often is the mark of a lazy reporter. The writer appears to be telling readers that they are not worth the writer's efforts.

> "'You must think I'm crazy,' Doris Jones said as she began the interview."

A better lede might be this one, which returns control of the story to the writer:

> "Doris Jones says she would understand why anyone might think she's crazy."

The lede is the reporter's responsibility. It is his or her job to craft the lede so it introduces the story to the reader — so it is aimed precisely at that reader. The lede is too important to be fobbed off onto the subject.

Ensuring the Lede Makes Sense

We'll talk more about eliminating wordiness and convoluted sentences in later chapters, but nowhere is it more important to have lean, clean prose than in the lede. These next two examples did not make it. Judge for yourself: Did what happened come through clearly the first time you read these two ledes? (Remember that a reader rarely gives the reporter a second chance.)

> A 21-year-old woman died Thursday afternoon of injuries suffered in a three-car accident five days ago that injured five others, including two children, on the South Side.

> Officials and village President Betty Madison found themselves under a federal corruption probe after they were secretly taped inside the town hall to investigate suspected political fundraising.

Murkiness of a different sort is becoming alarmingly frequent in many newspapers. Their editors appear to have made a conscious decision not to tell readers what the story is about — seemingly forever. Their thinking, apparently, is this: "We can't compete with the immediacy of radio and television news, so the best way for us to survive in the journalism marketplace is to get behind the breaking stories and concentrate on the story's environment and its *why*." This is an admirable goal, especially when most Americans get their news from television or the Internet, and when most TV newscasts use a headline-and-sound-bite style that doesn't provide viewers with much depth.

Often, however, instead of illuminating with background, the editors encourage their reporters to write long, slice-of-life ledes that can extend to eight or twelve paragraphs. Instead of providing solid description or unbiased analysis, the writers create a mini soap opera before they tell the reader what the story is about.

The editors of such newspapers defend their practice, saying that what they're doing is "magazine style." Perhaps this is true, but I would guess most well-written magazines would reject this type of reporting.

The "Nut-Graf" Approach

As in other forms of writing, it is dangerous to slavishly follow simple-sounding formulas; it inevitably results in hackneyed prose. But formulas do come in handy if used with restraint. If writers choose to follow a formula for writing ledes for a longer story, they would do well to review how newspapers known for the quality of their writing — including The Christian Science Monitor, The Wall Street Journal and The Washington Post — craft their ledes. The Wall Street Journal in particular has formalized what its editors call the "nut-graf" approach to its one-a-day, front-page features.

To make a broad interpretation, the editors of such newspapers tell their reporters to go wild with the lede paragraph, or graf, but make sure that by the third or fourth graf, the reader gets a payoff. By then, readers should know what the story is about and what's in it for them. The third or fourth paragraph is the "nut graf." It contains the nut, or the seed — the core of the story.

Take this example written by The Washington Post's Kevin Sullivan while he was in Burkina Faso in western Africa:

> OUGADOUGOU, Burkina Faso — After she woke in the dark to sweep city streets, after she walked an hour to buy less than $2 worth of food, after she cooked for two hours in the searing noon heat, Fanta Lingani served her family's only meal of the day.

First she set out a bowl of corn mush, seasoned with tree leaves, dried fish and wood ashes, for the 11 small children, who tore into it with bare hands.

Then she set out a bowl for her husband. Then two bowls for a dozen older children. Then, finally, after everyone else had finished, a bowl for herself. She always eats last.

Here is the nut graf:

A year ago, before food prices nearly doubled, Lingani would have had three meals a day of meat, rice and vegetables. Now two mouthfuls of bland mush would have to do her until tomorrow.

The Post story goes on for another 73 paragraphs, most of it about Lingani, but much of it about the plight of West African women during a developing food crisis.

How does a newspaper with the reputation of The New York Times handle a lede? Many journalists believe that while the Times can be brilliantly written, it is often overwritten. Its editors and reporters consider it the nation's newspaper of record (the paper's motto is "All the News That's Fit to Print"), so they are averse to cutting out detail that the normal strictures of newsworthiness would keep out of a story.

Getting to the Point

Many academic appraisals of journalistic writing dwell on the classification of ledes. They identify various subcategories of ledes — blind ledes, delayed-identification ledes, creative ledes and imperative ledes — and they spend many paragraphs defining each and providing examples.

Most people in the business, however, have at best fuzzy definitions of the array of available ledes. These pragmatists of daily journalism are more interested in finding a lede that works. Practical as they might be, these professionals know that a good lede is fashioned as much by the heart or the gut as it is by the head.

Hence this advice: If you spent half your time on the lede, even under deadline, you haven't wasted time. If the lede feels good — not just looks good or informs well, but feels good — then it can be counted on to do its job in organizing the rest of the story.

Even with the importance of the lede setting up the story for the reader, of providing a payoff by the fourth paragraph and of leading with irony when you can, the most common lede will be the one you use for a breaking story. This usually turns out to be a summary lede, if not a true inverted pyramid.

No matter how many questions you answer in the lede paragraph, the most newsworthy part of the story is usually what happened most recently, and this becomes the lede. Often a story grows what we are fond of calling "legs," meaning that it lasts days or weeks or months. Each new lede will still concentrate on the most recent details. For example, here are four paragraphs that began an earthquake story by Luis Cabrera of the Associated Press:

> SEATTLE — A powerful earthquake shook the Pacific Northwest yesterday, shattering windows, showering bricks onto sidewalks and sending terrified crowds into the streets of Seattle and Portland, Ore.
>
> At least 25 people were injured. At press time, CNN was reporting that at least one person died.
>
> The strongest quake to hit Washington state in 52 years temporarily shut down the Seattle airport, knocked out power to hundreds of thousands of people, cracked the dome atop the state capitol in Olympia and briefly trapped about 20 people atop a swaying Space Needle in Seattle.
>
> "Everyone was panicked," said Paulette DeRooy, who scrambled onto a fire escape in a Seattle office building.

This first paragraph is a classic summary lede. It has who (terrified crowds), what (the earthquake), where (the Pacific Northwest). It also implies when (yesterday) and how (shook). Cabrera managed to pack all that into one paragraph and still provide a lede that is graceful and moving. He doesn't answer an obvious question in the first paragraph — namely, whether anyone was hurt or killed — but he does answer it right away in the second paragraph.

Now let's examine how the same day's edition of USA Today led into the story. The reporter, Patrick McMahon, covers the four Ws and the H over two paragraphs:

SEATTLE — This business capital of the Pacific Northwest has been preparing for a big earthquake for more than 10 years. But when it finally struck Wednesday, it still jolted the city's psyche.

A midmorning 6.8-magnitude earthquake made skyscrapers sway, damaged overpasses, knocked out power, jammed cell phones and injured at least 25 people. One man died of a heart attack.

By avoiding a standard summary lede, McMahon has been able to inject a little color into his story, reminding readers that Seattle is a commercial capital for the region, and dealing with more detail in the second paragraph.

By anyone's standards, both Cabrera's and McMahon's ledes work. Cabrera's reflects the professional caution that a wire service must use to satisfy the diverse demands of the hundreds of newspapers that make up the membership of the Associated Press. McMahon has a little more leeway. His lede reflects the bright, lean prose for which USA Today — whose editors call it "McPaper" — is known.

Notice that both reporters mentioned a fatality. By quoting the Cable News Network, Cabrera saved himself the possible embarrassment of reporting the death himself and getting it wrong. McMahon wasn't so careful and, as it turned out, he got it wrong. No deaths were reported.

Now, let's compare how the AP and USA Today handled the second-day lede.

Another AP reporter, Gene Johnson, wrote the first few paragraphs of the next day's story from Seattle. He follows the dictum that, in a breaking story, what happened most recently is usually the lede.

SEATTLE — The damage estimate from the earth-quake that rocked the Northwest climbed to $2 billion yesterday as engineers inspected bridges, buildings, dams and roads. But the region congratulated itself for escaping far worse damage.

Most people went about their lives as usual, swapping stories about close calls during the most powerful quake to hit Washington state in 52 years. Few people noticed two minor aftershocks yesterday, and no additional damage was reported.

State emergency officials counted 272 injuries directly linked to Wednesday's magnitude-6.8 quake, but most were minor and none critical.

"The biggest news is that there is no news," Seattle Mayor Paul Schell said. "There aren't any fatalities. The damage, while serious, is not anything like what people would have expected."

McMahon continued covering the quake for USA Today. The next excerpt is how he handled the second-day lede, again concentrating more on writing a lede that would involve the reader and less on a traditional, what-happened-recently approach:

SEATTLE — City historian Walt Crowley made it sound like a good martini.

"Seattle," he said, "is shaken, not stirred."

His upbeat assessment captured the general mood in the Pacific Northwest on Thursday, a day after the region's worst earthquake in 52 years. People mostly went back to work, back to school and back to normal.

Still lingering were questions about when to expect a larger earthquake — one perhaps 1,000 times as powerful as Wednesday's 6.8-magnitude temblor. But there were few answers.

There are no inviolable rules for writing a breaking story that extends beyond its first day. In this case, both versions — one traditional and one not — were effective. As we read the first few paragraphs of each, it isn't difficult to figure out what went through each reporter's mind and how he addressed the needs of his audience.

Avoiding Lede Intimidation

The importance of writing good ledes can be daunting. It isn't difficult for the writer, who has spent effort and time trying to craft a quality lede without yielding results, to panic. To counter this, veteran journalists offer a couple of pieces of advice.

The first has to do with attitude. Despite the characterization of journalistic writing as an aggressive, direct, active form of communication, the pursuit of a good lede usually works best when it is the result of a passive process. Even on deadline, there is nothing wrong with sitting back, relaxing and letting the lede come to you. As indicated earlier, relaxing (as opposed to panicking) usually helps a writer meet the deadline.

Many journalists find it helpful to tell themselves to write the lede the way it wants to be written. They have faith that the lede is already there somewhere; it's just waiting to come out. Trying to force it will only make it more stubborn.

Robert Rhode, a highly respected journalism veteran and professor emeritus at the University of Colorado, said he would try this trick: As he drove back from covering a story, he would mentally compose the lede as he "saw" it on his visor.

What often works well is to lead with the weather. In a feature, the weather can set up the environment of the story as well as anything. Even in a breaking story, describing the weather in some detail and weaving it in with what happened most recently often works — as long as it helps move the story along. (We'll discuss this more in the next chapter.)

If all else fails, the best advice might be to write something — anything — just to get the story started. Then plow through the rest of the story before returning to the lede. When you've finished a draft, take a look at the second paragraph. Often that is where your real lede, or the core of the real lede resides. All you need do is tweak it, make it your lede, and dump the false lede you began with. (Computers are wonderful tools for accomplishing such a task. You can make a false start and just wipe it out — no penalty.)

Writing ledes goes back to basics. The story should, if nothing else, communicate. If the story is going to communicate, it must be introduced by a lede that illuminates, somehow sets up the rest of the story, convinces the reader to read on — or all three. If the lede is going to accomplish its job, it requires more of the writer's craft than any other part of the story. This usually requires paring down your words.

We'll talk about wordiness and how to surgically remove excess words in Chapter 5. But first, let's look at how solid ledes can help put whole stories together.

Chapter 3 Exercises

The following exercises are jumbles — news stories that have been separated into their parts and mixed.

A. Find the lede.

Keeping in mind that the most newsworthy part of a breaking story is usually that which happens last, find — or write — the most likely lede from among these series of facts and quotations. Then choose the two paragraphs that should follow the first one. For simplicity's sake, "today" is Saturday.

1. Bridge collapse

"A bus has fallen into the river," Gisela Oliveira, spokeswoman for the National Civil Defense Service, said.

According to local media reports, the bridge collapsed after one of its support pillars gave way under the pressure from river waters swollen by prolonged heavy rain.

As many as 67 people were feared dead after a bridge in northern Portugal on which a bus was traveling collapsed late Sunday, officials said.

Oliveira said two other cars had also fallen into the river Douro near the town and that one body had so far been recovered.

"We don't believe there are any survivors," Castelo de Paiva Mayor Paulo Teixeira told SIC television news.

Civil defense officials said a bus fell into the river near the town of Castelo de Paiva and that a local bus company reported one of its coaches with 67 passengers aboard was missing.

The town's mayor told SIC television he did not believe anyone could have survived the accident, which occurred at about 4 p.m. EST.

2. Storm warning

Experts said the brewing storm may not be the biggest blizzard in decades, but very well could become the biggest of its kind — a merger of two storms into a single massive one — in 35 years.

A meteorologist with the National Weather Service, Michael Eckert, called the late-winter storm highly unusual. It represents the combination of two mighty weather systems. "It's very rare. We just don't see things like this happen very often," he said.

Local officials from Virginia to New England faced the task of preparing for the approaching storm, while people flocked to stores to buy food and supplies. The storm had the potential to wreak havoc for air travelers and motorists, with the possibility of businesses, schools and government offices being closed on Monday.

Two major storm systems — a wet one trekking through the South and a frigid one moving down from Canada — were on a collision course on Saturday, threatening to spawn a massive snowstorm in northeastern and mid-Atlantic U.S. states the likes of which have not been seen since 1966.

"Just be ready," he said. "All you can do is be prepared for how this thing will evolve. Fortunately, we've got a lot of time. It's not like it's something that's jumping up at us from the middle of nowhere."

The National Weather Service said heavy snowfall could begin on Sunday afternoon and evening, blanketing an area from Washington, D.C. to southern Maine with at least a foot of snow, with some areas getting even more.

"What's going to happen is they'll eventually merge into one main system," he said. "You combine the extreme wetness of the system coming up from the South with the really deep, cold air of the North, and you've got the ingredients there for a major storm."

The rain could begin to turn into snow toward evening on Sunday near Washington — and perhaps as far south as Richmond, Va., Eckert said. The storm then is expected to track slowly northeastward up into southern New England through Monday and into Tuesday, dumping heavy snow all the way to Portland, Maine, he said.

4. The 4,000-year-old man

Professor Konrad Spindler of Innsbruck University in Innsbruck, Austria, says the corpse's teeth are well worn, consistent with those of a Bronze Age man.

Spindler and his colleagues flew by helicopter Wednesday to the 10,500-foot glacier. Scientists from Mainz University in Mainz, Germany, were to join the investigation.

The Iceman, as Austrian newspapers have dubbed him, lay undisturbed for about 40 centuries in a pass between Austria and Italy, mummified by the wind and preserved by the ice.

The exact age of the body is to be pinpointed using carbon-14 dating techniques. Scientists believe the man's age to be between 20 and 40. He was dark brown and measured 1.5 meters (5 feet).

Scientists say the Iceman had been nibbled by animals, but only slightly.

Climbers on the Similaun glacier in the Tyrolean Alps between Austria and Italy last week found the frozen corpse of a Bronze Age man believed to have died about 2000 B.C.

Spindler, who dated the body from a crude Bronze-Age ax clutched in a hand, says the remains, clothed and remarkably well preserved, were of "extraordinary scientific significance."

Scientists, worried that their find might rot before detailed examinations can begin, were busy Friday preserving the remains of a man believed to be 4,000 years old. They were using special chemicals for storage in a low-temperature container.

"The man wore weatherproof clothing of leather and fur, lined with hay," Spindler said in a written statement. "The fine leather is tanned, the pieces stitched together with fine thongs. His equipment consisted of a sort of wooden backpack, a leather pouch hanging from his belt with a fire flint, probably a bow, a stone necklace and a knife with a stone blade.

"But the most important discovery is an ax with a bronze head attached to a clef shaft," Spindler said.

The scientists' tests over the next few months are to include an examination of the contents of the Iceman's stomach to provide clues to the Bronze Age diet.

B. Lede Drills

Give yourself a minute to read each of the following stories. Then give yourself three minutes to write a lede for each.

1. Job fair

Summer jobs pay $7.46 to $13.12 per hour. Applicants can participate in on-site interviews for city positions at the job fair.

The city is seeking qualified job applicants for summer job positions that include lifeguards, lifeguard instructors, track and tennis coaches, parks workers, youth program leaders, youth program directors and assistant youth program directors for day camps, mobile playgrounds and the Youth Volunteer Corps program.

A city Summer Job Fair will be from 10 a.m. to 3 p.m. Saturday at the Civic Center, 950 Broadway.

Information about the job fair can be obtained by calling the Human Resources Department, 303-555-7245.

2. Postal rates

T.J. Robinson, an assistant postmaster general, issued a statement at a Washington news conference today.

He said the cost of running the postal service is constantly increasing.

"Further attempts must be made to cut costs," he said. "One of the plans under consideration is twice-weekly home mail delivery and thrice-weekly deliveries to businesses."

"Nothing is definite yet, pending further examination of options," Robinson said.

3. Shooting

Bernice Joyce, 32, who lives in San Marino, was arrested Friday evening at the home of her mother in New Dublin.

She was taken to criminal court and charged with shooting her husband, Coleman Joyce, during an argument Friday morning, according to New Dublin police.

Police officer J.N. Snodgrass said the two had quarreled over her plans to divorce him.

A fight ensued and he was shot.

Coleman Joyce is in critical condition at Kerry County Hospital.

The charge was attempted homicide.

4. Drive

Sharon Ann Gordon, president of the Brigham Estates chapter of the American Civil Liberties Union, has announced a new membership drive.

The chapter usually solicits members by mail and telephone.

Next month, the drive will be made person to person. The goal is to gain 50 new members.

Members and volunteers will be asked to invite friends to their homes to acquaint them with the goals of the ACLU.

"The chapter hopes to increase its membership to replace those who have dropped out or moved away," Gordon said. "If we cannot do so, we must discontinue the chapter."

4

Building the Story

How Not to Conduct an Interview

It was a warm but crisp day, not unusual for north central New Mexico in late fall. The sun glanced off Air Force One as it taxied down the runway and approached the bleachers that had been set up for the local news media. Half an hour later, and less than 100 yards away on a tarmac at the Albuquerque International Sunport, a reporter found himself standing alone.

The reporter had driven from Santa Fe, where he normally covered state government. Years later he could not remember how or why he was separated from the rest of the local media. But there he stood, with a tape recorder strapped around his left shoulder and a microphone in his right hand.

A white Cadillac limousine drove down the tarmac. It stopped in front of the reporter, and its right rear window rolled down. A familiar face appeared, and the reporter found himself facing the president of the United States.

Thinking quickly if not well, the reporter turned on the recorder, placed the microphone near the face of the president and said, "Uh, uh, welcome to New Mexico, Mr. President."

"Thank you," replied the president, sounding a little like Elvis Presley. "Thank you very much."

Up rolled the window, and away went the Cadillac to another part of the airport.

The year was 1972. The president was Richard Nixon, a Republican. He was in the middle of his bid for re-election against what appeared to be an anemic and badly organized campaign on behalf of South Dakota Sen. George McGovern, a Democrat.

There were many questions the reporter could have asked. The president had recently returned from China, where he had opened a government that had been closed to most of the outside world since 1949. Americans had just begun to hear about a "third-rate" burglary (as the White House press office called it) of Democratic headquarters in a Washington complex called the Watergate. The Vietnam War was consuming more and more of the resources and spirit of the United States.

Still more topics were newsworthy. Leftists had continued to display their anger, aiming it now not at Hubert Humphrey — Lyndon Johnson's vice president and the 1968 Democratic nominee — but at Mr. Johnson's successor, President Nixon. Also newsworthy was the campaign itself: Why was the president so eager to gather New Mexico's four electoral votes when it appeared all but certain that he would win re-election by a record landslide? (He did.)

But the reporter didn't ask questions about any of these topics. In fact, he ended up with about the same campaign news that every other reporter, local or national, did. And he kicked himself all 60 miles back to Santa Fe.

The memory of that encounter never faded with the author of this book. I was that reporter. To my credit, it took me only a heartbeat to realize how dismally I had failed to do my job. I had violated a basic principle of journalistic fact-gathering; I had ended up with no more information than I absolutely needed to file a story.

Why? Because I had allowed myself to be intimidated by a public official — another basic journalistic principle I violated.

The average reporter gets at least 90 percent of his or her information by interviewing people. When the reporter sits down to type out the story, the information had better be good — quantity as well as quality. No matter how strong or enticing the lede might be, if the reporter doesn't have more than enough information to develop the story, the reporter is in trouble. Most likely, a lack of information means that he or she blew the interview or failed to take adequate notes.

There is no attempt in this book to cover interviewing techniques; the world of journalism and writing is awash in books and articles addressing them. But I can say this: The attitude and the mind-set a reporter brings to the interview is as important, even more important, than the techniques themselves.

A reporter can act meek or flustered, as I did in my single encounter with a U.S. president, and miss getting the facts. A reporter can act arrogantly and miss getting the facts. A reporter can act bored and miss getting the facts.

But a good reporter approaches an interview subject the way a good writer approaches a reader: with respect, humanity and a modicum of professional distance. Unless you are digging in to "get" a public official who you suspect is violating a trust with the voters — as perhaps I should have done with President Nixon — you want to gain the confidence of the interview subject.

Reporters do this by meeting the subject at eye level, just as they meet the reader, listener or viewer. They are not arrogant: "I am so erudite and you are such scum," neither are they abjectly humble: "Oh, dear and gentle interview subject, please excuse me while I ask for a moment or two of your precious time."

As a good reporter, you approach the interview subject as one human being to another — one capable of sharing experiences with you that will be of legitimate interest to your audience. There's nothing wrong with liking your subject; most people like to be liked, and that's all right. It's no crime, nor is it a journalistic crime. But do keep a hint of professional distance. It is not the reporter's job to cheerlead any more than it is to pass judgment and mete out a sentence to the accused.

Another basic of tenet of interviewing is to ask open questions — ones that cannot be answered with only a "yes" or a "no," and instead force interview subjects to expand on their answers. Good interview questions often begin with "why" or "how" and a pair of follow-up phrases that are basic to good journalistic interviewing. For example, "What do you mean by that?" and "Give me an example."

One more thing: Listen. Listen closely. Don't make the mistake many novice television reporters make — don't concentrate so hard on fabricating the next question that you forget to hear the answer to the previous one.

So now you have the three principles of conducting a good interview: First, gain the confidence of the subject by approaching him or her as one human being to another. Second, be friendly, but keep a little professional distance from the subject. Third, listen.

Follow these principles and the finer techniques of interviewing will work themselves into position. A good interview will give you more than enough quality facts and information with which to build a solid news story.

Bringing the Story Together

The next chapters will address what to take out of a clause, sentence or paragraph to ensure a well-written story. But first, let's discuss what to include.

Recall the formula in Chapters 1 and 3: Start with a strong lede, try to have a direct quote as soon as the second paragraph and establish a dialogue with the reader. To someone unfamiliar with journalistic writing, this process might not be as easy as it sounds.

Once inexperienced reporters craft a decent lede, they should be able to go on to create a dialogue with the reader or at least deal out the facts of the story in descending order of importance. But often they lose their nerve and "tend to fall back on organizational devices learned in composition classes, such as chronological or climactic order," according to Walter Fox.

It's true that some newspaper features thrive on chronological or climactic order. But in a breaking news story, what Fox calls the "order of importance" is almost the same as asking the reader "What do you need to know next?" The imaginary reader establishes the order of importance, so it behooves the writer to keep listening. The important thing for a writer is to keep concentrating on the imaginary dialogue that follows a strong lede.

One excellent writer and teacher of nonfiction, William Zinsser, agrees. He puts it this way:

> Most of us are still prisoners of the lesson pounded into us by the composition teachers of our youth: that every story must have a beginning, a middle and an end. We can still visualize the outline, with its Roman numerals (I, II and III), which staked out the road we would faithfully trudge, and its subnumerals (IIa and IIb) denoting lesser paths down which we would briefly poke. But we always promised to get back to III and summarize our journey.
>
> That's all right for elementary and high school students uncertain of their ground. It forces them to see that every piece of writing should have a logical design that introduces and develops a theme. It's a lesson worth knowing at any age — even professional writers are adrift more often than they would like to admit. But if you're going to write good nonfiction you must wriggle out of III's deadly grasp.

If the reader can visualize Roman numerals in your copy, then something is wrong. Usually it means that the student writer has provided no bridges between some paragraphs. When readers don't get bridges, they see stop signs.

To fix the problem, go back to that dialogue with the reader. Ask the reader what he or she wants to know next, and make the answer to that your next paragraph. The dialogue method ensures that no stop sign will appear — unless the writer wants one to. Here's an example of what a story with a stop sign deliberately built in might look like:

The pilot went through her checklist as she always did. She learned anew that the propeller, the elevators and the rudder all worked; that the oil pressure was at a level it was supposed to be; that the fuel gauge was on "F."

But she didn't know about the bomb under the backseat.

Now the readers are stopped dead. But that's exactly the effect the writer wanted. Once the readers recover, they will read on and the dialogue will continue.

One Reporter's Example

In the following story by Tony Perry of the Los Angeles Times, readers need not wonder what the story is about. The straightforward, two-paragraph lede tells them:

> SAN DIEGO — At a conference dedicated to finding new ways to help Marines recover from post-traumatic stress and other disorders after serving in Iraq or Afghanistan, the Marines are looking to an ancient source: the plays of Sophocles.
>
> An audience of 250-plus Marines, sailors and healthcare professionals Wednesday night watched a dramatic reading by four New York actors from two plays that center on the physical and psychological wounds inflicted on the warrior.

In what might be considered a softened version of the nutgraf lede (see Chapter 3), Perry waits until the third paragraph to get to the point of the story and, in the best reportorial tradition, he lets an interview subject make the point — not the reporter.

> When it was over, Sgt. Maj. Tom Hall, who has served in Iraq and Afghanistan and will redeploy soon, said he could identify with Ajax.

"Ajax was infantry, just like me," Hall said. "The kinds of moral and ethical decisions he was facing are just the same as what Marines are going through now."

We can see how the subject gave the writer a nice, cogent statement of the point of the story. Now the reader is most likely looking for an example of the decisions Marines are facing. Perry goes to another interview subject to provide this:

> Retired Lt. Col. Jay Kopelman, who fought in Fallouja, Iraq, was taken by the scene in which Philoctetes and a younger soldier, Neoptolemus, talked of comrades killed in combat. Kopelman said he's seen Marines have similar discussions.
> "That is something all warriors can relate to," Kopelman said. "It bonds us and makes us even tighter."

If the newspaper didn't sell much advertising that day, or if it was a heavy news day and a copy editor couldn't squeeze any more room for the story, what the readers have witnessed so far is adequate. They do get the point. But they could not be blamed if they felt a little cheated, as if they missed some fleshing out of the story. Perry provides this next, in the form of yet another point of view:

> The readings from "Ajax" and "Philoctetes" were presented by the New York-based Philoctetes Project, whose artistic director and translator is Bryan Doerries, who has a master's degree from [the University of California at] Irvine. The group has done numerous readings for literary gatherings and recently at the Cornell University medical school.
> When the chance arose to bring his troupe to the Marine Corps Combat Operational Stress Control Conference, Doerries did not hesitate. "I think there is no better audience in the 21st century to be hearing these plays," he said.

For Perry's readers who might have nodded off during a discussion of Greek drama in a literature class, he includes a brief description of the author, Sophocles, and one of the main characters, Ajax (who first earned his literary reputation in Homer's "Iliad"). Perry takes the opportunity to reinforce the point of the story: Ajax and his buddies act and sound like modern-day warriors.

> Sophocles (circa 496 B.C. to 406 B.C.) was an elected general of the Greek forces during decades of constant war. Military service was compulsory. As a result, almost all the men in his audiences were combat veterans.
>
> The character of Ajax, Doerries said, "is an ancient textbook description" of post-traumatic stress disorder [PTSD]. Ajax feels cheated of honors due him, betrayed by the generals and alienated from his wife and the society he fought to protect. "Incurable Ajax," the chorus says, "his mind infected by divine madness."
>
> Philoctetes, marooned on an island after suffering a debilitating injury, also feels betrayed by an army that tossed him aside when he was of no further use.

Most newspapers don't include morals to the stories in their reportage. Journalism doesn't require them, and a good story will enable readers to figure out the moral on their own. But Perry has provided a little extra with this story. What we might call a moral, he calls a "take-away." He suggests that he didn't supply the take-aways; the conference planners did.

> The "take-aways" from the two plays fit the principal themes of the conference: PTSD and other maladies are real; the military and society need to better prepare the warrior for combat and then help him readjust afterward; and the warrior has to accept help, even if he has lost faith in his family and fellow soldiers.
>
> As the chorus says in "Ajax," anger and violence will not relieve a soldier of his demons: "We will not cure evil

with evil, for if we try, the pain will only grow worse than the illness that brought it upon you."

Ajax takes another path. He kills himself by falling on a sword given to him by Hector, "my deadliest enemy." Some scholars see his death as a purifying act, but Marshele Waddell takes away a grimmer meaning.

"By giving up, we fall on the enemy's sword, and the enemy has it their way," said Waddell, whose husband, a Navy SEAL, has done four combat tours and been diagnosed with PTSD.

Not all scholars agree on the meaning of Ajax's death, and this is newsworthy to readers who might assume that there is no disagreement on the subject. Perry picks up on that assumption and enriches his story by quoting an interview subject, Marshele Waddell, who challenges it. He continues to bring forth more people, as we'll read. They serve to reinforce the point of the story — that over the centuries soldiering hasn't changed much — by highlighting not just any wars, but specifically 21st-century wars.

The parallels between the Trojan War and the current wars were striking, said retired Sgt. Maj. Eduardo Leardo, who fought in Fallouja. "The combat stress, the inner conflicts, the loss of your self, all are the same," he said.

Perry isn't through introducing new characters, but as we've seen, they do more than occupy space in the Los Angeles Times. They advance the story. If they didn't, a responsible editor would make sure they never appeared. In addition, it makes sense that the reader would want to know what the actors in the play think about their experimental drama.

For the actors, it was new kind of audience. All have substantial film and stage credits: Bill Camp, Jesse Eisenberg, David Strathairn and Heather Raffo. Raffo, whose father is from Iraq, used an Arabic-style accent in the role of Ajax's wife, Tecmessa.

Eisenberg, who played the chorus and Neoptolemus, said the audience was one of the most attentive the group has ever had, including a recent tony gathering on New York's Upper East Side. The Marines responded at the finale with a prolonged standing ovation.

Strathairn, best known for his Oscar-nominated role as Edward R. Murrow in "Good Night, and Good Luck," said the civilian and military worlds exist side by side in U.S. society but rarely interact.

"This is kind of an extraordinary moment for us as artists to be able to apply our craft" to this military world, he said.

Perry makes sure this report is more than what glib news professionals often call a "think piece." He reports some of the action:

> The actors sat at a table and read from scripts. They wore no costumes, but their powerful voices filled the hotel ballroom. Some of the lines seemed to have particular resonance, as when Tecmessa recounts being told by Ajax to shut up: "He turned to me and firmly said: 'Woman, silence becomes a woman.'" Said Waddell, "I've heard that — in other words."

> Retired Navy Capt. William P. Nash, part of a panel discussion that followed the readings, pointed to the scene in which Tecmessa says of Ajax, after he has flown into a violent rage, "there is nothing more troubling than to discover an evil crime of which one is the culprit."

> That line, Nash said, reminds him of a Navy corpsman [the Marine version of an Army medic] tortured by the fact that he killed Iraqis in ways outside the rules of engagement.

> "That is the corpsman's burden: how to forgive himself," Nash said.

As does any good journalistic writer, Perry has put aside a good quotation to end the story. This isn't always a good strategy if a reporter works for a newspaper whose editors cut from the bottom, but apparently the Los Angeles Times is not one of those newspapers. In this case, Perry might have saved not only a good quote, but his best:

> Navy Lt. Cmdr. James Johnson, a chaplain set to deploy to Iraq with Marines from Camp Pendleton, said the moral from the two plays is simple.
> "War really hasn't changed in 2,500 years, whether the troops are in chariots or Humvees," he said.

When to Stop Describing

One effective way to enliven a story is to sprinkle it with some solid noun-and-verb description — as long as it moves the story along. As the well-established writer of fiction Barnaby Conrad put it, "Too much description can kill a story." Journalists would do well to heed his admonition. Here, in shortened form, is a list of what Conrad calls the four deadly sins of description:

> Don't let your description, no matter how beautifully written, bring your narrative to a halt.
> This must be kept in mind by the writer of fiction: Do not overdescribe anything, whether it be the Grand Tetons or the sunset or zebras on the beach at Waikiki; your narrative thrust will suffer for it, and you will put your reader's attention in jeopardy. ...
> Don't spend too much time describing nonessential surroundings. [A journalist should spend *no* time on nonessential surroundings.] ... It would be a waste of space to include it in a novel, much less a short story. ...
> Don't squander the reader's attention by focusing on an inconsequential action. This is a more common fault among beginning writers than you might think. ...

> Don't generalize — be specific. ... Not a drink but a
> martini; not a dog but a poodle; not a flower but a rose; ...
> not a cat but an Abyssinian; not a gun but a .44 Colt on a
> frontier frame; not a painting but Manet's "Olympia."

We'll discuss this further in Chapter 7 under the subhead "A
Passion for Accuracy: Be Specific."

Developing the Breaking Story

When reporting breaking news, journalists often find themselves
using a summary lede. They might even revert to the inverted
pyramid, which summarizes at the top and then recounts the
facts of the story in descending order. For a story that's already
broken but is still too newsworthy to ignore, writers can use the
second-day lede, as Ben Fox did in this 2002 Associated Press
story:

> EL CAJON, Calif. (AP) — An 18-year-old student ac-
> cused of shooting five people at his high school made a
> reference to the Columbine High massacre in class earlier
> this year and simulated guns with his hands, a classmate
> said yesterday.

Now the dialogue with the reader begins. The reader wants
to know who the student was. It also wouldn't hurt to remind
the reader where the shooting occurred. In this second paragraph, Fox explains the shooting's "why" and what is likely to
happen to the suspect.

> Authorities also said Jason Hoffman, 18, was targeting
> a vice principal in Thursday's shooting at Granite Hills
> High School and that he will likely be charged with at-
> tempted murder and assault with a deadly weapon.

"All right," the reader might say, but then ask, "How have the authorities learned about the reported reference to Columbine High?"

> Bernadette Roberts, 18, said girls were making noise in a classroom in January when Hoffman appeared to become frustrated, put his hands in the shape of guns and stated, "I wish I could do Columbine all over again."
> "When he said it, it really shook me up," Roberts said.

"What did she do about it?" the reader might ask. But first, Fox reminds readers about the Columbine High massacre mentioned in the lede graf. Most likely, most readers remember the tragedy, but the reporter should not assume so.

> In 1999, two students at Columbine High School in Littleton, Colo., killed 12 students and a teacher and wounded 23 before killing themselves.
> Roberts said she told her teacher and met in February with Vice Principal Dan Barnes, who asked if she needed protection. She said she declined and did not know what steps the district took.

The reader would quite likely ask, "What steps did district officials take?"

> Officials at Grossmont Union High School District did not return phone calls seeking comment yesterday. Police Chief James Davis said investigators were aware of the report but declined further comment.

When officials don't respond to questions about a breaking story, it often means they haven't talked with their lawyers yet. A no-response can be frustrating for the news media as well as the public they are expected to serve.

Prosecutor Paul Pfingst said Barnes was the target of the attack.

"All we can say about the motive is that by virtue of the charges, the focus of this individual was the vice principal," Prosecutor Paul Pfingst said.

That is a good quote because it shows how carefully the prosecutor has couched his own statement. His legal language doesn't enlighten the reader much, though. (And whoever edited this article forgot to eliminate the fact that Pfingst is named by his title twice in two paragraphs.) Readers are more likely wondering what happened to Barnes, which Fox addresses next:

Barnes was not harmed, but three students and two teachers were hit by shotgun pellets, none seriously.

Note that the victim count had been updated. The total count was three on the day of the shooting. The reader might be asking why the current count wasn't inserted higher in the story. The reader might also be asking, "What about the suspect? Was he hurt or killed?" Fox provides an answer to these questions:

Hoffman remained hospitalized with a broken jaw and a wound to his buttocks. He was shot by a police officer at the school.

At the time this was written, very little detail about Hoffman had been released. But Fox was able to come up with an interesting item of his own. We might wonder why it didn't go higher in the story.

The Associated Press learned yesterday that Hoffman assaulted a middle-school classmate several years ago and was ordered to attend an anger management class.

Hoffman was 14 when he struck the student in the head with a racquetball racket, according to a source familiar with the case who spoke on condition of anonymity.

The victim was not seriously injured. Case records are sealed because Hoffman was a juvenile at the time, but the source said a charge of assault with a deadly weapon was reduced to a misdemeanor and Hoffman was given probation and ordered to attend the anger class.

It's a shame that the only way Fox could get this information was from an anonymous source, but anyone who has covered a story that even hints at politics knows that anonymous sources are sometimes the only option. When a reporter must use such a source, an editor has every right to make the reporter jump through some hoops. For example, The Washington Post requires its reporters to get at least two anonymous sources who independently verify the facts before printing the information. (Bob Woodward and Carl Bernstein did that when they broke the Watergate story that doomed the Nixon administration.)

Fox ends the story by using a technique proven to be effective — a good quote:

"Nobody picked on this kid because he was so intimidating," student Sean Connacher said.

When many reporters winnow through their notes, they look for a bright, pithy or ironic quotation with which to end their story. Even though many lazy copy editors cut from the bottom, ending with a quote is worth a try because it gives readers a send-off; they are much more likely to think about the story as they walk away from it.

Developing an Issue by Using Specifics

Moving the story along, layer by layer, works just as well in a light feature as in a heavier one. Here is a piece by Mary Klaus of The Patriot-News of Harrisburg, Pa. Klaus' story handles quotes — direct and indirect — especially well; they drive the story.

It's called The Best Little Cat House in Pennsylvania.

But lately, this feline hospice in West Hanover Twp., also a home for abandoned domestic rabbits, has seen an overflow of bunnies.

"And it's not even Easter," said Lynn Stitt, owner.

"I am swamped with rabbits," said Stitt, walking among cages of white, brown and black rabbits. "Last year, a lot of people got rabbits who shouldn't have. We've had poor adoptions this year."

Long considered a popular symbol of Easter and spring, rabbits take center stage this time of year. Some parents put a real bunny in their child's Easter basket and, a few hours later, realize that the cute, warm and cuddly gift is a lot of work.

"We start getting calls by Easter afternoon from people who decide they don't want to keep their rabbits," said Stitt. "Most people should buy stuffed rabbits for Easter baskets. Rabbits are not disposable animals."

The Best Little Cat House, the final home for many terminally ill and handicapped cats, began accepting rabbits a few years ago. Now, rabbits and cats coexist peacefully, the rabbits in individual, roomy cages and the cats freely roaming the facility.

On a recent morning, all 31 domestic rabbits seemed peaceful, a variety of Dutch, New Zealand, Fuzzy Lop, Red and Californian, along with several mixed breeds.

"People see rabbits as cute, cuddly, cheap pets," said Sandy Nevius, BunnyPeople capital campaign coordinator. "People often buy rabbits on impulse, without knowing that the maintenance of a rabbit is as much or more as a dog or cat."

Sometimes, she said, parents buy a rabbit to teach their kids responsibility. Once the novelty wears off, the rabbit is neglected "and either ends up here or is let loose in the woods, where it can't survive because it isn't fast and doesn't camouflage easily."

Occasionally, the center gets an abused rabbit, Stitt said, pointing to Zeus, a 3-year-old rabbit whose owner would fight with his girlfriend and then beat up Zeus.

The center also has Tack, a white 1 1/2-year-old New Zealand rabbit experimented upon in an animal laboratory. "We had Tick, Tack and Toe from that lab," Stitt said. "Tick and Toe were adopted, but we still have Tack."

Tammy Paull of York Springs, [Pa.,] president of BunnyPeople, said that rabbits aren't for everyone. Bunny-People is a Harrisburg-area organization promoting responsible ownership and care of rabbits.

"Rabbits don't follow commands and may not be as affectionate as dogs or cats," she said. "You can't pick them up like you do a cat, although most like to be petted."

Domestic rabbits live an average of 10 years, are sexually mature by six months and can have litters of eight every several weeks.

Stitt said that pet rabbits should be spayed or neutered to control the population and to calm them down.

These days, Stitt is busy planning an 18-by-22-foot rabbit addition to the shelter. She hopes to break ground for it this fall.

Meanwhile, she keeps accepting unwanted domestic rabbits from some people and adopting rabbits out to others.

The Feature: Writing about How and Why

That last story fits under the general heading of features, which freelance writer Beth Ryan describes by contrasting it with a straight news story. "The news story tells the audience what happened," she writes online for the SNN Newsroom Web site. "The feature will tell them why and how it happened, how the people involved are reacting and what impact the decision is having on other people."

One fine illustration of how a feature can bounce off a news story — or a whole package of news stories — appeared in

Sports Illustrated the week after the 2008 Summer Olympic Games ended in Beijing. Writer Tim Layden begins with an anecdotal lede that gets almost all its energy from action verbs:

A golf cart raced through wide, clean tunnels under the Bird's Nest, Beijing's Olympic Stadium. Volunteers jumped aside, lest they be flattened. Banners flapped in the little vehicle's slipstream, and passengers gripped tiny handrails. Usain Bolt slid right and left on the cushion of the passenger seat, the fastest man alive going even faster. He wore Jamaica's colors — green, yellow and black — on a T-shirt, and from his neck hung the Olympic 100-meter gold medal. "We should race a 100 in the car," said Bolt's agent, Ricky Simms, and Bolt laughed in a youthful baritone from deep in his chest.

"That would be fast, man," he said. "Very fast." They whipped around a corner, buzzed up a concrete ramp and into the warm China night, bound for a car that would drive Bolt back to the Olympic Village.

Fast has a new meaning now. Bolt did not just win the gold medal last Saturday night, he ran away from the field in 9.69 seconds and broke his 11-week-old world record by .03 of a second, despite letting up and celebrating the final 10 long strides, making a joke of the concept of competition and record-keeping. Not 400 meters across a concrete courtyard where Michael Phelps had redefined greatness in water, Bolt did likewise on dry earth. "They are both freaks of nature; there is no other way to put it," said Donovan Bailey, the Jamaican-born Canadian who won the 100 meters at the 1996 Olympics and whose Olympic-record time of 9.84 Bolt obliterated. "Usain is amazing, absolutely amazing."

Now Bolt, just 21 years old and 6'5", stepped from his undersized chariot in a parking area lit by tall, ornate streetlamps. Volunteer workers in logo shirts stared and whispered. "This is why you run," Bolt said. "Definitely, man. All the time I've been running, I dreamed about

getting on the biggest stage and being a champion someday. Here it is. Big feat, man, big feat."

The writer has introduced a story with four, mostly long
paragraphs that give the reader a vignette — a little drama
within a story. This technique works well for a magazine such
as Sports Illustrated, but not so well for many newspapers that
try to emulate magazines.

As the story continues, Layden fleshes out a main character
whose personality has already been illuminated by some choice
direct quotations. Notice that Layden also provides snatches of
history as background:

He is young and at the same time old for the game. A
Jamaican schoolboy legend (no small title on a sprint-cen-
tric island) in his early teens and a world junior champion
in the 200 meters at 15, Bolt did not attempt the 100 on a
world-class level until last summer and broke the world
record in only his fourth final. The Olympics were just his
eighth final, and he is speeding the evolution of the event
just as Bob Beamon advanced his (the long jump in 1968)
and Michael Johnson his (the 200 in '96). "We're looking at the future," said four-time Olympic medalist and
NBC sprint analyst Ato Boldon. "This kid is something
like we've never seen before."

The 100 meters was not nearly the conclusion of Bolt's
Olympic work. He was scheduled to run the 200-meter final on Wednesday night, and Johnson's 12-year-old world
record of 19.32, once thought untouchable, was expected
to receive its first serious assault. "If he gets someone to
push him through the corner, we could see something
unbelievable," said Bailey. "I'm thinking between 19.22
and 19.26."

Bolt is also expected to anchor Jamaica's 4x100-meter
relay on Friday night. He laughed when he looked ahead,
pulling on the brim of a Jamaican team baseball cap. "I feel
very good, man," he said. "Yeah, yeah. I feel strong."

Layden then introduces what a fiction writer would call a subplot. This technique also works well in nonfiction.

> On a breezy evening some 24 hours later, a trio of Jamaican women added a punctuation mark to Bolt's feat when Shelly-Ann Fraser won the women's 100-meter gold medal and Sherone Simpson and Kerron Stewart finished in a dead heat for silver, the first women's 100-meter medal sweep in Olympics history. Despite having three sprinters in the field, the U.S. was denied a spot on the podium for the first time since 1976 (although 2000 became a shutout when Marion Jones was later stripped of her gold medals for admitted steroid use).
>
> "The Jamaicans showed up and we totally didn't," said Lauryn Williams, the defending silver medalist who placed fourth. "It's very humbling."
>
> Fraser ran a ripping 10.78 with calm winds, the fasted final time in Olympic history. (Florence Griffith Joyner ran a wind-aided 10.54 in 1988 and Jones a vacated 10.75 in 2000.) While many Jamaican sprinters have attended college and run track in the U.S., Fraser, like Bolt, instead stayed home to train with growing MVP Track Club in Kingston. She came to prominence while running barefoot in the Jamaican primary schools' (12-and-under) championship, and her Olympic time was a personal best by .07. "It was the performance of a lifetime," Fraser squealed afterward. "I can't stop smiling; my braces are hurting me."

In the next paragraph, Layden brings readers back to the main subject. (Note that in the second sentence, Layden employs an odd use of the word "chalk," without explanation. Potentially unfamiliar terms should be explained or avoided.)

> Bolt's title was the first for Jamaica in the Games' signature sprint. (Like Bailey, Linford Christie of Great Britain, the gold medallist in 1992, was born in Jamaica but

competed for another nation; Jamaicans have won three silver medals.) Bolt came to Beijing as chalk. This depth of the favorite's role depended on a handicapper's belief that Tyson Gay of the U.S. and Asafa Powell of Jamaica were capable of turning the race into the three-man showdown that track fans had anticipated since spring.

But there were big issues for both. Gay, the 2007 world champion and U.S. Olympic trials winner in an American record 9.77 seconds, was trying to regain sharpness after injuring his hamstring in the 200 meters at the trials on July 5 and missing four weeks of hard training. But that hill was too steep to climb. Gay struggled through the first two preliminaries. Expert observers saw a shell of the old Gay. "The guy who could pressure Bolt is Tyson," said former Olympic sprinter Darren Campbell on Saturday. "But the Tyson who's here isn't really Tyson."

Gay was eliminated in the semifinals. Afterward, his voice catching, Gay said, "I gave it my best; I just didn't come through. I just didn't have that pop like at USAs. I feel like I let [my family] down." Gay could still run for the U.S. in the 4x100-meter relay, a unit that will have its hands very full with Jamaica.

Powell, 25, was visited by old demons. Fifth in the 2004 Olympics as the favorite, second in the '07 worlds as the favorite, he had hoped to shed his Olympic insecurities in Beijing. "Asafa is the baby of six children, so he has taken time to be strong," said Powell's older brother, Donovan, before the Games. "But I think it will be different this time." Alas, it was not. Powell, who had beaten Bolt at a race in Stockholm in late July, ran tight and finished fifth.

This is one of several places where Layden's article could have ended. But it is a magazine feature, and he keeps layering on new information. And it works because each paragraph moves the story along.

Bolt, meanwhile, treated the Games like a night in one of the Kingston clubs he loves. He roomed with Jamaican decathlete Maurice Smith in the Olympic Village. "All I did was relax," Bolt said after the 100. "I chilled, I focused. That's all it is."

Bolt's mother, Jennifer, was the only family member who went to Beijing. His father, Wellesley, stayed home, in the north shore parish of Trelawney. "My dad is not into getting on airplanes," said Bolt. "It's O.K. I know the whole country is behind me."

Bolt easily won his semifinal heat in 9.85 seconds into a slight headwind, the fastest semifinal in Olympic history. As in each of his preliminary races, uncatchable even is a low gear. "If you add up all four of his races, he barely ran a full 100 meters," said Bailey. "He expended very little energy." Before the final, Bolt stayed loose on the training track adjacent to the stadium. His coach, the relentlessly grumpy Glen Mills, jokingly leveled the threat that Bolt most fears. "If you don't win the gold medal, I'll make you run the 400," said Mills.

"They were like little kids before the race," said Simms. "No nerves at all."

With the aid of a couple of good quotes, Layden goes on to detail the race itself, effectively giving readers the feeling that they are watching it in slow motion. Note how, mainly with verbs, he describes Bolt's actions just before the race began.

Minutes before 10:30 p.m. in China, the stadium pulsed with the emotions that always precede a 100-meter final. "Groundshaking," said Walter Dix, the 22-year-old U.S. sprinter who would run to a bronze medal, three months after his graduation from Florida State. Bolt ran through a series of comical, self-motivating gestures, firing imaginary six-shooters, pointing with two fingers at the JAMAICA on his jersey, pulling his hands apart high and low as if shooting an arrow into the night sky. He recalled the words Bailey told him last spring: "The crowd is your friend."

Bolt came away clean if not brilliantly fast. Thirty meters out he was in a close fourth place, but his transition to top speed was otherworldly. "I felt myself pulling away from the rest of the field, and Usain was accelerating away from me," said Richard Thompson of Trinidad, who ran at LSU. Short of 50 meters, Bolt was in front and in open daylight. At least 15 meters shy of the finish, he turned to his right and spread his arms wide as if to embrace the roaring noise. He beat his chest once at the line and as the clock first flashed 9.68, and then adjusted to 9.69, Bolt raced around the bend to the backstretch. He didn't instantly see the record time and didn't care. "I had the record, I still have it. Now I have a gold medal too."

This is another place where Layden could have ended the story. But now he gives himself the chance to do something that magazine journalism can do so well — to tell what it means. Note how he allows interview subjects to do the analysis of Bolt's accomplishment for him.

His ascendance has been swifter than even his countrymen imagined. "I knew he would run fast if he tried the 100 meters," said Michael Frater, a silver medalist at the 2005 world championships who finished sixth in Beijing. "But to run like this, with no wind behind him, I didn't think he would run that fast." (Of course, it is an unfortunate sidebar to every world record that Track Nation waits nervously for the result of Bolt's every drug test; Powell complained before the competition that all Jamaicans had been blood- and urine-tested too often, as if targeted.)

Behind Bolt, Thompson held together for second and Dix closed impressively. A year ago Dix had shocked observers (and cynics) by turning down lucrative offers to turn professional and instead returned to Tallahassee for his senior year. He struggled with hamstring injuries through the spring. "If you had told me in April that I'd get the bronze in the Olympics, I would have been shocked," Dix said. "It's sweeter now that I'm here." The bronze is consolation for the U.S. but an auspicious start to the international career of Dix, who was also scheduled to run the 200.

Meanwhile, Jamaica rocked. The race was broadcast live in the country at 9:30 a.m. on Saturday; expatriates living in the U.S. asked islanders to put phones up to their televisions so they could listen. (NBC showed the race on tape delay, more than 13 hours after its conclusion.) Shortly after the finish, street-side sound systems blasted music into the afternoon, commencing a long party. In an even larger demographic, two of the 100-meter finalists were Americans, but the other six were from the Caribbean, stunning dominance from a tiny corner of the world.

But Bolt stands alone, a subset of one.

Writing for Magazines: A Category in Search of a Definition

A generation ago, the category called magazines was reasonably well-defined. It included feature magazines with names such as Life, Look, Collier's, The Saturday Evening Post and The New Yorker. (Life and The Saturday Evening Post still exist but in an abbreviated state. The New Yorker remains one of the most successful general-readership magazines.) The category also included weekly newsmagazines — Time, Newsweek and U.S. News & World Report are still strong — although their "news holes" have shrunk along with the size of the magazines, and a greater percentage of space reflects commentary, not news — as well as specialized consumer magazines such as Popular Mechanics, Ladies Home Journal, Argosy, Better Homes & Gardens, Field & Stream, True Romance and True Detective.

Parade magazine fell into this category; it still comes along with a newspaper in nearly every market of any size. The larger daily newspapers all printed their own Sunday magazine. Some still do.

In the past, a few magazines fell under the heading of "trade publications," or magazines covering a particular industry or type of management within an industry. (Industries weren't nearly as self-conscious as they are now, and there seemed to be a stronger sense of "Why should I tell my competitors?")

The Reader's Digest took up, and still takes up, a category unto itself. The Digest reprints articles (in an abbreviated form) from other magazines or from newspapers and specialty publications. It also publishes some original articles.

Today, the magazine category includes many of the older magazines and a new magazine for nearly every special interest, geographic area, political persuasion, age group and several varieties of how-to. Airline in-flight magazines have taken up some of the general-readership slack left by Life, Look, Collier's and The Saturday Evening Post. Today the required writing styles for magazines vary nearly as much as the publications available.

As an example, take one robust group of magazines that caters to corporate business. Fortune or Forbes might take an approach considered typical magazine style. This usually means the lede will be more languid than one in a newspaper. It will certainly be softer and longer than anything you see or hear on radio or television, unless the story is an in-depth report you're hearing on National Public Radio's "Morning Edition," "All Things Considered" or a documentary you're watching on television. Most will, however, include the occasional page comprising a number of two-or-three-paragraph news briefs, written in the staccato style of a newsletter.

Despite the hard image of the corporate world that many business people seem to enjoy promoting, an article in a magazine such as Fortune might strive first to provide the reader with a mood or an environment. It might begin with an anecdote that somehow illustrates the point of the article. Or it might begin by launching into a state-of-the-industry article, with a synopsis of how the industry has grown or withered or changed during the past five or 10 years. Another magazine, Business Week, might imitate the clipped, often snappy, sometimes snide style of one of the general weekly newsmagazines.

Once a corporate magazine finds itself catering to a particular industry, however, the writing style might be less important than how specific the content is to the audience. For instance, the subcategory of corporate computing is saturated with niche publications, most in magazine formats. Two weekly publications have dominated. One is actually a newspaper, Computerworld, and the other is a newsmagazine, InformationWeek.

A third magazine, Business 2.0, boasts that it focuses on what it calls "business strategies and disciplines, and the integration of the Internet and other technologies into various industries." Another monthly, Software magazine, stopped publication for a time but was reborn as a quarterly with an attached electronic newsletter. Either of these magazines could be considered a publication of record for their field. From a somewhat different angle, another magazine, Upside, says it focuses on "executives and investors in digital technology companies."

Within the subcategory of corporate computing, there are several niche magazines. One monthly is Application Development Trends, a publication aimed at developers of systems that perform specific-user functions (as opposed to systems developers, who concentrate on the systems that in turn provide applications). One of its competitors is Enterprise Systems Journal, which appears only on the Internet.

A couple of magazines address computer and software security. Two are Information Security and SC Magazine, both of which are aimed at top decision-makers in corporate Information Technology, or IT. These include chief information officers (CIOs), security officers, information-systems managers, network administrators and data processing auditors whose job it is to protect a company's information assets. Information Security says it is "an industry trade publication that provides news, analysis, insight, and commentary on today's infosecurity marketplace."

Other niche magazines include those for developers and users of particular computer languages or operating systems, such as Java Developers Journal or XML Journal. All these publications live in a corporate computing subcategory — just one example of how diverse magazines have become.

The Magazine Feature

One thing most magazines have in common is that their feature articles are usually longer than those of a newspaper. Magazine features involve more interviews with more people, cover a subject with more breadth and depth and include more of the environment surrounding the story.

This next article is a good example of how to set up an environment. In this Smithsonian magazine story about Stonehenge, David Roberts takes special care to employ the reader's senses as much as possible.

Steady rain fell diagonally, driven by a raw wind out of the north, and I narrowed the hood of my parka. With neither tent nor bag, I faced an unpleasant night on southern England's Salisbury Plain. At least my vigil would not be solitary. Around me a boisterous crowd of some 7,000 was camped on the turf at Stonehenge, the enigmatic circle of towering sandstone slabs capped with heavy lintels, whose origins lie in the Neolithic age, some 5,000 years ago. "The most celebrated prehistoric monument in the world," the distinguished archaeologist Sir Colin Renfrew called Stonehenge.

In 2000, fifteen years after the British government closed it to large groups of revelers — following desecration of the site and the death by the drug overdose of a young woman in 1984 — Stonehenge was reopened to groups, and a long tradition of celebrating the summer solstice resumed. Now, as I huddled in my foul-weather gear, I observed an odd assortment — neo-hippies, self-styled latter-day Druids in white cloaks, Goths in black,

New Agers of all persuasions, tattooed bikers, drunken "brew-crew" louts of the sort that have given English football a bad name, along with suburban-looking families with young kids, and elderly couples. For hours, people played drums, zithers, horns and didgeridoos; hugged the stones, eyes shut in beatific trance; kissed each other as they stood inside the trilithons (as the assemblies of uprights and lintels are called); and danced upon the recumbent boulders. There were drugs, drinking and a little nudity, but came a bleak, misty dawn and no one was arrested. The celebrants had even picked up their trash.

Once Roberts paints this word-picture, he is free to go anywhere he wants with his magazine article about Stonehenge. He chooses to talk about the great stone circle's influence on a million visitors each year, which brings him to what English composition teachers would call his "thesis statement." (In journalistic translation, this is the payoff sentence of a long lede.) He writes, "Despite a century of serious archaeology, we still have only the foggiest idea about why and how Stonehenge was built."

Roberts most likely wrote several drafts before his article appeared in the Smithsonian. It is rare that a full-blown feature does not require at least one top-to-bottom rewrite. In an attempt to avoid rewrites, editors require writers to query the magazine with story ideas — even if the writer is a regular employee of the publication. If the editor accepts the story (a big "if"), he or she is likely to respond with a detailed outline of how the magazine would like to see the story developing in content, organization and style.

Although not necessarily for those reasons, writers should get comfortable with considering their freshly written story as not the finished piece, but as the first draft. In "Magazine Article Writing," Betsy P. Graham looks at the first draft of an article as a psychological tool, especially for the new writer:

You'll face a blank sheet of paper or an empty computer screen with less dread ... if you remember that your first draft is indeed private. It doesn't have to be correct, much less artful or brilliant, for no one will see it but you. ... Writing the first draft is simply a matter of putting on a computer screen or paper what you are bursting to say. The stronger the urge to tell someone about your topic, the better. Writing it should be no more difficult than telling your best friend about it. You need only make your point, in whatever words tumble out.

This is good advice not only for magazine writers, but for anyone who faces that demon known as writer's block. Graham provides more tips:

Before beginning your rough draft, think once again about your audience and the purpose of your audience. Are you writing to persuade, to entertain, to amuse, or to inform? If you're sure the readers will be keenly interested in getting needed information from the article, the natural mode of writing will be exposition, a clear and logical presentation of facts. Entertainment digressions or embellishments may not be appropriate; in fact, the reader may be annoyed by such distractions. How-to articles, for example, often consist only of a clear set of instructions given in chronological order. No stylistic frills. No amusing anecdotes. If, on the other hand, your purpose is to entertain, examine your notes for opportunities to use narrative and thus insert anecdotes.

Once the first draft is written — and probably rewritten — the rest should be easy, but it rarely is. The next step is a period during which the draft usually goes back and forth between writer and editor, especially if they have not worked together before. This is because the writer's conception of the article, seen from a personal point of view, can be at odds with the way the editor perceives it from the broader, better-defined view of the whole magazine.

The lede might change several times. Whole paragraphs and pages are likely to be deleted or find themselves next to pages and paragraphs they have never formally met. If the editor is good, he or she will ask the writer to clarify points that are perfectly clear to the writer but, as written, will mean nothing to the reader. On occasion, it's time to go back to the outline — to make sure the editor and writer agree on the fundamental reasons to publish the story.

If a draft is successful, the writer then carries the editor or editors through the organization and details of the story. If not, or for reasons that might have nothing to do with the quality of the article but with the internal politics or financial status of the magazine, the story can be killed. If the writer is a freelancer, the magazine might or might not pay a "kill fee" — usually a quarter or half the original payment offered.

One way to ensure that the deadly subject of a kill fee never comes up is to write with as much life, skill and economy as you can — to show your mastery of the craft in a smooth, powerful form of English that conforms to the set of norms known collectively as journalistic style. In the business, this set of norms is also called AP style, named after the wire service (the Associated Press) that first compiled and formalized it. They continue to update The AP Stylebook for news organizations across the globe.

With this in mind, we'll discuss AP style in the next chapter.

Chapter 4 Exercises

The following story by Marcia Dunn, aerospace writer for the Associated Press, begins with a lede and four short grafs. The fourth paragraph is a direct quote. The rest of the story is jumbled; the paragraphs are not in the order they appeared in the story. See if you can put them in an order that responds to a dialogue with the reader.

Here are the grafs that make up the lede:

CAPE CANAVERAL, Fla. — Spacewalking astronauts gave the Hubble Space Telescope a better view of the cosmos by installing a new high-tech instrument Saturday, then tackled their toughest job yet: fixing a broken camera.

It was the third spacewalk in as many days for the shuttle Atlantis crew, and it was expected to be the most challenging ever performed because of the unprecedented camera repairs. Astronauts had never before tried to take apart a science instrument at the 19-year-old observatory.

Hubble's chief mechanic, John Grunsfeld, deftly opened up the burned-out camera and plucked out all four electronic cards that needed to be replaced.

"Somehow I don't think brain surgeons go 'woo-hoo' when they pull something out," one of the astronauts observed from inside Atlantis.

Now, here are the jumbled paragraphs (not all stand alone; in some cases two grafs are joined as they are in the original story):

Fixing the 7-year-old camera was far more complicated. The instrument — called the Advanced Camera for Surveys — suffered an electrical short and stopped working two years ago. Ground controllers had been able to eke out a minimal amount of science but hoped to get it back into full operation before it broke, the surveys camera provided astronomers with the deepest view of the universe in visible light, going back in time 13 billion years.

NASA considered this repair job — and one set for Sunday on another failed science instrument — to be the most delicate and difficult ever attempted in orbit. Neither instrument was designed to be handled by astronauts wearing thick, stiff gloves.

Earlier, Grunsfeld and his spacewalking partner, Andrew Feustel, accomplished their first chore, hooking up the $88 million Cosmic Origins Spectrograph.

They made room for the new supersensitive spectrograph — designed to detect faint light from faraway quasars — by removing the corrective lenses that restored Hubble's vision in 1993.

Hubble was launched in 1990 with a flawed mirror that left it nearsighted. But the newer science instruments have corrective lenses built in, making the 1993 contacts unnecessary. The latest addition, the cosmic spectrograph, is expected to provide greater insight into how planets, stars and galaxies formed.

To NASA's relief, everything was going well and the astronauts were even running ahead of schedule for a change. The first two spacewalks ended up running long because of unexpected difficulties encountered with Hubble, last visited seven years ago.

The daunting job unfolded 350 miles above Earth. Orbiting so high put Atlantis and its astronauts at an increased risk of being hit by space junk. NASA had another shuttle on launch standby in case a rescue was needed.

Grunsfeld unscrewed 32 fasteners to get to the camera's electronic guts, all the while working around a corner that prevented him from seeing everything he was doing. He used long tools designed just for the job.

"This activity is dedicated to studying the behavior of tiny screws in space," he joked.

"This is really pretty historic," Grunsfeld said as he and Feustel hoisted out the phone booth-size box containing Hubble's old contacts.

If all goes well, the fifth and final spacewalk is set for Monday, and the telescope will be released from Atlantis on Tuesday.

This last mission to Hubble cost more than $1 billion.

NASA hopes to keep Hubble working for another five to 10 years with all the improvements. No one will be back to Hubble, so everyone at NASA, the seven astronauts included, wants to squeeze in as much repair work as possible. Already, they have given Hubble an improved wide-field planetary camera, fresh batteries and gyroscopes and a new science data unit to replace one that broke last fall.

The switch — taking out the 7-foot-long box containing the corrective lenses and putting in the spectrograph — proved to be straightforward. It's exactly the kind of replacement work astronauts performed on four previous repair missions.

The Craft

The Rewards of Murky Writing

The story wasn't big, so when it appeared, it measured only a few column inches and carried no byline. Apparently the piece received only passing attention from the editors who handled it. The story passed through two respected news organizations, one known for the integrity of its reporting and the other for the brightness and economy of its writing. Yet the reporting was apparently not thorough; I say "apparently" because the murky way it was written camouflaged any good reporting that might have been accomplished.

The lede of the USA Today story, which was picked up from the Associated Press, became a murky start to a murky story. The lede sentence was so complex that it carried a dependent clause, and that clause carried a dependent clause of its own.

> The U.S. transplant network has agreed to share with Mexico its experience in distributing organs, opening an information exchange that officials hope will boost Mexico's less developed system and give the U.S. system insight into increasing Hispanic donations.

Let's go over this again. The network that distributes organs in the United States is going to share the results of its experience with officials in Mexico. All right, that makes sense. Whoever rewrote the story had enough information at that point to craft a sentence that stood on its own.

"Why would they do that?" we imagine the reader asking. The writer could respond, "To help boost Mexico's less developed system and [here comes the murk] give the U.S. system insight into increasing Hispanic donations."

What exactly does that mean? "Insight" is a vague term. Does the U.S. system want to understand why Hispanic donations are increasing? The information is not clear.

Maybe the writer meant that an increased understanding of Mexico's system would help increase the number of donations coming from Hispanic countries. If this is true, it's too bad that isn't what the writer wrote. Let's look at the second paragraph:

> The formal agreement, signed Friday in Mexico City, was not necessary from the American point of view, given that the U.S. network regularly shares information with other nations.

Phrases such as "from the American point of view" and "given that" make it seem as though a band of bureaucrats has stolen some poor reporter's ability to write in English. To put it more clearly, "Officials from the two countries signed the agreement Friday in Mexico City. Americans said it would be of no direct benefit to the United States since the U.S. network regularly shares information with other nations."

The next paragraph explains that Mexican authorities might want to do more than simply share information. Mark Rosenker, a spokesman for the United Network for Organ Sharing (UNOS), says the Mexicans are seeking a formal relationship with the U.S. transplant network, whose system distributes donated hearts, lungs, kidneys, livers and pancreases.

There wasn't anything particularly wrong in the paragraph. A direct quote from Rosenker would have worked better, but the paragraph is understandable. The next paragraph is a direct quote, which works well:

"We have much to teach and much to learn through this exchange," says Walter Graham, executive director of UNOS.

Notice that there are no quotes, direct or indirect, in the next paragraph:

The agreement is not expected to lead to the exchange of actual organs. Rather, the agreement is meant to help Mexico's National Transplant Council develop a nation-wide system for distributing organs. For example, the agreement calls for an information exchange on how to certify transplant centers and professionals.

Why is the reporter filtering all this information? Readers may as well believe that the reporter made it all up. The fog factor — the abstract quality of the copy, enhanced by so many latinizations — is huge.

Graham might have been a source. If so, the reporter could have written, "Graham said no one expects the agreement to lead to an actual organ exchange between the two countries; but it is meant to help Mexico's National Transplant Council build a nationwide organ distribution system. The agreement calls for the United States to give Mexico information about how to certify transplant centers and professionals."

Murkiness is what happens when a reporter, writer or editor gets lazy and stops demanding the most direct English available. As is, the story is dull and mostly incomprehensible.

Direct English calls for the skills of a craft. This chapter focuses on many results of good craftsmanship.

Separating the Craft from the Profession

Journalism is called a profession even though it requires no formal course of study or the completion of examinations, unlike the professions of law, medicine or accounting. The freedom-of-the-press clause in the First Amendment pretty much forbids such an infringement. Journalism is a profession when we look at how it exists in the society in which we practice it, the interpretations of the Constitution that govern its practice (libel law, copyright law, privacy law) and the academic atmosphere in which journalism is taught.

But when the term "journalism" is applied to newspapers, magazines, newsletters, radio and television newscasts and documentaries, journalism is much more a trade and a craft than a profession. As a craft, journalism ensures that the best writers are those who make the most economic use of language without losing meaning or flavor. It requires eliminating a lot of words.

For journalists, regardless of medium, craft means pare, pare, pare. Getting rid of even a two-letter word — if it fails to carry its weight — should represent a tiny triumph. If writers don't pare, they risk inflicting sentences such as this one on their audiences:

> At the end of the alley, there were two construction workers surrounded by orange cones wearing brown overalls and gloves drilling a hole from the end of the alley to the middle of the street.

Let's examine this 35-word sentence for a moment. We can't fault the writer's observational skills, but the sentence is wordy. It's needlessly complex. It portrays cones wearing overalls and gloves drilling a hole.

Now read it again, after a rewrite:

> Orange cones surround two construction workers wearing brown overalls and gloves. The workers are drilling a hole from the end of an alley to the street.

Twenty-six words are now split into two sentences. We've pared nine words, or 26 percent, of the original sentence with no meaning lost, no flavor changed and nothing of value left out. In other words, we've eliminated some wordiness. We've also clarified the meaning by getting rid of dangling modifiers.

Avoiding Wordiness

Let's look at an example of how to choke the life out of English. Steve Rubenstein of the San Francisco Chronicle wrote about how one corporate spokesman did his best to distort the English language to a nefarious end. Rubenstein explained that as the new century emerged, Cisco Systems Inc. was one of the leading corporations connected with the Internet and was one of the darlings of Wall Street. In 2001, as the so-called "dot-com bubble" burst, Cisco executives saw much of their business and profits evaporate. They announced that they were eliminating the jobs of 8,000 employees. This is when the spokesman got involved. He "declared that the employees were to undergo 'normal involuntary attrition.'" (See "Be Honest: Avoid Euphemisms" in Chapter 7.)

Rubenstein quoted Julian Boyd, an emeritus professor of English at the University of California at Berkeley, who called the phrase "comical. It's someone trying to avoid blame. It's someone trying to say this thing is doubly not my fault."

A spokeswoman for the California Employment Development Department said she didn't know what "normal involuntary attrition" meant. "Each one of the words I have heard before," Suzanne Schroeder told Rubenstein. "They're English. Put them together, I'm not sure."

The phrase might be English, but plain English — good, solid, clear, unambiguous, forceful English — it isn't.

Not that journalistic plain speaking originated from loving attention to clarity and honesty. The often brutal emphasis on brevity and word economy that characterizes much journalistic writing did not stem from a desire to improve communication so much as it stemmed from the need to save money, time, ink and trees.

In the United States, the Civil War is credited with inspiring much of today's spareness of news copy. Americans on both sides used the world's first wire service, Agence France Presse (AFP), as a model. AFP showed journalists how to cover the war for dozens of newspapers that were members of the wire service. The only link the reporter had to the member newspapers was an expensive telegraph wire, and the only language the wire recognized was Morse code.

To get coverage of a story about, for example, the Battle of Gettysburg in southern Pennsylvania, the new system required that a reporter covering the Union side of the conflict to send a messenger to an authorized telegrapher a dozen miles away in Taneytown, Md. There the messenger would wait impatiently for army officers to complete its dispatches and then wait further as the reporter's prose was translated into dots and dashes. It became obvious that the fewer words a reporter wrote, the shorter the wait and the less the expense.

The tradition continued through at least six more wars, with publishers devoting much of the time in between to worrying about the price of paper, which even now comes from expensive trees in faraway places such as northern Canada. Paper prices also influenced a reporter's brevity.

Regardless of their motives, there is little question that by using this process, reporters and editors have enhanced the ability to communicate in English. Avoiding wordiness and using plain English, which began as a mechanical writing and editing function, has become an art form as well.

Sometimes getting rid of an unneeded word is simply a matter of changing an adverb into an adjective — in this case, the word "not."

Police have not found any witnesses.
Police have found no witnesses.

Here are more examples, followed by edited versions:

He considers himself a supporter of the Republican Party. He did not, however, support its choice of John McCain.
He says he is a Republican, but he did not support John McCain.

People were sitting in the restaurant, eating and conversing.
People sat in the restaurant, eating and talking.
(Or)
In the restaurant, people ate and talked.

She is hoping to organize a service project.
She hopes to organize a service project
(Or, to assure the reader that the reporter isn't making it up:)
She said she hopes to organize a service project.

Our footsteps fell lifeless, and void of synchronicity.
Our footsteps fell lifeless, out of sync.

We had an ample supply of time to get to know each other.
We had ample time to get to know each other.

The budget plan will stem the skyrocketing deficit by $496 billion through raising taxes on individual and corporate income.
Raising individual and corporate income taxes will reduce the deficit by $496 billion.

People become disoriented from their friends due to their preoccupation with their significant other when they should be preoccupied with relationships with friends, it shifts to concern about their significant other's happiness as well as their own happiness.
(Rewriting this example is difficult, as the meaning is lost.)

I find myself zipping up my leather jacket and struggling with cold hands to fasten the metal snap at its neckline.
I zip up my leather jacket and struggle with cold hands to fasten the metal snap at its neckline.
(Sometimes you can achieve word economy simply by using a more direct verb form.)

He spends the majority of his time with his girlfriend.
He spends most of his time with his girlfriend.

When high school coaches encourage this atmosphere of free agency, they are endorsing the sense of randomness in teenagers that leads some of our city's youth to drop out of high school to join gangs instead of remaining committed to their schoolwork.

By encouraging free agency, high school coaches contribute to a sense of randomness among teenagers. This lack of direction can lead them to drop out of school, even to join gangs.

She competed in the Olympic swimming trials and just barely missed a spot on the team.

She competed in the Olympic swimming trials and just missed a spot on the team.

Neither of them saw it as a permanent move, they said.

Neither saw it as a permanent move, they said.

With the patents, inventions and discoveries she has developed for the pharmaceutical business, it seems that the ideas and planning have been great, however the rewards have not been equivalent to the effort. She says she wants to find a way to improve her job or remuneration both financially and personally.

She appears proud of the patents, inventions and discoveries she has developed for the pharmaceutical business. She says she wants to improve her job financially and personally.

One way to avoid wordiness is to replace a string of adjectives or adverbs with a noun or a verb. For example, in the Southwestern United States, you can look up into a summer sky and see a "big, black and gray, anvil-shaped cloud," or you can define it with a single noun familiar to Southwesterners: thunderhead.

The journalist can write that police believe the suspect "beat the victim repeatedly over the head with a blunt object." Or, the journalist can write that police believe the suspect "bludgeoned" the victim.

As we mentioned in Chapter 1, English has an Anglo-Saxon base. The Anglo-Saxon gifts to the language usually are shorter and punchier than their latinized equivalents. In "On Writing Well," William Zinsser points out that paring often means working on the size of a word as well as the number of words. He asks why people insist on using "assistance" when "help" will do nicely. The same for "facilitate" instead of "ease," "numerous" instead of "many," "individual" instead of "man" or "woman," "remainder" instead of "rest," "initial" instead of "first," "sufficient" instead of "enough," "attempt" instead of "try" and "referred to as" instead of "called."

"Beware of all slippery new fad words for which the language already has equivalents," Zinsser warns. He includes "overview and quantify, paradigm and parameter, optimize and maximize, prioritize and potentialize. They are all weeds that will smother what you write. Don't dialogue with someone you can talk to. Don't interface with anybody."

When you're counting not only the number of words but the number of characters, the importance of paring words gets magnified. This should be obvious to the writers and editors of the ticker running along the bottom of the television screen of a 24-hour news show. Space is critical on those tickers. It became apparent one day in 2008, however, that someone at MSNBC didn't get the word, literally and figuratively.

The ticker was trying to keep track of Hurricane Ike, which went on to wreck much of coastal Texas. At one point it told viewers, "CENTER OF EYEFALL EXPECTED TO MAKE LANDING AT 1-2 AM EST." It was 56 characters total, spaces included. The writer must have fallen into a vat of weather jargon, because "center of eyefall" can, and should, be replaced with "eye." In addition, "make landing" can be replaced with a simple present-tense verb: "land."

Our rewrite now reads, "EYE EXPECTED TO LAND AT 1-2 AM EST." It has 34 characters, or about 60 percent of the length of the original sentence. We've eliminated four words without changing the meaning of the sentence.

Caution: Concise Writing Doesn't Always Enhance Clarity

Even the most concise writing isn't going to communicate facts, thoughts, ideas or opinions if chopping away at a sentence renders it unreadable. Washington Post humor columnist Gene Weingarten illustrated this point in a half-serious review of the Web site Twitter, which forces its correspondents to limit themselves to 140 characters per message. He then ends his article with a 140-character parody of Lincoln's Gettysburg Address:

> I suppose it could be argued that by limiting the length of its members' posts, Twitter is actually performing a service: forcing people to better marshal their thoughts, limiting senseless blather and, in fact, improving the general level of discourse through ruthless self-editing. To argue that, however, you would have to believe that even complex or subtle thoughts can be reliably reduced to 140 characters.
>
> I decided to test this theory by condensing into Twitter length a piece of writing that is already famously concise. I kept feeding my version into the Twitter edit box, and cutting, until I got this sucker down to the prescribed format.
>
> Here we go:
>
> 87 years ago, our dads made us free. Yay! Still want free, but hard! Fighting, dying, burying! Need more fight tho, so dead be happy.

Eliminating Redundancy

Redundancy is a wonderful thing to have in a space vehicle: One computer system goes down, another takes its place, the mission lives and so do the astronauts. But while redundancy might keep a space vehicle aloft, it can sink a sentence.

Redundancy is defined as the quality or state of exceeding what is needed or normal. In English, redundancies do serve a couple of useful purposes. For example, they provide fodder for a chapter in a book that talks about how to write better. More often, they provide comic relief.

I saw a slight hint of light.
(How slight can a hint get?)
I saw a hint of light.

the Catholic pope
the pope

He was promoted in the organization to handle the newspaper's layout, design and photography.
He was promoted to handle the newspaper's layout, design and photography.
(Unless "the organization" is a group dedicated to organized crime, we can safely assume that he works for the newspaper.)

The smell of burnt charcoal loomed in the air.
The smell of burned charcoal loomed.
(Where else would it loom? Also, in the United States the preferred usage is *burned*. "Burnt" is a British usage.)

Remember the old adage …
Remember the adage …

The beating victim can now dress himself and brush his own teeth.
The beating victim can now dress himself and brush his teeth.
(Before he was the victim, he must have been able to brush other people's teeth.)

... a private school which is located in Simsbury, Conn.
... a private school in Simsbury, Conn.
(More often than not, "located" is redundant.)

He continued on in the tradition of DePaul University, where he has obtained both a BS as well as an MBA from the School of Commerce.
He earned a Bachelor of Science and a Master of Business Administration from the School of Commerce at DePaul University.
(This sentence isn't long enough to use "both" and "as well." In addition, "earned" is a more precise word than "obtained." And when did DePaul University get a patent on this tradition?)

Besides pursuing an internship in the field of journalism, he is in a band.
Besides pursuing an internship in journalism, he plays in a band.
(Notice the change to an action verb: "He plays in a band.")

5 a.m. in the morning.
5 a.m.

Bond was set at $900,000 Wednesday for an 18-year-old man charged with killing two men dead and wounding another.
Bond was set at $900,000 Wednesday for an 18-year-old man charged with killing two men and wounding another.
(Are there different levels of dead?)

His desire to get better and improve is a major reason for his success.
His desire to improve is a major reason for his success.

The mayor says she wants to talk about the town's poverty-stricken slums.
The mayor says she wants to talk about the town's slums.
(Slums are, by definition, poverty-stricken.)

He moved like an unstoppable tornado.
He moved like a tornado.
(As opposed to a stoppable tornado.)

In addition, he also edits the yearbook.
In addition, he edits the yearbook.

In school, he says he enjoyed history the most out of his subjects.
In school, he says he enjoyed history the most.

He is an avid traveler who has, in the past, written a number of travel stories.
He is an avid traveler who has written a number of travel stories.
(He must not have had time for them in the future.)

The temperature in the barn had reached a smoldering 115 degrees.
The barn's temperature had reached 115 degrees.
(Most would agree that 115 degrees is smoldering.)

Among her most favorite destinations is London.
Among her favorite destinations is London.

I feel the majority of people want to be well-liked and popular.
Most people want to be well-liked.

Not only has she competed in Chicago, but also around the nation.
Not only has she competed in Chicago, but around the nation.
("Also" simply takes up space. You might be tempted to over-edit and reduce the sentence to "She has competed around the nation," but you would lose some of the rhetorical flavor of the sentence.)

Photography has also become another of his passions.
Photography has become another of his passions.

Pennsylvania Hall stands among the large trees, casting its own unique shadow.

Pennsylvania Hall stands among the large trees, casting its unique shadow.

Compounding the Sentence with Complexity

For this next section, let's quickly review some grammar terms, specifically compound and complex sentences. A compound sentence is two complete sentences joined by a conjunction (and, but, for, nor, or, yet). A complex sentence contains at least one clause that acts as an assistant to the main part of the sentence. Clauses aren't supposed to stand by themselves. (A clause has its own subject and predicate, but it's still part of a larger sentence.)

There is nothing particularly wrong with compound or complex sentences. Ideas are often hard to convey without their help. It is when these types of sentences are not needed that they create problems for the conscientious writer — journalistic or otherwise.

When extra sentence elements (words, phrases, clauses) appear, red flags should go up, reminding the writer to ask, "Do I really need this?" If you do need it, keep it in. But more often than not, it just gets in the way.

The easiest way to reduce complexity is to divide the sentence and transform it into at least two sentences. Take this one, for example:

Her Wednesday playwriting course will be directly impacted by this class, as some of the basics can easily be transformed from journalism to theater writing, she believes.

She says journalism will have a direct impact on her Wednesday playwriting course. The basics will transfer easily.

Sometimes you can boil down the sentence by rewriting it. In this example, the rewritten sentence still fits the definition of "complex," but it's much less complicated than the original:

In Europe during her semester abroad, there are many places she has not yet visited. She explained that, although she was afforded the chance to travel throughout, there are still many places there she wants to see.

She says she saw much of Europe during her semester abroad, but she still wants to see more. (Notice the use of passive voice in "she was afforded" and the needless "there are." Both bog down this sentence.)

Here are additional examples:

The price of gas and a Whopper can be discerned by gazing at the corner of State and 12th, where a BP gas station with a Burger King restaurant stretches out a quarter of a block.

A BP gas station and a Burger King restaurant take up a quarter of a block. One displays the price of a gallon of gasoline; the other, the price of a Whopper.

Residents in the subdivision have formed an action group called AWARE (Amber Grove — We're Against Road Expansion) and they have spent the last three weekends picketing the developer's sales office at Amber Grove, carrying signs that read "Ask before you buy" and "Trucks + Traffic = Tragedy" in below-freezing temperatures.

Subdivision residents formed an action group, AWARE (Amber Grove — We're Against Road Expansion). They have spent the past three weekends in freezing temperatures, picketing the developer's sales office with signs: "Ask Before You Buy" and "Trucks + Traffic = Tragedy." (Readers can be forgiven if they concluded from the first example that group members believe road expansion is all right during the summer.)

The icy wind, making itself felt through my mittens, reminds me of the lake's incredible power over this city at all times.

The icy wind makes itself felt through my mittens. It reminds me of the lake's incredible power over this city at all times.

Whole chapters — whole books, even — have been written about what a sentence is and what it isn't. For our purposes, a few principles will suffice. So far we've seen simple sentences and those adorned with extra phrases and clauses. Because good newspaper or magazine writing can be informal and conversational, sentence fragments are often allowed. They must make sense, however, and the reader must be able to conclude that the writer wrote the fragment on purpose.

What you should not see in newspaper writing are run-on sentences — two complete sentences that, because they are not separated by a period, resemble a head-on train wreck. Like this one:

There was no one who could help me, I was devastated.

No one could help me. I was devastated.

(Also note that we do not need "there was." We can take it out and turn a being verb into an action verb. See Chapter 9 for more on this topic.)

In this next example, the writer again supplied punctuation in the right place, but the sentence needs a period, not a comma.

Football immediately caught his eye, filled with desire and self-discipline, he knew he would excel.

He took to football immediately. With desire and self-discipline, he knew he would excel.

("Caught his eye" is a cliché, and an inapt one at that. See Chapter 8 for more on this topic.)

Correctly Using "That" and "Which" (and "Who" and "Whom")

Although discussions of when to use "that" and when to use "which" often verge on the comical, this is a bigger problem than grammatical hairsplitting. The banter would not be necessary if more writers used "that" or "which" correctly to begin with, but many don't. Using these words incorrectly affects meaning, so the problem is real.

It involves the use of restrictive and nonrestrictive clauses, which sounds forbidding, because the discussion veers so closely to grammatical pedantry.

For this reason, the editors of The Associated Press Stylebook chose instead to use the terms "essential" and "nonessential" clauses, and this is what we will call them in this book. In simplest terms, essential clauses use "that" without a comma. Nonessential clauses use "which" with a comma. Essential clauses are required information for the sentence to make sense. Nonessential clauses are less critical to the sentence; they can be removed without rendering the sentence unintelligible.

When we're talking about people instead of things, either type of clause can use "who." Use it without a comma in an essential clause and with a comma in a nonessential clause.

Here are some examples of essential and nonessential clauses.

Essential: *Mountains that rise less than 10,000 feet in altitude are considered hills in Colorado.* (Only those that rise less than 10,000 feet are considered hills.)

Nonessential: *Mountains in the Appalachians, which do not exceed 6,000 feet in altitude, would be considered hills in Colorado.* (You could delete the information inside the commas and the sentence would still make sense.)

Essential: *Men's shirts that have red tags are 20 percent off.* (Shoppers get the discount only if they buy red-tagged shirts.)

Nonessential: *Men's shirts, which have attached collars, are 20 percent off.* (If it's a men's shirt and it's on display, it's on sale, no matter what color tag it might have. The ones in this store just all happen to have attached collars.)

Essential: *The National Football league team that wins the American Conference goes on to play in the Super Bowl.* (If your team hasn't won its conference championship, there is no way it is going to play in the Super Bowl.)

Nonessential: *Super Bowl teams, which represent the best or luckiest of the 16 teams in each conference, meet each other in early February.* (Often nonessential clauses are separate thoughts or asides to the main thrust of a sentence.)

If we're talking about people, instead of mountains or shirts for football teams, we use "who" instead of "that" or "which." This means that the only difference between these types of essential or nonessential clauses is whether they use commas. The AP Stylebook editors use this apt example:

Essential: *Reporters who do not read the stylebook should not criticize their editors.* (This sentence says that only one class of reporters — those who do not read the stylebook — should avoid criticizing their editors. It seems the other reporters may criticize editors if they want to.)

Nonessential: *Reporters, who do not read the stylebook, should not criticize their editors.* (Notice the difference a pair of commas makes. This sentence says that not a single reporter has read the stylebook, and none of them should criticize their editors.)

Let's discuss "who" versus "whom." Strictly speaking, if the word you're using who/whom for is the subject of the sentence — if it is doing the action or portraying a state of being — it is who. If the word is receiving the action, it is "whom." For example, "Who is throwing a baseball at whom?" the announcer asked. But in American English, using "whom" can sound awkward, even pompous: "Who do you know here?" really should be "Whom do you know here?" By that measure, the famous reference books that appear under the title of "Who's Who" should actually be entitled "Who's Whom."

Suppose you and a friend arrive at a party. You are invited in and, as the door closes behind you, you look over the crowd, then at each other. "With whom are you acquainted here?" you ask.

In reality, you probably don't, at least, not if you're an American living in the 21st century. We don't talk that way. Maybe 100 years ago we did, but not since World War I has such correctness entered the conversation of any but the most pedantic of Americans. You most likely asked, "Who do you know here?"

What many Americans do to avoid sounding pompous (or wrong) is replace "who" with "that." Unfortunately, though, they have forced a choice between pompous and sloppy. Using "that" places human beings in the same category as chair legs — as inanimate things. Let's look at some examples of how to correct this:

I know it was Jackson that had just been shot.
I know it was Jackson *who* had just been shot.

A person that excels in academics is not necessarily interested in other areas.
A person *who* excels in academics is not necessarily interested in other areas.

She said she knew of no one that could have successfully pulled off such a heist.
She said she knew of no one *who* could have successfully pulled off such a heist.

Writing with Precision

If wordiness implies the use of too many words, imprecision implies the use of the wrong word. In Chapter 1, we discussed what an asset English's huge vocabulary is when the writer is looking for the precise word to convey an idea to the reader, nuances intact. It also works the other way. The best way to appear to be a sloppy thinker is to write and speak without precision.

As Mark Twain put it, "The difference between the almost-right word and the right word is really a large matter — it's the difference between the lightning bug and the lightning." Look at the following examples; each is imprecise enough to make the reader wonder what the writer is writing about. And speaking of bugs, the next example illustrates one of the most misused words in the English language, especially among those who would impress people with their vocabularies.

Most bugs are hideous and make me nauseous.
Most bugs look hideous. They make me *nauseated.*
(Note the change to an action verb. Also, the correct word is nauseated. If you are *nauseous*, you make other people feel sick.)

Sometimes, as with the following example, the reader simply laughs.

The house displayed peeling pants and weathered roofs.
The house displayed peeling paint and a weathered roof.

Here are some more examples:

He had a chance to run through the various vendors.
(But better judgment overtook him and he kept his sword in its scabbard.)

The father's gait is unusually large.
("Gait" usually refers to something a horse does, but "large gait" still sounds funny.)

A walk down the sidewalk revels large black and gray garbage cans.

A walk down the sidewalk *reveals* large black and gray garbage cans.

("Revel" usually implies a party.)

The proposal would allow residential permit parking on streets with businesses and residences after 8 p.m., and on streets and residences on one side and business on the other after 9 p.m.

(On occasion, the reader is simply tempted to respond with a "Huh?")

People finished all there gossiping.

People finished all *their* gossiping.

A flock of yellow cabs soar north like vultures looking for passengers late for work.

("A flock of yellow cabs" is apt and not bad imagery. But the reader has a hard time believing they soar.)

A few cars with curious passengers drove past us.

Curious people drove past us.

(Otherwise it sounds as though the cars were driving themselves. Also, the fact that the people driving were in cars is implied.)

There were many nights were I had a lot of work to do.

On many nights, I had much work to do.

(The writer wrote "were" instead of "where." But even with that correction, the sentence looks sloppy.)

… a seemingly congruous addition to the area already redolent of elitism and the pursuit of knowledge.

(It is impossible to edit something if the meaning is entirely unclear.)

I was excepted to a few different schools.

A few schools *accepted* me.

(Also, use active voice. See the next chapter for more on this.)

He is embarked on himself being first from now on.
(Embarking is something you do from a boat or a ship. This sentence is just unclear.)

He is not a person who is often taken serious.
He is not a person who is often taken *seriously*.

There is much more to life then academics.
There is much more to life *than* academics.

The car suffered minor damage.
(People suffer injuries. Cars usually sustain damage.)

As new generations are coined, those claimed to be a part of them may feel the urge to rebel.
As new generations grow up, some of their members might feel the urge to rebel.
(How do you "coin" a generation? In addition, "might," not "may," implies probability. "May" implies permission.)

His ideal predicament would find him employed in the research and development area of the pharmaceutical industry.
The ideal job for him would be to work in pharmaceutical research and development.
(A "predicament" is a difficult or trying situation. I don't think that's what the reporter meant.)

After Boston, she attended Northwestern University.
After she left Boston, she attended Northwestern University.
(Otherwise readers may wonder if Boston is no longer with us.)

In the next example, the problem is not with word precision, but with staying in the same tense.

Not only did he devote himself to music and politics, he has also excelled in athletics. (Note the redundancy of "also.")

Not only did he devote himself to music and politics, he excelled in athletics.

You wouldn't think that too many people would get the words "ancestor" and "descendant" confused. But apparently many do. Syndicated columnist James J. Kilpatrick found six articles that brought someone's ancestors back to life:

In Olympia, Wash., a newspaper headline reads, "Geronimo's ancestors face a million-dollar question."

In Columbia, S.C.: "Ancestors of Civil War veterans protested the removal of the Confederate flag from the state capitol." (Kilpatrick calls it "a haunting story.")

In Salmon, Idaho: "A century after prospectors prowled the mountains looking for gold, their ancestors walk the same trails."

In St. Augustine, Fla.: "An ancestor of Christopher Columbus canceled a speech here and returned to Spain." (Kilpatrick's comment: "And high time, I'd say.")

In Dearborn, Michigan: "Founder's ancestor named Ford executive."

In the dairy industry, making a living can be impossible "for American farmers 100 years ago" and "their ancestors today."

In another article, Kilpatrick pointed to a story in the Las Vegas Sun in which the reporter wrote, "Here is a synthesis of what happened."

"Synthesis?" Kilpatrick asked. "Maybe, to synthesize is to combine various elements into a single entity, but ... I suspect the reporter wanted 'synopsis.'"

Using Parallel Structures; Making Your Numbers Agree

When you write a sentence that uses a series of clauses, make sure they start and end the same way grammatically. If you don't, you destroy whatever rhythm you've tried to establish. More importantly, if you use parallel structures, your readers will have a more enjoyable time absorbing and understanding your facts, ideas and concepts.

Let's look at a few examples. In the first one, the writer used the same verb form — present participle — in three clauses but switched to straight present tense in the final clause. (The writer has also implied that Peru is in Europe. Note that the rewritten sentence eliminates all reference to Europe without sacrificing meaning or content.)

She has spent time in Europe participating in programs to benefit people in need, which included working with Albanian refugees, working in Peru as part of a community development program and in Greece, where she studies anthropology.

She has spent time working with refugees in Albania, taking part in community development in Peru and studying archaeology in Greece.

Sometimes a subject switch makes a sentence confusing. In this series of commands, the subject, "you," is implied, but suddenly "the treasure" takes over as the subject. This throws off the reader.

Take 12 paces to the north, take 20 paces to the east, dig a four-foot hole and the treasure will be there waiting for you.

Walk north 12 paces, go east 20 paces, dig a four-foot hole and discover the treasure.

Here's another example:

If you can't seem to find a lede that works, sit back, take a deep breath and the lede will come to you.

If you can't seem to find a lede that works, sit back, take a deep breath and let the lede come to you.

News professionals cite what they call "the rule of threes" to explain how best to communicate with the reader. It works like this: The writer makes an assertion and then backs it up with three examples. Not two or four — these sound funny. Three. For some reason either mystical or deeply psychological, three works well. It's the same case with parallel structures. They are most powerful and persuasive when they come in threes.

"When you read your copy aloud, you make sure your rhythms are right, your words are necessary and your sentences are direct."

"First, look up the police records; second, pick out those that appear newsworthy; third, set up interviews to flesh out possible stories."

"Driving through New York City can be frustrating, frightening — and thrilling."

Agreement of a different sort becomes an issue when writers try to match singular nouns with plural pronouns or vice versa. Take this example: "One of the most challenging writing tasks are to pare a sentence without changing its content or flavor." This sounds strange, and rightfully so, because the subject of the sentence isn't "tasks," it's "one." Once we've identified the subject, we see that "one" is singular but "are" is plural. The correct sentence would read: "One of the most challenging writing tasks is to pare a sentence without changing its content or flavor."

As obvious as this problem appears to be, it is invading American speech and writing patterns. The problem usually occurs when a prepositional phrase follows the subject of the sentence:

"The group of students spent their second week on an educational excursion to the Sea Islands off the coast of Georgia."

This sentence seems all right. After all, "students" is plural, and so is "their." But "students" isn't what "their" is referring to. The real subject of the sentence is "group." It is followed by the prepositional phrase "of students," which is not the subject, but a modifier of the subject. It tells you what type of group — a group "of students."

Now let's make the sentence grammatically correct:

"The group of students spent its second week on an educational excursion to the Sea Islands off the coast of Georgia."

This sentence is grammatically correct, but it too sounds strange. Where you once had several students sailing off the coast, now you have a clump, an "it." I don't think students like to come in clumps any more than anyone else does.

We'll need to find a new solution. Why not change the subject?

"Several students spent their second week on an educational excursion to the Sea Islands off the coast of Georgia."

But have we changed the meaning? Have we left something out? "A group of students" implies that the students were members of something: a class, an assembly, a team. Now we have some students who might have come together only by chance.

It seems that all we've succeeded in doing is proving that a grammarian can split hairs that would send a lawyer screaming. But the answer to whether or not the students have become part of a greater whole is most likely covered somewhere else in the story.

As we shall see, however, making words agree in number can create problems elsewhere.

Sexist Language versus Good English

One excuse for violating the agreement-in-number rule is that you must to avoid sexism in your writing. For example:

"A student can spend his week on an educational excursion to the Sea Islands off the coast of Georgia."

In this example we can apply the most universal antidote to sexist language: pluralization.

"Students can spend their week on an educational excursion to the Sea Islands off the coast of Georgia."

Why is sexism a problem? Because for nearly 200 years, Americans — and many other speakers of English — have acquired the habit of taking a noun representing a person or a number of persons, and referring to that noun with the pronoun "he," "him," "his" or "himself."

"Everyone in school knows when it's his time to deliver his senior thesis."

"Each manager in the bank knows what he has to do in case of a robbery."

"He who laughs last, laughs loudest."

Sentences such as these reinforce the gender stereotypes that are often derogatory towards females. Sexist language supports the sexist behavior of denying women access to positions other than teacher, librarian, nurse or flight attendant. These occupations, which in the not-so-distant past were a female's only career options, seemed to automatically attract the pronouns "she," "her," "hers" or "herself."

Within the last century, it became apparent that the use of sexist language was indirectly helping to keep women from high-level positions in business, such as supervisor, manager or executive, and other professions such as physician, lawyer or engineer. Today, more women have entered all of these positions, but the use of sexist language has tended to retard the willingness of people to hire them.

It's easy to change the sentences we just looked at to remove sexism. In the first one, you simply eliminate each "his."

Everyone in school knows when it's his time to deliver his senior thesis.

Everyone in school knows when it's time to deliver a senior thesis.

In the second example, get rid of "he has," and you have not changed the meaning of the sentence at all. In fact, you've improved it.

Each bank manager knows what he has to do in case of a robbery.
Each bank manager knows what to do in case of a robbery.

In the third example, all you need do is pluralize this old and stale proverb.

He who laughs last, laughs loudest.
They who laugh last, laugh loudest.

One way to eliminate sexism in old proverbs is to simply ax the "he" without replacing it. Doing so can add a poetic feel to the phrase. One person who apparently agreed with this was George Norlin, whose name adorns the library of the University of Colorado at Boulder. Beneath the carved letters identifying the Norlin Library is an equally impressively carved "Who knows only his own generation remains always a child."

Unfortunately, Norlin didn't get rid of the "his," but he lived in a time when sexist language had not yet become much of an issue. Let's see what we can do with the pronouncement. First, let's try it his way:

"Who knows only one's own generation remains always a child."

The main problem with this solution is that the use of "one" as a pronoun, although quite acceptable among the British, sounds needlessly stiff in conversational American English. Let's apply another remedy for sexist language:

"Who knows only his or her own generation remains always a child."

We are forced to use the phrases "his or her," "he or she" or "him or her" once in a while, but such a combination tends to stop the reader dead in his or her tracks. So now let's try the plural solution:

"They who know only their own generation remain always children."

We lost some of the poetry, didn't we? You could also re-place "they" with "those" for a slightly different effect.

There appear to be times when, because of the peculiarities of American English, we are forced to use a variation of "he or she." For example:

"Everyone had the identical expression on their face."

Here, pluralizing simply doesn't work because "everyone" (and "everybody") is technically a singular pronoun. If you want to see lovers of correct language cringe, just stick "their" into a sentence that begins with "everyone" or "everybody". We could use "his or hers" or "hers or his," but the usage would be awkward enough to interrupt the flow and rhythm that keeps the reader with us.

Regardless, what we cannot do with these kinds of sentences is use "his" by itself. Instead, we need to opt between our four choices: "their," which can be bad English; "his or her," which can kill elegant use of the language; and "one," which can sound unnecessarily stuffy and rewriting the sentence to avoid singular pronouns.

An American Dilemma?

Other countries seem to have an easier time using nonsexist language. It seems to be acutely an American issue.

The British, for example, have an easier time pluralizing than Americans do. The reason is that the British treat collective nouns as inherent plurals.

For example, Americans might find it awkward to say, "The government has come out in favor of motherhood, and it says it will continue to do so," because the government is an abstract administrative group. Using "it" to refer to "the people in the government" sounds strange, especially when "it" speaks.

The British, however, would say, "The government have come out foursquare in favor of motherhood, and they say they will continue to do so." It's understood that the government is — the government are — made up of a bunch of people who, apparently in this case, all agree. Similarly in Great Britain, corporations takes the verb "are" and the pronoun "they." In the United States, such constructions would be considered poor English.

Like Americans, British treat "everyone" and "everybody" as singular pronouns. Perhaps this is because of the way they treat collective nouns, so that "everyone ... are ... they" doesn't sound as jarring to them.

Other Germanic and Romance languages don't seem to have quite the same problem with gender specification because their languages regularly use singular, gender-neutral pronouns. As we discussed, "one" can sound stuffy in English — as in, "one should brush one's teeth regularly." However, in many languages, this type of pronoun is part of everyday speech. (Even though they deal with gender nouns all the time, that doesn't mean they're not concerned with sexist issues, too.)

Other languages also deal with sexist language differently because many of them are riddled with gender references already. In Romance languages, for example, nouns take on genders seemingly at random. In Spanish, the table ("la mesa") is female. In French, the table ("le table") is masculine, as it is in German ("der Tisch"). None of the gender tags for nouns seem to carry any psychological weight.

So until American English uses gender-neutral pronouns naturally, the formula is this: Pluralize whenever you can, use variations of "he or she" when you must, but avoid sexist language. (See Chapter 8, toward the end of the "Business Jargon" section, for more on this topic.)

In her book "Origins of the Specious: Myths and Misconceptions of the English Language," Patricia T. O'Connor writes,

> What we need is an all-purpose pronoun for people that can be masculine or feminine, singular or plural. As it turns out, we once did have such a word. For hundreds of years, people used "they," "them," or "their" to refer to people in general, whether one or more, male or female. ... Great writers, including Shakespeare, Defoe, Swift, Fielding, Richardson, Goldsmith, and Johnson all made great use of the sexless, numberless "they/them/their" without raising eyebrows.

O'Connor, a former editor of The New York Times Book Review, refers to a grammarian, Lindley Murray, who in 1795 determined

> that it was a violation of good English to use the plural pronouns "they" and company to refer to technically singular words. ... He insisted "their" should be "his" and "they" should be "he." The idea caught on with other popular grammarians, who saw English in black and white, and were uncomfortable with the gray area occupied by "they."

O'Connor, who wrote the book with her husband, journalist Stewart Kellerman, reports that the 11th edition of Merriam-Webster's Collegiate Dictionary "already includes the singular 'they' as standard English," but The American Heritage Dictionary of the English Language does not.

"Eventually, the fate of 'they' will be decided by the ladies and gentlemen of the jury — the people who actually speak the language," she says. O'Connor admits that she goes through some "verbal contortions" to "deal with the problem."

Your Antecedents Are Showing: Dangling Participles and Misplaced Modifiers

As the section on redundancy demonstrates, it isn't difficult to use the English language in a comical way, but writers usually prefer not to be the subject of their readers' laughter.

When writers violate rule 20 in Strunk and White's The Elements of Style (which is "Keep related words together"), they risk falling into the most ludicrous pitfall in the English language. In a complex sentence, if the subject does not closely follow the antecedent (the word, phrase or clause that begins the sentence) strange things can happen.

The writer can end up with a misplaced modifier. The most common is a dangling participle. (A participle is a word that can function as a verb or an adjective, and it usually ends in -ing.)

Some well-known examples of dangling participles come from Strunk and White, this time as examples of how to violate their rule 11: "A participial phrase at the beginning of a sentence must refer to the grammatical subject."

Here are three famous examples of misplaced modifiers from Strunk and White:

Being in a dilapidated condition, I was able to buy the house very cheap.

Wondering irresolutely what to do next, the clock struck twelve.

As a mother of five, with another on the way, my ironing board is always up.

Here are some examples loosely translated from some student papers, with a little advice on how to make them come out right.

Once defrosted, we add pumpkin to the other ingredients.
Once the pumpkin is defrosted, we add it to the other ingredients.
(We couldn't have done it earlier, when we were frozen.)

Police said a patrol officer was issuing tickets when he noticed a Jeep Cherokee with Minnesota license plates wanted in a double homicide.
Police said a patrol officer was issuing tickets when he noticed a Jeep Cherokee with Minnesota license plates, apparently driven by a suspect wanted in a double homicide.

Lighting a cigarette, a small prop plane passed overhead.
As she lit a cigarette, a small prop plane passed overhead.

Occasionally, you hear a car drive by. It could be another bad muffler.
Occasionally you hear a car driving by. It could be another one with a bad muffler.

Admitting that there were many questions concerning the body that would never be answered, the body gives many clues to scientists.
Many questions about the body will never be answered, but the body does give scientists many clues. (Is the body capable of confessing anything?)

The following misplaced modifiers come from a Northwestern University law professor, Steven Lubet, who collects misplaced modifiers as some people collect Elvis memorabilia.

"The late astronomer Carl Sagan began researching the origins of life in the 1960s."

"Sen. Richard Durbin (D-Ill.) pledged to work for increased gun control in his campaign."

Lubet notes that a foundation advertised that it had been "working to make economics understandable for 50 years." He says he'd be happy "if someone would make economics understandable for half an hour."

Another list of misplaced modifiers comes from "The Suspended Sentence" by Roscoe Born:

From Fortune magazine: "Hewlett-Packard has just introduced a $4,995 personal computer for engineers with a nine-inch electro-luminescent screen."

From the Los Angeles Times: "In 1935 he joined the embryonic Basie Group and remained with what many consider the greatest jazz organization until 1948."

From The Boston Globe: "As lead singer Paul Redman pranced on the stage, a woman, perhaps 70, smiled and watched, her hair drawn back in a tight bun and dressed in a widow's black."

From The Detroit News: "Feikens is to make a final decision on how the contractors, Vista and Michigan Disposal Inc., can continue to haul Detroit sludge in a meeting next Monday with their lawyers."

Writing Directly, Without Apology; Avoiding Tiptoe (or Weasel Words)

Just as the pompous writer loses the trust of the reader, so does the writer who treats the reader as a god. If writers can't or won't communicate with readers at eye level, one human being to another human being, they risk losing those readers.

Pomposity turns off readers for obvious reasons. Few people like to be preached at or told they aren't as good or erudite as the writer. The writer who is subservient to the reader sends a message that is more subtle, but no less damaging. This message says, "I am afraid to be honest with you, so I'm going to tiptoe." Vague words such as "sort of" are not often accurate descriptions of a degree of similarity. The honest writer writes directly to the reader, without apology.

We'll talk more about honesty — and the appearance of honesty — in Chapter 7. But here are some examples of how to avoid using tiptoe words, or "weasel" words:

Teachers need to be motivated to teach a little better than they are doing.
Teachers need to be encouraged to teach better.
    (Or)
Teachers need a reason to teach better.

The wind came from the north. It almost seemed to dance through the tree branches.
The north wind danced through the tree branches.

The lawn mower seems to have created its own sculpture with its uneven movements.
The mower's uneven movements have created their own sculpture.
(Note the misplaced modifier in the example. According to the writer, the sculpture is moving.)

Compared with her neighbors, she is relatively new to the West.
Compared with her neighbors, she is new to the West.

The National Weather Service predicts showers around 100 percent likely on Friday.
The National Weather Service says it is 100 percent sure Friday will bring showers.
(Bettors of sure things wouldn't want to risk their money on something that was "around" 100 percent. Also, "around" is a geographic term. If a word is necessary to measure a quantity, "about" works better.)

She says she is a little nervous.
She says she is nervous.

She kind of shelved some of the hopes she had.
She shelved some of her hopes.

Other tiptoe words include "aspect," "area," "numerous" and "probably," plus cute versions of "a little" such as "a tad," "a skosh," "a hair" and "a wee bit."

Replenishing the Word Supply

As noted in Chapter 1, English's huge vocabulary can be the language's curse because it gives pompous, dishonest or sloppy writers so much opportunity to misuse words. But if you have the opposite problem — your vocabulary is lean — then don't feel alone. Work to strengthen it. Here are some examples of imprecision:

And Jesus healed the leopards.

The governors kept the king on his thrown.

Fans pay exuberant *sums of money to watch NBA games.*

The hurricane reeked *haddock.*

He was at her every beckon call.

... the trill *of victory*

Only your tows *are touching the mat.*

Many pro-life supporters believe that life begins at contraception.

The strict dress code was the one stat chute *he didn't regularly abide by. Often* dawning *the torn slacks and wrinkly undone cotton dress shirt, he appeared to be dressed in the fashion of characters in Oliver Twist.*

To avoid these mistakes, writers should work to improve their practical vocabularies. One technique is to develop a meaningful relationship with a dictionary and to place a copy of Roget's Thesaurus within reach of your keyboard.

I would add an additional piece of advice: Get in the habit of working crossword puzzles. Start with easy ones. Solving crossword puzzles isn't an efficient way to add to your vocabulary — among the words you learn will be dozens you'll never use — but it will make you more skillful in coming up with the right word on demand. As many copy editors will tell you, crossword puzzles provide excellent language calisthenics.

We'll be doing some more fine-tuning of deathless prose in Chapter 9. In the next chapter, however, we'll examine two ways of writing with strength, economy, clarity and integrity: the use of active voice and action verbs.

Chapter 5 Exercises

A. Wordiness.

Edit or rewrite these sentences to eliminate unneeded words.

1. The ice has melted, and the water has taken on the kind of bright blue color that is more likely to be seen in the South Pacific.

2. We are starting to approach the library, which I notice is quite a large building.

3. We can see that whether or not you feel like adding salt to the pot of soup, the salinity level will be more than we need to establish that sodium poisoning can be a possibility.

4. She made the decision to vote in favor of the liquidation of the corporation.

5. She is in fact interested in the broadcast media; this idea came about by a stray remark made by one of her high school teachers. She felt high school was "definitely" a place that this all started when the teacher said, "You have the nicest voice I've ever heard."

6. He has often been giving reviews of movies.

7. He does not believe that many people think that language skills are of much value.

8. I would like to call your attention to the fact that, in spite of the fact that this mountain highway is curving, your car is in the process of going straight.

Sometimes wordiness and redundancy amount to the same thing. Here are a couple of examples for you to edit or rewrite:

9. They are considering San Antonio as a possible home for the future.

10. Dr. Malone is currently at the hospital, where he is engaged in the delicate surgery involved in removing a patient's tonsils.

B. Misplaced modifiers.

See if you can straighten out these sentences and place the modifiers where they belong.

1. Lighting a cigarette, a small prop plane passed overhead.

2. Two people, including a 15-year-old boy who was in critical condition, were shot as they walked along an Atlanta street Thursday.

3. Turning the corner, the jackhammer grew louder and louder until we were hit by a shattering crescendo.

4. Single, no children, age 28 is thinking of children at a later time in her life.

5. Since 1927, it's been illegal in Maryland to shoot waterfowl under the influence of drugs or alcohol. (Source: the Chesapeake Bay Maritime Museum, St. Michael's, Md.)

6. Once defrosted, we add pumpkin to the other ingredients.

7. The late Carl Sagan began researching the origins of life in the 1960s.

8. While touring the Louvre, the paintings of several French impressionists came into his view.

9. U.S. Sen. Mitch McConnell (R-Ky.) pledged to fight campaign finance reform during his campaign.

10. In 1935, he joined the embryonic Basie group and remained with what many consider the greatest jazz organization until 1948.

C. Redundancies

Edit or rewrite these sentences or phrases to eliminate redundancy.

1. Some of these projects include:

2. The Defense Department spokeswoman said the Army is not sure at this stage how it will integrate the new tank program.

3. She lived overseas for five years and crisscrossed Europe and Asia as well.

4. She says she hopes to eventually own her own magazine in the future.

5. Walking by the alley, he got the unpleasant smell of garbage.

6. He has obtained both a bachelor's degree at Pepperdine University as well as Master of Business Administration at the University of Michigan Graduate School of Business.

7. He grew up in Salt Lake City throughout his lifetime.

8. A circuit court judge set a $900,0000 bond Wednesday for an 18-year-old man charged with killing two men dead and wounding another.

9. In addition, he also edits the sports pages.

10. Not only is the play still showing in London, but it is also on tour in the United States.

Active Voice, Action Verbs

The Relationship of Active Voice and Action Verbs

Active voice might be the least understood element in English that people mistakenly think they understand. It's even more common to get using active voice confused with using action verbs. Many editors have difficulty keeping them straight.

The two aren't actually related; they just sound as if they are. It doesn't help that a sentence written in active voice can include a "being" (or action) verb:

"Assam is an Indian state."

And a sentence written in passive (non-active) voice can include an action verb:

"Nicholas O'Herlihy was named after his maternal grandfather, a Russian."

Active voice and action verbs do have one thing in common: They contribute to strong, honest, direct writing.

If the agent of a sentence performs the action, the sentence is in active voice. Active voice is the exact opposite of the sentence-wrecker known as passive voice. Here's an example of passive voice: "The truck was struck by the train."

The truck is the subject of the sentence, but the train is the creator of the action. This means the sentence is in passive voice. Here's the same sentence in active voice: "The train struck the truck."

Now the subject has switched roles. No longer is it receiving the action. The train has become the subject, and it is creating the action. This is active voice.

Notice that by switching to active voice we have eliminated a verb, "was," and a preposition, "by." Together these words made the sentence 40 percent longer. This is not an unusual result of passive voice and is one reason good writers avoid it when they can. There are at least two other reasons for using active voice.

For example, you come across a convoluted sentence that seems to start off in several directions and ends up going nowhere. Take a close look at it. The writer probably began writing the sentence in passive voice. Few other forms of sloppy writing produce such muddiness.

Working on newspapers even allowed him to open up other opportunities, such as being a reporter nominated by his teacher for a news company to the Republican National Convention the year it was held in Minnesota, where he had grown up.

This sentence does begin in active voice, but in the second clause, it falls down. Try dividing it into three sentences:

Working on newspapers allowed him other opportunities. A teacher nominated him to report for a news organization from the Republican National Convention the year it was in Minnesota. That's where he grew up.

Active Voice and Honesty

Another reason to use active voice is that it's more honest. Active voice makes the agent responsible for the action. Passive voice is a way to avoid responsibility. At least three recent U.S. presidents — Ronald Reagan, Bill Clinton and George W. Bush — have used the identical, passive-voice phrase in an attempt to deflect criticism and embarrassment and to avoid responsibility: "Mistakes were made." What this phrase means is, "It wasn't my fault. I didn't do it. Someone else did."

In "When Words Collide," Lauren Kessler and Duncan McDonald offer two situations in which passive voice must be used. First, passive voice is justified if the receiver of the action is more important than the creator of the action. They use this example:

"A priceless Rembrandt painting was stolen from the Metropolitan Museum of Art yesterday by three men posing as janitors."

Here, the Rembrandt should remain the subject of the sentence even though it receives the action. The painting is obviously more important — thus more newsworthy — than the three men who stole it.

The second reason for using passive voice is if the writer has no choice. This occurs when the writer doesn't know who or what the creator of the action is. Here's the example Kessler and McDonald use: "The cargo was damaged during the trans-Atlantic flight."

Air turbulence? Sabotage? Was the cargo strapped in properly? The writer doesn't know, so the voice must be passive.

One final note, a specialized one: When reporting a police or court event during which someone is charged with a misdemeanor or felony, we usually deliver the word "charged" in passive voice. It's possible to say "police charged a woman with murder," but this is usually inaccurate because the police aren't doing the charging.

Charging is a process that involves prosecutors. In the United States, this means district attorneys or state's attorneys or their assistants. Since the journalist most often does not know exactly who is doing the charging, it's considered proper to say, "The woman was charged with first-degree murder," even though the sentence is in passive voice.

Active Voice, Clarity and Crispness

Active voice is direct, honest and economical. But mostly, active voice is considerate of readers, of their limited time and of their need for clear, crisp, concise information. Passive voice is one reason many people swear off how-to books on computing, carpentry or cooking; they come across instructions such as this:

> First, a pair of chopsticks is placed on top of a pot of water. Then, the asparagus is put inside a wicker basket and the basket is placed on top of the chopsticks. The water is brought to a boil, and the asparagus is steamed for no more than 10 minutes, so a slight crunchiness is retained.

Passive voice seems to take so long to get it out. But when you turn these instructions into commands, using active voice, they become much more crisp and clear. The writer addresses the reader directly, with "you" implied.

> Place a pair of chopsticks on top of a pot of water. Put the asparagus inside a wicker basket and place the basket on top of the chopsticks. Bring the water to a boil and steam the asparagus for no more than 10 minutes, so it retains a slight crunchiness.

Here are some more examples of how active voice creates clarity:

After my clothes were on, I drove to the firehouse.
After I put my clothes on, I drove to the firehouse.

State lotteries are used to fund education.
State lotteries support education.

When examined in independent university studies with other leading cellular industry products, its high-efficiency design has been scientifically proven to reduce dropped calls and failed call attempts.
Independent university researchers compared it with other leading cellular products. They proved that its efficient design reduced dropped calls and failed call attempts.

You're driving to work and it is announced on the radio that the company you work for is completely breaking apart.
You're driving to work and the radio news reporter announces that the company you work for is breaking apart.
("Completely" is redundant. Review Chapter 5 for more on avoiding redundancies.)

Nothing but his heavy breathing can be heard by him, and only the distant oaks can be seen in the darkness.
He can hear nothing but his heavy breathing, and he can see only the distant oaks in the darkness.

The previous summer was spent by him at Exxon Mobil Corp.
He spent the previous summer at Exxon Mobil Corp.

Each week a different musical theme would be supported for a different cosmetic brand.
Each week a new musical theme would support a different cosmetic brand.

Passive voice not only robs sentences of clarity and economy, it buries the subject of the sentence. The reader finds it difficult to learn who or what is doing the action in a passive construction. It's the writer's job to make sure the subject is obvious.

By using chemicals and preserving the corpse at low temperatures, the necessary tests were conducted.

Pathologists preserved the corpse at low temperatures and used chemicals to conduct the necessary tests.

(Who is using the chemicals and preserving the corpse? In this case, the reporter knew but didn't say.)

Big words often are used to impress readers.
Writers often use big words to impress readers.

He was called into his supervisor's office.
His supervisor called him into her office.

Action Verbs and Imagery

In Chapters 1 and 5 we made a case for avoiding pompous writing, namely, sneer at your readers and they will make a point of avoiding what you write. One great way to write pompously is to use being verbs to drain the energy from your sentences, as done in these examples:

"I am hopeful that that solution to your predicament will prove to be an effective resolution to your problem."

What is this writer trying to say? The sentence was in trouble from the beginning. It starts with a being verb and a latinized adjective, "am hopeful." The writer could easily have replaced it with the action verb "hope." We also have "that that." Grammatically this is all right, but it's awkward. Then we read "will be an effective resolution to your problem." What is that clause doing there? The writer can write the sentence much more clearly this way: "I hope that solves your problem."

According to grammarians, action verbs and their opposites, being verbs, don't exist. What writers informally call action verbs, grammarians divide into two categories: transitive verbs and intransitive verbs. Transitive verbs move the action from the subject to the object of the sentence. Intransitive verbs sound active but have no object.

Transitive: "He drove the car."
Intransitive: "He swam."

What writers call being verbs, grammarians call linking verbs, because they link the subject with the object to describe a state of being: "You are beautiful."

It isn't a bad idea to become familiar with the nuances of transitive, intransitive and linking verbs. For the practical writer, however, it's enough to know that action verbs do things while being verbs simply are. Since action verbs add energy to sentences and being verbs usually sap sentences of energy, good writers prefer action verbs — transitive or intransitive.

Being (or Linking) Verbs

Being verbs are, were or have been. But they simply won't do.

Major League Baseball was the first sports organization to institute the concept of free agency for its players.
Major League Baseball created free agency.
(This sentence was also too wordy.)

Action verbs serve English best when they replace a noun — especially one that just sits there as a reflection of the subject and the beneficiary of a being verb. (Grammarians call this type of noun a predicate nominative.) In the next example, the verb "edits" takes the place of the predicated nominative: the editor. In the replacement process, we also manage to extract another freeloader: the preposition "of."

He is the editor of two magazines.
He edits two magazines.

We can't always depend on action verbs to eliminate words. Sometimes they actually add words but, as in the next example, allow a little paring later in the sentence.

Officials of the Air Line Pilots Association and United Airlines expressed satisfaction Friday with an almost unanimous vote by pilots in favor of a four-year wage agreement.
Officials of the Air Line Pilots Association and United Airlines said Friday they are satisfied by the pilots' near-unanimous vote for a four-year wage agreement.

Here are more examples:

She is a self-proclaimed renaissance woman.
She calls herself a renaissance woman.

Every year there is a race along the Inca Trail.
Each year a race takes place along the Inca Trail.
(See "Special Red Flags" in Chapter 9.)

She is still in need of instruction and practice.
She still needs instruction and practice.

The next example obviously has much going against it, and the use of an action verb won't solve the larger problem of a clumsily written sentence. But we can begin the editing process by using an action verb, "cite." Let's pick our way through it and see if we can make this sentence make sense:

Officials with the Attorney Registration and Disciplinary Committee have said similar representations of tax clients in which city officials opposed the city, even indirectly, have been found against legal ethics.

Officials of the Attorney Registration and Disciplinary Committee cite similar cases. When lawyers who hold civic office file legal action against the city, they will be found to have violated legal ethics — even if their involvement in the lawsuit is indirect.

But let's back up for a moment. Can our pickiness doom journalistic prose?

Creativity Killers?

Journalists aren't supposed to make things up, but this doesn't mean they can't be creative in the way they present their facts. A slavish, literal adherence to the rules (such as those in this chapter, Chapter 5 and Chapter 9) can kill creativity.

Consider how one of the 20th century's great wordsmiths, H.L. Mencken, put it in "A Book of Prefaces." For someone "with an ear for verbal delicacies who: ... searches painfully for the perfect word, and puts the way of saying a thing above the thing said — there is in writing the constant joy of sudden discovery, of happy accident."

A dictum such as this, from a man whose fame derived from the way he wrote editorial columns — he admitted he was not an unbiased reporter — might provide a quandary for journalists today. It would seem that good journalism dictates that content reigns — that the "thing said" should always outrank the "way of saying it." But we can take solace from the fact that the two rarely collide. Any perusal of Pulitzer Prize-winning articles will convince the reader that fairness and good writing need not compete.

Mencken could simply be saying that writers should never get so picky with their content or prose that they kill the great joy that comes from writing and discovering that they have developed that elusive thing called "style."

Few of the rules of journalism are so absolute that they cannot be ignored or broken. If you do break a rule, though, make it a conscious crime. Make sure you know why you're doing it. One definition of professional journalists — or any professionals — is that they know the rules well enough to know when to break them.

Chapter 6 Exercises

A. Passive to active voice

Edit or rewrite the following sentences, changing the voice from passive to active:

1. The suspects were arrested by California Highway Patrol officers.

2. The Oscars were provided by the Academy of Motion Pictures Arts and Sciences.

3. The report concluded that perhaps $10 billion a year is added to the U.S. economy by immigrants, legal and illegal.

4. It would be illegal and unfair for welfare recipients to be forced to work for less than the minimum wage, according to labor unions and advocates for the poor.

5. A soul-infused tone was set by the singer for the evening.

6. Penalties against the National Basketball Association team were upheld Friday by a U.S. district judge, hours before the players faced the sixth game of their NBA playoffs finals.

7. The quality of apples in southern Pennsylvania is enhanced by the state's soil and climate, she said.

8. The book said the threat of war is often used as intimidation.

9. The operation of the commuter airline has been suspended by the Federal Aviation Administration.

10. An increase of more than 600 points was registered by the Dow Jones Industrial Average as the result of reports of a recent upsurge of mortgage lending by major banks.

B. Being verbs to action verbs

Edit or rewrite the following sentences and transform the being verbs into action verbs without altering the meaning of the sentences.

1. The president said he is hopeful the talks will lead to an accord.
2. Privately, officials say they are doubtful that the two sides will ever get together.
3. She has been a teacher for 14 years.
4. The blood bank is in need of more donations, especially of "O" negative.
5. He is the self-proclaimed first citizen of the new regime.
6. The forest fire was being contained by smokejumpers from the Oglala Sioux nation who were flown in. [This sentence needs active voice as well as an action verb.]
7. It is "more than likely" that there was a conspiracy, according to the prosecutor.
8. County officials are in review of records of a day care center where a 10-month-old boy died from what they believe was shaken-baby syndrome.
9. The Milwaukee Brewers are in anticipation of winning a National League championship, but their goal is bigger than that.
10. Journalists are sworn to say that no matter what goes wrong, it isn't their fault.

An Appearance of Honesty

Journalistic Ethics: An Oxymoron?

To many people who are not in the news business — and to some who are — "journalistic ethics" is an oxymoron, a contradiction in terms. Many go after the cheap scoop, especially when in pursuit of celebrity melodrama. So we might excuse readers, viewers and listeners for wondering what reporters give up in exchange for their scoops, and whether ethics aren't at the top of that list.

In fact, for most of the mainstream news media, journalistic ethics do exist. They are even spelled out and enforced. Reporters and editors lose their jobs if they violate those ethics. Most good journalists carry a gut-level, regardless-of-consequences, raw sense of honesty with them — some carry it to the point of being rude.

Professional reporters and editors must be unwaveringly honest; it's a job requirement. But because of a strange path that logic takes, it's even more important that their writing have the appearance of honesty. Honesty and the appearance of honesty are not always the same thing. From an ethics standpoint, honesty is obviously more important than the appearance of it. But readers, viewers and listeners have no idea if the writer is honest or not. They can only respond to appearance. Because of this, the appearance becomes more important.

What sounds honest sometimes isn't, and history is littered with charlatans who took advantage of people who didn't know the difference. These charlatans typically use clear language — the kind that is encouraged for good writing — to defraud and misguide their followers. Sometimes it isn't even conscious fraud. Many writers and orators don't know the difference themselves, and they have managed to gull themselves as well as their followers.

Most recently, such chicanery has found its way into journalism, and it has not restricted itself to tabloid newspapers. At its most raw, supermarket tabloids use it to trick unsophisticated readers into believing stories about aliens or celebrities or people with strange growths on their bodies. Style can overcome credibility in the nation's most sophisticated newspapers, not just "attitude" tabloids such as the New York Post. Even the stately New York Times has recently found itself following after the coverage of sensational news by tabloids such as the National Enquirer, whose "reporters" blanket such stories.

Training people in the art of using language to sound honest is not the same thing as teaching them to be honest. Doing so might be akin to teaching miners how to use explosives, knowing that a few miners might go on to become terrorists. In this sense, clear, informal, conversational language is a tool, just as explosives are. Honest-sounding words and expressions can be used for good or ill. But there is something else we can be sure of: Pompous, overblown English is an inadequate tool for communication, honest or otherwise.

A Passion for Accuracy

Nearly a century ago, someone at the City News Bureau of Chicago (which was a prime training ground for new reporters) coined a phrase that has since become a newsroom cliché: If your mother says she loves you, check it out. Most people in the news business take dictums such as this quite seriously. Many journalists remember instructors who reacted to a single misspelled word by calling it an error of fact and giving a student an "F" for the whole story.

To a professional journalist, few things are more embarrassing than inaccurate copy, and few should be. The key ingredients of accuracy are honesty, specificity and depth of questioning and investigation. The chief opponents of accuracy are dishonesty, exaggeration, overgeneralization and the shallow acceptance of what appears to be factual — most often in pursuit of an unrealistic deadline.

Some inaccurate reports are simply a matter of typographical errors that the computer's spellchecker could not be expected to highlight. For example, one student recently referred to a well-known civil rights leader as "Martian Luther King."

Here are more examples of inaccuracies:

The common cold infects more than 1 billion people a year in the United States.
(The U.S. population is about 300 million.)

Haystacks were a favorite subject of impressionist painter Claude Manet.
(It was Claude Monet. The impressionist with a similar name was Edouard Manet.)

...Mainz University in Austria.
(Mainz is in Germany.)

In many countries such as Africa, AIDS has become an epidemic.
(If Africa is a country, what continent is it on?)

Gettysburg was the greatest battle ever fought, not only in Virginia, but in the Western Hemisphere.
(Gettysburg is in Pennsylvania.)

Before Sept. 11, 2001, experts called the Cashmere region between India and Pakistan the greatest potential threat to world peace.

(It's the Kashmir region.)

The Giants won the superball.

(Super Bowl)

He has visited several foreign countries, such as Canada, France, Germany and New Mexico.

(If you need help with this one, find a map of the Southwestern United States.)

The New Deal was a populist political and economic plan offered by the administration of Theodore Roosevelt.

(Right family, wrong president. It was Franklin Roosevelt. They were distant cousins.)

A Goodrich blimp flies overhead, advertising Sea World.

(It's the Goodyear Blimp.)

Sometimes it's obvious that a typo prevented the reporter from writing the right sentence. In this case, the writer might be excused if he or she were anything but calm:

A clam slowly fell over me.

Avoiding Generalizations, Assumptions, Pomposity and Overblown Statements

Getting the facts right is only one way to be accurate. To be truly accurate, the presentation of facts must be as concrete as it can be, with as little ambiguity as the writer can manage with the subject. The less specific the subject matter is, the more a writer must work to avoid ambiguity.

A political consultant once confided to a reporter that when his colleagues talked with journalists, they would double the estimated size of the crowds that greeted their candidates. Why? Because they knew that skeptical journalists would automatically take their head counts and cut them in half. This particular consultant, however, did not share their enthusiasm.

"That's ridiculous," he said. "What they really should do is not estimate the crowd at 5,000, but go for a specific number, like 4,568. That's more believable, and you guys will accept it."

Moral of the story: Reporters should take their own head count and not rely on political operatives to do their work for them. But the point is still made; the more specific the information, the more believable it seems. This is a philosophy that underlies journalistic writing; it shuns the generic and goes for the concrete. Here are some examples that lack this level of specificity:

He attends Queens University in Ontario, Canada.
(Ontario is a province, like a state in the United States. Where in Ontario?)

She wrote a freelance story for the local paper.
(What is the newspaper's name?)

His basic training was in Texas. Then he was stationed in California.
(The writer picked the two most populous states in the union, and both are geographically diverse. Tell the reader where in Texas and where in California.)

Tennis players fill the lighted court with activity.
("Activity" is a generic word. Describe it, and do it with nouns and action verbs, not adjectives and adverbs.)

Euphemisms: When Tact and Truth Don't Agree

One way to avoid total honesty is to use euphemisms. The New Webster's Dictionary and Thesaurus of the English Language defines euphemism" as "the use of a pleasant, polite or harmless-sounding word or expression to mask harsh, rude or infamous truths."

Journalists take pride in avoiding euphemisms, and as a result they are often considered harsh and rude. But it is true that news professionals avoid reporting that someone "passed away" when a person died. Instead, journalists often snicker at the ostentatious use of politically correct terms, such as referring to the blind as "visually challenged." One inside joke is to call someone "mendacious" when what we really mean is "liar."

In "The Language of Argument," Daniel McDonald and Larry W. Burton call euphemisms "purr words," as opposed to "snarl words."

> For generations, minorities have been insulted with snarl words. They were called *niggers*, *spicks*, *broads*, *queers*, *fatties*, *old geezers*, *retards*, *gimps*, and so on. To avoid this (and, indeed, to compensate for it), academics, ethnic voices, and social critics have produced a new vocabulary to discuss minority groups. We now speak of *African-Americans*, *Hispanics*, *spokespersons*, *people of color*, *alternative life styles*, *senior citizens*, *people of size*, and individuals who are *physically challenged* or *intellectually challenged*.

> As a writer, you can expect problems in this area. Of course, you want to use politically correct language where you can. First, because it is the civilized thing to do, and second because there is a broad audience that expects it. It's a mistake to offend someone you don't want to offend.

> But don't let political correctness cripple your prose. You still want to write with specific details. You want to sound like a speaking voice. Therefore, you shouldn't write, "At

school yesterday, I talked to an African American, a senior citizen, and two people of size. One had a child who is physically challenged." This language calls too much attention to itself, and your reader won't know what you're talking about. You can do better than this.

Political correctness is a worthy goal, but it can be a minefield for writers and persuaders. Walk with care.

(You can review this topic in the "Sexist Language versus Good English" section of Chapter 5.)

A fine but fuzzy line exists between being polite and being dishonest. As the late S.I. Hayakawa demonstrated in his classic book on semantics, "Language in Thought and Action," Americans have a history of keeping the line fuzzy.

Words having to do with anatomy and sex — and words even vaguely suggesting anatomical or sexual matters — have, especially in American culture, remarkably affective connotations. Ladies of the nineteenth century could not bring themselves to say "breast" or "leg" — not even of chicken — so that the terms "white meat" and "dark meat" were substituted. It was thought inelegant to speak of "going to bed," and "to retire" was used instead. In rural America there are many euphemisms for the word "bull"; among them are "he-cow," "cow-critter," "male cow," and "gentleman cow." But Americans are not alone in their delicacy about such matters. When D.H. Lawrence's first novel, "The White Peacock" (1911), was published, the author was widely and vigorously criticized for having used (in innocuous context) the word "stallion." "Our hearts are warm, our bellies full" was changed to "Our hearts are warm and we are full" in a 1962 presentation of the Rodgers and Hammerstein musical "Carousel" before the British Royal Family.

Hayakawa did find some redeeming social value in verbal taboos. He wrote that uttering forbidden words "provides us with a relatively harmless verbal substitute for going berserk and smashing furniture; that is, the words act as a kind of a safety valve in our moments of crisis." (I can say with some authority that Hayakawa obviously never enlisted in the U.S. Navy, where sailors apparently face continual moments of crisis.)

In "Copy Editing for Professionals," Edmund Rooney and Oliver Witte define euphemism as a "polite expression for an impolite idea." They continue:

Euphemisms are offenses against plain speech and clear communication, which is why bureaucrats and the politically correct love them.

Only the CIA could make laughable a chilling expression like *terminate with extreme prejudice*. Even *intelligence* is a euphemism for *spying* and perhaps also for *killing*.

When words become polluted, we discard them and move on to pollute new words.

Opposed to war? The United States abolished it a long time ago when the *War* Department was renamed the *Defense* Department. Its mission hasn't changed, but somehow people are more comfortable for what it does. The AP takes a middle position: Don't call it *defense spending*, the Stylebook warns; say *military spending*.

Having fouled *Welfare*, we renamed the department *Human Services* and everyone feels good better about giving and receiving *public* assistance.

Perhaps those who have been fired from their jobs would be more accepting if they understood that they participated in corporate *downsizing*. It didn't take long for *downsizing* to acquire a bad name (*down* has an unfavorable connotation), so the term became *rightsizing*.

1995 marked the year genocide was banished; now it's called *ethnic cleansing*.

Athletes at one university no longer play games; they engage in *athletic competition*, according to mail from the athletic department.

You don't have an obsolete computer; you have a *legacy* computer.

Fudge Marks: How Not to Embellish Your Prose

Embellishing your copy with **boldface,** <u>underlining</u>, *italics*, ALL CAPS and exclamation points!!! are sure ways to make the reader doubt your sincerity. Instead of persuading readers that your report is important, you're telling them, "I'm too lazy to come up with the precise word that will communicate the idea, concept, opinion or emotion I want to convey, so I'm going to design my message to shout at you." Such usages are akin to going to war in cardboard tanks. It is the way you put words together, not their ornamental embellishments, that determines the strength of your copy.

A more practical reason exists for the journalistic prohibition of underlining and italics. In the days before computers, it was impossible to convey such embellishments in Morse code or, later, on the keyboards available on a Teletype machine. Even now, these typographic designs are not available on all typesetting equipment.

Another way to lose your readers is by misusing quotation marks. They should only be used for quotations or to highlight terms that the writer is defining and pretty sure the reader is not familiar with. Most other uses of quotation marks tell the readers that you don't really mean what you're saying. Retailers are especially fond of misusing quote marks. The phrase "We Aim to Please," embellished with quote marks looks like an ironic statement; they're just saying that, or they're quoting someone else who is saying that.

Yet another way to persuade readers that you don't know what you're talking about is to use some form of "et cetera," "etc.," "and so on and so forth" or "and stuff." By adding this type of appendage to a list, you're telling the reader, "I can't think of anything more, but I can fool you into thinking I can."

Of Opinion and Ethics: The Elusiveness of Truth

Journalists take themselves seriously. They talk about their mission to communicate the truth and their duty to report with objectivity. Truth, however, is elusive. Because truth deals with conclusions and values, each person has a different interpretation of what truth is.

It is journalism's job to provide facts, concepts, ideas and emotions — as we sense them — but not conclusions. Conclusions are what the reader, listener or viewer comes to.

Objectivity, supposedly the soul of journalism, simply does not exist. The moment a reporter uses his or her sense of newsworthiness to decide what to keep in a story and what to leave out, objectivity has vanished. (You can review this in Chapter 2.) What passes for objectivity becomes the reporter taking the job of a tape recorder — methodically taking down what was said and making no effort to check its veracity. Nor does such a "reporter" make any effort to get another point of view.

Better that we, as journalists, pursue attainable goals: accuracy, balance and fairness without bias. That we can do. Not only can — we must.

There is, however, a place in the news for honest opinion. In most newspapers, opinion takes three forms: editorials, letters to the editor and the op-ed pages. The opinions of the publisher, editor or editorial board become editorials, which are typically four- to five-paragraph statements of what the newspaper executives believe. Often on the same page, letters from opinionated readers find their way into print; they're usually labeled as "letters to the editor." On the op-ed page are columns that are local and nationally or internationally syndicated, written by staff writers and freelancers. These pieces might or might not agree with the newspaper's own opinions.

But only the most biased or irresponsible publications allow their opinions to slop over into the news pages.

Don't Editorialize Unless You Are Writing a Column or Editorial

Here are some examples of editorializing seeping into news:

Anyone who has been to the State Driver's License Bureau suspects that this is where the winners of both political parties have deposited loyal supporters who were not qualified to do anything else.

(This is quite an assumption, and a plausible one, but it isn't the reporter's job to make assumptions of any kind. It would be better to get this opinion as a quotation from someone who has just walked out the Driver's License Bureau door, then get someone in the bureau to refute it.)

Whether in trading, public relations or marketing, she will do fine. She has youth and perseverance on her side.

(Seasoned journalists will tell you it's dangerous to predict anything — she could get hit by a truck tomorrow. The folly was compounded by a reporter who had just met his subject and couldn't have predicted how she would do.)

During the past few months, a gaggle of corporate executives have succeeded in their attempt to encourage the investing public to turn their backs on Wall Street. Today, the machinations of yet another have emerged.

(First, "gaggle" is a gathering of geese. Although many a corporate executive might have earned the epithet "silly goose," using "gaggle" has convicted them all. Second, to imply that even the most avaricious of the executives wanted to discredit Wall Street is absurd; the slick ones count on people believing that the investment community is incapable of wrongdoing. Finally, by using the loaded word "machinations," the reporter has played judge and jury by convicting the most recent wrongdoer. None of that is the reporter's job.)

However — and this is a big "however" — don't be afraid to provide some analysis if you're covering a complicated issue. Just be sure of two things: that you truly understand the issue and that you back your analysis with assertions from people you've interviewed.

Here's a solid analytical lede from USA Today's Jim Drinkard and Kathy Kiely:

> WASHINGTON — Under a withering lobbying campaign that included calls from some of their biggest donors, Senate Democrats on Thursday shelved an attempt to tighten rules on the accounting treatment of stock options.

Without showing bias, Drinkard and Kiely combined two facts that apparently did belong together. The first was that lobbyists, including big donors, were busy working on Senate Democrats. The second was that the Senate majority party backed off from rules that might restrict the actions of such donors. Notice that the reporters refrained from writing that one caused the other; they left the conclusion to the reader.

Sometimes editorializing doesn't display the writer's opinion so much as it assumes that all people — writers and readers alike — think the same. The problematic implication is that anyone who doesn't think this way is obviously of a lower social order. One of the best examples of this kind of bad writing came in 2001 from Entertainment Weekly's EW.com. (It was so bad that the site has apparently since mended its ways.)

> Hollywood's newest power couple Cruised — or is that Cruzed? — the red carpet at last night's LA premiere of the new World War II romance "Captain Corelli's Mandolin." The erstwhile Mr. Kidman arrived with his gal pal, "Corell" ingénue Penelope Cruz. The two gleefully embraced and flashed miles of smiles to a wildly cheering crowd. And Cruz's onscreen leading man, Nicholas Cage, created a stir of his own, meeting up with his rumored new squeeze, Lisa Marie Presley.

"It's a little weird and kind of unnecessary," said Oscar winner and age buddy James Coburn ("Affliction") of all the love-life hoopla. "But I guess the gossip people and all those magazines just love this kind of stuff."

The biggest problem in this example is that the reporter didn't report, she gushed. Cruised and Cruzed? Avoid trying to impress readers with puns. "The erstwhile Mr. Kidman," is an insider reference to Tom Cruise's ex, Nicole Kidman, which haughtily implies that readers should already know the back-story. The phrase "flashed miles of smiles" is cliché. (You can review clichés in Chapter 8.) And then there is more breathless gushing over two more celebrities, Nicolas Cage and Lisa Marie Presley. At least the writer showed an awareness of the plastic in her own profession by including the Coburn quotation.

Respect the Reader

Making judgments and indulging in conclusions can have a deadly effect on your writing as well as your reputation for fairness and balance. It can lead to generalizations that make your copy bland and riddled with stereotypes. For example, if you begin by describing a youth as a "typical teenager," you abandon any attempt to later describe the youth's individual characteristics. Such a judgment, Hayakawa says, "prevents us from seeing what is directly in front of us, so that clichés take the place of fresh description."

Here are some examples of conclusions drawn unnecessarily for readers:

It is clear that while her career has been very challenging, it has also been extremely demanding.

(The writer should give examples and let the reader decide how challenging and demanding it is.)

American confidence is more than a state of mind; it is a mus-cle, a westward-ho-ing, atom-splitting, moon-landing muscle, and Osama bin Laden's autumn ambush, designed to break it, seemed only to make it stronger. The markets reopened within a week af-ter Sept. 11, swooned and then revived, and even as the fires still burned downtown and the soldiers headed off to war, more Ameri-cans said they believed the country was on the right track back in October than felt that way last week. Is it possible we could do to ourselves what our worst enemies did not manage?

The corporate criminals among us, the swindlers and the profi-teers, are now described in language once saved for bin Laden's le-gions. Business professors are staggered by the suicidal audacity of top executives — did they really think they would not be caught?

(In this example, the conclusion begins the actual story. The reader gets the feeling that the reporter is trying too hard to come up with an enticing lede. Rhetorical questions help to soften the writer's conclusions, but it's obvious what the writer believes.)

This sensitive, intuitive people-person feels that she has a cre-ative side that isn't being fully utilized.

(The writer should have quoted the interview subject and let the reader decide.)

People become disoriented from their friends due to their preoc-cupation with their significant others when they should be preoc-cupied with relationships with friends. It shifts to concern about their significant others' unhappiness as well as their own happi-ness.

(What does "it" mean in the last sentence? Here's a case in which the writer's attempt to draw conclusions leads only to confusion.)

His education includes a number of noteworthy accomplish-ments.

(Tell the reader what those accomplishments are and let the reader decide if they are noteworthy.)

She made the bold decision to quit her job and pursue academics full-time.
(Let your readers know what her circumstances were, and they can decide whether her decision was bold.)

Tragically, her father died when she was three.
(The reader is capable of determining that a father's death is tragic.)

There are 12 people playing tennis and, surprisingly, all are male.
(Why is that surprising?)

Students wander by. They have athletic builds, suggesting a fitness-minded generation.
(It also suggests a writer who belabors the obvious.)

The law school has a strange-looking blue piece of artwork in its lobby.
(Describe it in detail, and let the reader decide if it's strange.)

She has dabbled in things that few of us would even think of.
("Try me," we imagine the reader responding.)

Make Sure the Reader Knows What You're Writing About

There is a point when many reporters begin speaking a language that is not shared by the audience. This seems to happen most frequently with reporters who cover beats such as the police or politics for a long time. These writers begin to adopt the language of the people they are covering — a bureaucratic idiom that makes sense to them but few others.

Here are lede paragraphs from the normally well-written Washington Post. You may want to read it over more than once:

The FBI's inquiry into the leak of intercepts related to the Sept. 11 attacks began to focus on members of Congress after a government agency told the FBI that news reporters had claimed to have received the information from lawmakers, according to sources close to the investigation.

When FBI agents visited one national security agency several weeks ago, officials provided detailed accounts of conversations they had had with at least two reporters who, officials said, revealed their sources to be members of Congress. The government agency, which insisted it not be named, gave agents copies of phone records that confirmed the date and time of day these conversations took place.

Reporting the doings of two bureaucracies plus some members of Congress cannot be easy, especially when the reporter is forced to name unnamed sources. (The Post's stated policy requires confirmation by two independent sources before the newspaper will run an unnamed-source story.) However, the two reporters who wrote this story could at least have defined a "leak of intercepts." The terms aren't explained until 10 paragraphs later, and even then not very well:

The leaked information, parts of which had been reported in The Washington Times in late September 2001 and then again by other news outlets in mid-June, contained snippets of conversation intercepted by the NSA on Sept. 10 in which people, speaking in Arabic, said "The match is about to begin" and "Tomorrow is zero hour."

The size of that sentence alone is an indication of the fogginess permeating this story. The story's most serious problem is that it is potentially compelling — linking members of Congress to information that might have helped prevent the actions of September 11 — yet the readers can't comprehend it. Most readers won't find the story compelling because the reporters didn't bother to explain what they were talking about.

Here are some shorter examples by writers who made unfair assumptions about what their readers would know:

The lawn is cut in a circular moiré pattern.
(I had to look up "moiré" in the dictionary. And then I learned I was pronouncing it wrong.)

He was a bar back at a local bar.
("Bar back" is a regional usage from the eastern United States. It means a bartender's assistant.)

The press today is often accused of being liberal. He would agree with that assessment.
(He would agree that the press is too liberal? Or that the press is accused of being too liberal?)

Quotations and Attributions: Taking the Onus off the Reporter

One distinguishing aspect of journalistic writing is the use of the direct quotation — the word-for-word repetition of what the subject said. Quotes make the story appear more honest. They take the onus off the reporter; the writer can truthfully state, "I didn't say it. The subject of my story said it."

As in a research paper, direct quotations can be citations of written statements, but most journalistic quotes are spoken. Journalists use verbal statements more often than most other kinds of writers.

Newspaper writing, which remains at the core of all journalistic writing, has developed certain traditions for dealing with quotations or "handling a quote." Broadcast writing handles them differently (see Appendix A for more on that subject).

Here are the basic principles for how quotes are usually handled in newspaper writing:

- In the first reference, use "according to" or "says" or "said," followed by the name and title of the source.
- In the second reference, the name comes first, followed by "says" or "said."
- The attribution comes at the end of the first quoted sentence.
- A direct quote begins a new paragraph.

Here's an example of how these principles would work in a lede:

> The crash was vivid, according to Sam Jones, curator of the Museum of Demolition Derbies.
> "The smell of rubber sure was awful," Jones said. "It was even worse than that time in Talladega when four cars all came together."

Striving to find a new way to attribute a quotation can make the writer sound silly. This is why attributions are usually a prosaic "said" or "says" (depending on tense), and not "cited," "stated," "averred," "opined," "noted," "enthused," "reflected" or "chortled." If sticking with "says" or "said" sounds monotonous, that's because you're the writer. The reader rarely notices.

He cited that he liked children.
He said he liked children.

She opined that the good old days just aren't what they used to be.
She said the good old days are gone.

"This is going to absolutely be the best time we ever had," she enthused.
"This is going to absolutely be the best time we ever had," she said.
(The words she used make it obvious she's enthusiastic.)

Sometimes attributions add a tint of color or bias that the writer didn't intend. If, for instance, you use "claimed," you are automatically casting doubt on the statement and the person who made the statement. By contrast, "declared" gives the statement some authority it might not warrant. Declarations are usually formal, not conversational.

Here are more examples of how such words can be misused:

"I went into medicine because I love people," she claimed.
("Claimed" makes it sound as if she really went into medicine because she liked poking people with needles and listening to them squeal.)

"Good writers all start somewhere," he admitted.
(What did he do wrong?)

"I had a tuna salad sandwich for lunch," she declared.

Exceptions do exist. If a prisoner confesses in court, it is more precise to use "she confessed" or "she admitted" than "she said." If the verb is specific and more accurate than a mere "said" or "says," then use it. If he insisted that his wife wear a seatbelt, then that's how the attribution should read. Or if she argued that despite spending cutbacks, the department budget would still be out of balance, then use "argued." If he screamed, and didn't just say, "I'll kill you if you ever try that again!" then "screamed" was what he did. (And the exclamation point stays there.)

Sometimes writers try to get around what they think is the monotony of using "said" by substituting "pointed out." The problem is that if you write, "She pointed out that the whole world agrees with her," then you have acknowledged the apparent truth of what she said. She pointed it out, and there it was.

One solution is to change "pointed out" to "pointed to" — now you're simply acknowledging the direction in which she is pointing. Or you could write, "She noted that ..." but this still comes close to affirming that she spoke the truth. Better yet, go with "said." The reader rarely notices "said," allowing the quote to speak for itself.

An important note on the punctuation of attributions: The end quotation mark comes after the final comma, period or question mark:

"The ballot is stronger than the bullet," Lincoln said.

Is the Reporter Making this Up?

If an interview subject states an opinion, expresses an emotion or reports a perception of the senses, then the quotation — direct or indirect — needs to carry an attribution. Otherwise, the reader can accuse the writer of mind reading. If the reporter writes, "He felt sad," then the reader has every right to ask, "How did the writer know that?"

It's very likely the reporter did one of two things: listened to the subject or observed how the subject looked or acted. But if there is no apparent reporting of that, the reader is resigned to believe the reporter is simply reading the subject's mind.

She hopes to find a career that would offer her both the financial rewards and personal satisfaction she is looking for.

(How does the writer know what her hopes are? The interview subject must have stated them. The comment needs an attribution.)

He enjoys the occasional trashy novel.
He says he enjoys the occasional trashy novel.

She finds great fulfillment in her volunteer work.
She says she finds great fulfillment in her volunteer work.

After living in New York City a couple of years, he was concerned about moving to Chicago, a city with substandard cultural offerings.

(According to whom? The writer needs to attribute both the comment of concern and the opinion about Chicago's cultural offerings.)

Her abundant enthusiasm and thirst for knowledge forces her to move on.

(The writer can report her apparent enthusiasm; that's observable. But her thirst for knowledge is a matter of opinion. It must carry an attribution.)

The Power of the Direct Quote

There is no particular reason to use a direct quote of a mundane informational statement — "I was born in a hospital in Portland, Ore." — but if the quotation has some life, try to get it verbatim.

A decent quote can ensure the power of a story. Direct quotes tell the reader more about the interview subject than does attire, body language, facial expression, tone of voice or diction. You are what you say.

Each of the following examples indicates what the direct quote might have been.

He likes argumentative, meaningful conversation.
"I like argumentative, meaningful conversation," he said.

Although he has no plans for the future, he hopes to see the world. He would also like to attend graduate school, but right now he would just like to graduate from college and see where his life goes from there.

Although he says he has no plans for the future, he wants to travel. "I do hope to see the world someday," he said. "But right now I would just like to graduate from college and see where my life goes from there."

(There would be no reason to transform all of this into direct quotations, but the writer does need to establish that the opinions are the interview subject's.)

She talks about nearly being eaten by a lion and some baboons. She is the only person she knows who has been urinated on by a leopard.

"I could tell stories about being nearly eaten by a lion and some baboons," she said. "And I'm the only person I know who has been urinated on by a leopard."

After Sept. 11, it's been perplexing for him to witness nothing but blind patriotism smeared throughout America's media and political bodies.

"Since Sept. 11, it's been perplexing to witness nothing but blind patriotism smeared throughout America's media and political bodies," he said.

She is very athletic and enjoys jogging, even though she recently sprained her ankle while running in Lincoln Park.

She says she is very athletic. "I enjoy jogging, even though I just sprained my ankle," she says. "I was running in Lincoln Park when it happened."

When he was a high school senior, he was fortunate to experience one of the coolest moments of his life. The event was a tour of Air Force One.

"When I was a high school senior, I experienced one of the coolest moments of my life — a tour of Air Force One," he said.

Sometimes a quotation is good because it's bad. Many journalists make a point of collecting not-meant-to-be-funny quotes, prizing those that come from prominent people. One such quote, from New York Yankees great Yogi Berra, has been repeated so often that it has become a cliché. Many people who say it (and then giggle) have no idea where "It was déjà vu all over again" came from. Berra also is credited with saying, "You can observe a lot by watching" and "The game ain't over 'til it's over."

But Berra is by no means alone. During the infamous 1968 Democratic Convention, when police went after political activists without much restraint, Chicago's Mayor Richard J. Daley said, "Get this straight once and for all: The policeman isn't there to create disorder. The policeman is there to preserve disorder."

Former Vice President Dan Quayle: "We are now ready for any unforeseen event that may or may not occur."

The late film magnate Samuel Goldwyn: "Anybody who goes to see a psychiatrist ought to have his head examined."

Former President Gerald Ford: "If Lincoln were alive today, he'd roll over in his grave."

Keep the Reporter Out of the Story

The reporter's role as a conduit means that most of the time he or she should remain invisible. Sometimes, though, the writer feels the need to report that a response was in reaction to a question. This can be accomplished by beginning with a rhetorical question:

How does he handle the financial uncertainty that is part of freelancing? "The first rule is to have a spouse with a steady job," he says.

Often you don't need such a device; the interview subject's answer usually implies what the question was. Here are some examples with rewrites that illustrate this:

When questioned as to the immediate benefits of such a course, other than increasing his ability to write concisely, he found little or no connection to his current occupation as a sales representative.

Except for increasing his ability to write concisely, he said he finds little to connect writing with his current occupation in sales.

When asked what writer inspired him, he said it was Joseph Conrad. Regarding Conrad, he said, "I am struck by the way he put words together."

He said he is an enthusiastic reader of Joseph Conrad; "I am struck by the way he put words together."

On this balmy summer evening, I had the pleasure of interviewing Ms. Miller and I must say I received more than an interview. I received a trip through her childhood to her present state.

Miller looked out at the balmy summer evening and recited a trip that began with her childhood and ended with who she is now.

(Not only did this reporter insert herself needlessly into the story, the writing is gratuitous and cloying.)

Originality's greatest foe is the cliché, which we address in the next chapter.

Chapter 7 Exercises

No one expects a student or young journalist to know enough trivia to win "Jeopardy!" but we should expect them to know at a shallow level facts and concepts that we expect the average educated American to know.

Hence the 20 inaccurate statements below. Below them is an exercise designed to give you some practice in quoting people in a way that only implies that someone asked them questions. Doing so saves words and assumes the reader is bright enough to figure out that the quote came in response to a question. Whether or not a question was asked is irrelevant — or, at most, of minor newsworthiness. Nor is there any reason to take the attention away from the subject and direct it toward the reporter.

A. Find the inaccuracies

1. The ambassador then introduced the speaker of the U.S. Senate.

2. Since it was attacked, the grounds of the New York Commerce Center have become a shrine to those who lost their lives on Sept. 11, 2001.

3. Hurricanes most frequently cut a swath through a territory that extends for north Texas through Oklahoma and Kansas.

4. The Eiffel Tower in St. Louis was once the world's tallest human-built structure.

5. Theodore Roosevelt was confined to a wheelchair throughout his presidency.

6. President Barrack Obama appointed former New York Sen. Hilary Clinton as secretary of defense.

7. In the Galapagos Islands, now a territory of Peru, Charles Darwin began to develop the idea that would lead to the theory of evolution.

8. Since the demise of the Soviet Union, Stalingrad has reverted to its original name, St. Petersburg.

9. During the modern era of American basketball, the American League has won many more All-Star games than the National League.

10. Cardiologists specialize in the diagnosis and treatment of lung disease.

11. The Battle of Gettysburg in Virginia is considered the turning point of the U.S. Civil War.

12. Canada is, at least in theory, bilingual. The two primary languages of Canada are English and Spanish.

13. Iraq is the modern name of the country once known as Persia.

14. The stock market was mixed today, as the blue chip Dow Jones Industrial Average lost five points and the tech-heavy Standard and Poor's 500 gained eight points.

15. A hydrogen atom contains a single proton and two electrons.

16. Only Liverpool, England could have created the personalities of John Lennon, Paul McCartney, George Harriman and Ringo Starr, who as the Beatles changed popular music forever.

17. Monterrey is the capital of Mexico.

18. The capital of Tennessee is Memphis.

19. The military dictatorship now called Myanmar was once the former British colony of Thailand.

20. The state of Washington shares borders with two states, Oregon and Montana.

B. Rewrite these statements:

1. When asked about strife between the East and the West, philosopher Martin Buber replied, "The real struggle is not between East and West, or capitalism and communism, but between education and propaganda."

2. I asked poet Carl Sandburg if he thought slang corrupted the language. To my surprise, he answered, "Slang is the language that rolls up its sleeves, spits on its hands and goes to work."

3. When asked what effect language had on him, V.S. Pritchett said, "I am under the spell of language, which has ruled me since I was 10."

4. I asked mystery writer Agatha Christie what compelled her to avoid clichés in her writing. "For one thing, clichés aren't always accurate," she said. As an example, she cited "necessity is the mother of invention." "I don't think necessity is the mother of invention," she said. "Invention, in my opinion, arises directly from idleness, possibly also from laziness; to save oneself trouble."

5. When asked what he thought of word economy, poet Henry Wadsworth Longfellow replied, "Many a poem is marred by a superfluous verse."

The Eternal Cliché

Word Exhaustion and the Death of Originality

Words get tired. More precisely, people get tired of words and expressions that have lost their meaning because they are worn out — some were meaningless to begin with. When writers, especially journalists, find themselves becoming rhapsodic and searching for that one modifier that will send the audience into a swoon, they are approaching danger. Soon any originality will die.

When William Shakespeare wrote, "Parting is such sweet sorrow," the words were as fresh as the play from which they came.

When Benjamin Franklin first penned, "A penny saved is a penny earned," the phrase must have struck his fellow colonials as the ultimate in pith, innovation and wisdom. It might even have impressed a few British.

When Winston Churchill coined the term "iron curtain," the term was lively enough to be used by journalists and politicians across the English-speaking world.

It has been more than half a century since Churchill uttered his words at Westminster College, in Fulton, Mo., and the iron curtain has gone the way of the Soviet Union. Two and a half centuries have passed since Franklin created pithy sayings for his "Poor Richard's Almanac," and most of them have lost their pith. Four hundred years separate us from "Romeo and Juliet," and our parting from many of the tired lines has proved more sweet than sorrowful.

Avoid the Empty and the Trite

There's nothing particularly wrong with the following lede, but it represents wasted space. It adds nothing to what most people already know.

> KANSAS CITY, Mo. — More and more Americans are recognizing the importance of community-level action in order to improve the health and well-being of their communities and countries.

You can practically hear the reader saying, "Yes, so what's the point?" In this case, the point was that 120 national organizations had formed a coalition dedicated to improving the health of communities across the United States. But readers had to get through the empty lede first, and not many would have hung around long enough to learn what the story was about.

Here's what the lede would look like if the writer reported what happened:

> KANSAS CITY, Mo. — Members of 120 national organizations met Monday to try to improve the health and well-being of communities across the United States.

Rhapsodic utterances generally make for poor journalism (and most other forms of writing). In general, they haven't been considered good writing since the Romantic Age of the 19th century. Here are a few more examples:

Nothing is more beautiful than a fall evening in Chicago. Fall is a wonderful time of year. It indicates the end of summer and the beginning of a new season. Seasons are a part of city living.

One look into the soulful eyes of a Basset Hound will tell you that dogs are a man or woman's best friend. The noble and loving dog is eternally devoted to you and wants to be with you forever. Even when a dog is scratching him or herself or when he or she is working on gnawing at a bone, he or she is always thinking of you, the master or mistress of your earnest and lovable canine companion.

Our employees are the true professionals who have exhibited dedication and commitment to the highest level of expertise in their respective areas.
(As opposed to the untrue professionals? See "Business Jargon" later in this chapter.)

The Making of a Cliché

Many journalists believe that if a cliché describes what you want to say, then you should use it — if the cliché fits, wear it. A couple of problems come with this belief.

No matter how well the cliché fits, readers, listeners and viewers have probably heard it so often that they're tired of it. By barely "hearing" it in their minds, they miss its meaning. A second problem results from the perception that the writer has not bothered to find a more original way to communicate the fact, concept, idea, opinion or emotion — it tells readers that the message wasn't very important. The reader may perceive the writer's laziness as an insult.

Some clichés live long enough that they get recycled. A few of the meaty sayings in the King James Bible seem to be on their way back into vogue. For example, during a time when personal sniping, nuisance lawsuits and petty celebrity scoops get more and more publicity, the phrase "Judge not lest ye be judged" is finding a new audience. But this is rare.

Other clichés make the journey from freshness to triteness in record time. In 2001, President George W. Bush first used the phrase "axis of evil" to describe Iran, Iraq and North Korea. Now the phrase is often used sarcastically — a good indication it has developed cliché status.

It hasn't been very long since it became fashionable for a public official, corporate executive or athletic coach who faced imminent dismissal to say, "I have resigned to spend more time with my family."

Not too long ago, "Think outside the box" was a command to avoid clichés of thought. Now it has become a cliché itself.

So remember that whatever the message — no matter how apt the cliché sounds — there is almost always a better way to say it.

Clichés to Avoid

Not only did the taxi driver overcharge her but, *adding insult to injury*, he left her at the wrong address.

We try to give you the training you need but, once on the job, it's *sink or swim.*

The U.S. soccer team scored seven minutes into the match, but the goal turned out to be *a drop in the bucket*, and the Mexico team won 5-2.

We're behind you *110 percent.*

Dear to your heart

Rome wasn't built in a day.

She was *catching some z's.*

"An apple a day keeps the doctor away" is so old it harks back to a time when physicians routinely made house calls.

He's history.

Has the *cat got your tongue?*

Rise and shine.

Finally the astronaut faced *the moment of truth* as she opened the hatch and began her space walk.

The sky's the limit.

Busy as a bee

You can't teach an old dog new tricks.

A chill ran down his spine as he looked down and saw an underground river 50 feet below.

The early bird gets the worm.

The team that Enron assembled appeared to be the industry's *cream of the crop.*

That's how the cookie crumbles.

When she met adversity, she just *kept plugging away.*

Follow your heart.

Like, you know

Knowledge is power.
(This might be true, but figure out a less stale way of stating that truth.)

The new Miss America *has it all.*
(List her qualities and let the reader decide.)

There was an unbelievable *hustle and bustle* along 42nd Street.
(Describe the activity in detail, with strong nouns, action verbs and a minimum of modifiers, including "unbelievable.")

Winning isn't everything. It's the only thing.
(Here's a case in which the late football coach Vince Lombardi took a cliché and refreshed it, only to have his refreshing line itself become a cliché.)

Party leaders said it was *a little late in the game* for the president to be changing his position on sanctions against China.
(Here's a rewrite: Party leaders said it was too late for the president to change his position on sanctions against China.)

She could not decide if the job's benefits would outweigh its liabilities. Finally, her husband said to *go for it.*
(Finally, her husband said she should take the job.)

He *has a way with words.*
(Instead, quote him and let the reader decide if he's articulate.)

Don't give up the ship.

Where the fun never sets

The more things change, the more they remain the same.

No problem!
(Just reply to "Thank you" with "You're welcome.")

He's got attitude.

"Sheer" can refer to stockings or cliffs, but it's a cliché if you're referring to a state of mind, such as *sheer idiocy, sheer lunacy, sheer folly* or *sheer madness.*

The marathoners have been drinking water *like it's going out of style.*

He *couldn't care less.*

Been there, done that.

Chocoholic or *workaholic*

She's *losing it.*

He *flew the coop.*

A meltdown situation

The answer is *yes to all of the above.*

All was not lost.

It *runs the gamut.*

She had her *head squarely on her shoulders.*

Full speed ahead

He was *at a crossroads in his life.*

Any port in a storm

Ahead of the game

Out of sight, out of mind

A meaningful relationship

Give credit where credit is due.

A sad state of affairs

She was *cut out for ...*

Back on track.

He's *right on target.*

There's no stopping him.

Avoid clichés *like the plague.*

Take a chance.

How do you like them apples?

Some clichés arise from the fact that a particular modifier almost always precedes the same one or two nouns, prepositional phrases or set of synonyms. For example, "fraught" is almost always followed by "with peril." The same is true with "one fell swoop." "Fell," in this sense, used to be an adjective that applied to anything that was dread or deadly, but now it's almost never used with any noun except "swoop." "Whirlwind" almost always comes with the nouns "tour" or "campaign." (See "Journalese" later in this chapter.)

Apprentice Clichés and Slang

In his book, "The Suspended Sentence," Roscoe Born asks why those who are so eager to denounce clichés are so apt to keep on using them. He concludes that students make a mental note of the list of clichés they have read, but do not remain on guard to avoid new clichés. Train yourself to spot new clichés before they are fully grown. Always use caution before using a trendy phrase; chances are it's an apprentice cliché.

Some phrases die without ever attaining the level of a true cliché. A few examples include: *Get out of town* (as in "You don't say," or "You're kidding"); *Oh please!* (in reaction to a suggestion that sounds ludicrous); *Chill!* or *Chill out!*; *Show me the money*; *Get a life*; *Go figure*; *Wake up and smell the coffee.*

Often trendy, short-lived catchwords come from entertainment media. For example, the now-classic movie "Wayne's World," spawned phrases such as "Party on" that quickly graduated to a full-blown cliché.

Since the 21st century began, some new apprentice clichés have crept into the vocabulary of young men and women. (Chances are this list is already old.)

My bad (meaning "it's my fault" or "my error").

That's so quality. (A form of praise.)

I'd rather chew broken glass. (The newer apprentice clichés are often sarcastic.)

I googled it.

That's so gay. (This is not a reference to sexual preference. It means "That's so stupid" or "That's so silly," but is falling out of favor because of its homophobic implications.)

I'm bouncing. (Let's leave this place.)

Investors are reluctant to *catch the falling knife.*

Keep things on the DL. ("DL" refers to "down low," and it means to keep something from becoming widely known.)

Ya' think (in response to an obvious observation).

I've got your back.
(Don't worry. You have my support against *them.*)

As with every generation, there's an entire list of phrases meant to imply the goodness of something. Recent slang includes "sweet," "phat," "sick," "hot," "slammin'," "bangin'" and "fly."

Born offers this warning:

> The cliché factory works around the clock. A writer with any pride — and there are no real writers without it — will brace himself constantly against some other writer's trick phrase or odd use of a familiar word. A phrase that a writer admires may indeed be worthy, but he must resist the temptation to adopt it as his own, first because it would be a shameless theft, and second because a thousand other imitative writers are sure to do the same. That is the way to avoid clichés. And the writer who shuns the fashionable will always be in style.

Juggling Jargon: the Mark of a Lazy Writer

One sure way to avoid being original is to get caught up in the jargon of a business or profession. Just as clichés do, jargon provides a comfortable escape for the lazy writer. It's easy for writers to parrot the expressions they hear each day and not expend any brainpower or energy thinking up new ways to say things. The trouble is that intelligent readers know flat, jargon-riddled copy when they see it, and they have ways of getting back at its author — they have an irritating habit of moving on to something else if the copy doesn't keep their interest.

As mentioned in the first chapter, jargon does play a legiti-mate role among colleagues in the same industry or profession. It helps professionals communicate with a great deal of preci-sion, because the originator and consumer of the message both recognize exactly the same definition for each word of jargon. To two physicians, a shinbone is a "tibia." It simply cannot be defined as a "lower leg bone," or it could be confused with the "fibula" — the other lower leg bone.

When professionals use jargon on people who aren't in the same profession, they get in trouble as writers (and as com-municators). This is particularly true in the realm of business, especially big corporate business.

Business Jargon

Big corporations employ many Americans who spend at least half their waking hours behind a desk in a cubicle, so it becomes tempting for these businesses to assume that everyone shares their language and their (cliché alert) corporate culture.

The result of business jargon going unchecked and traveling beyond the corporate door includes reports such as this one, which concerns the merger of two broadcast holding companies:

> The sales are consistent with the station divestiture and portfolio optimization initiatives being undertaken in con-nection with the formation of the media corporation. At the time the merger and acquisition agreement were an-nounced, the two companies indicated that they would sell stations in markets where the combined entity exceeded current Federal Communications Commission ownership limits.

Aside from the unnecessary use of passive voice, this para-graph glistens with jargon: "optimization initiatives," "merger and acquisition" and "the entity" or, in this case, the "combined entity."

Comic value aside, it was exactly this type of language that covered up creative accounting and hid true revenues from stockholders in several corporations during the 2002 economic downturn and the 2008 economic disaster. As we have painfully learned since then, financial reports need to appear transparent so shareholders and bondholders can see how the numbers were put together. This requires writing that uses as little jargon as possible.

Another way to misuse jargon is with business euphemisms — a term that has itself been used as a euphemism for business lies. By now, we've lived through a quarter of a century of corporate writing that first used "downsize" to describe massive layoffs. Corporate writers used "downsizing" to the point that it became a dirty word. They replaced it with "restructuring," then "re-engineering." Both of these terms have legitimate definitions, but neither is an adequate substitute for massive layoffs.

Misuse caused "restructuring" and "re-engineering" to grow stale. Then, corporate writers came up with "rightsizing" and "rationalizing the workforce," which was really just another way of saying "conducting massive layoffs."

Some elements of business jargon are benign. Business jargon can simply be a matter of wordiness. For example, we can easily replace "The list of bidders for the project are as follows" with "Here are the project's bidders" without changing the meaning.

Some additional nuggets of business jargon are:

as per your request

Enclosed please find ...

the bottom line

a sudden downturn

dynamic (as a noun)

access (as a verb)

impact (as a verb)

service (as a verb with an object, usually a customer or an account). *Serve* or *maintain* works much better.

implement (as a verb)

initiate (legitimate, but overused)

on the fast track

turnkey (This usage began as an imaginative way to define an entire working system that came in a single package — all you had to do was turn the figurative key to make it work. But overuse has turned the concept into a cliché.)

scalable (What's wrong with "measurable?")

move up the ladder

repropose

state of the art

cutting edge, leading edge or bleeding edge (Someone suggested I call this section "Cutting Edge Clichés.")

infrastructure

paradigm

in the event of

corporate meltdown

best-of-breed

freefall (a noun describing stock prices in a bear market)

window of opportunity

The business world (and nearly everyone's world) includes the widespread use of a couple of words that normally are not clichés or jargon. But corporate technology has pushed "system" and "program" to the point that they are, if nothing else, overused.

There is one usage that should not be used outside of business, but frequently is: CEO, or chief executive officer. The CEO can be the chairperson of the board or the president or both. This distinguishes the top executive from the chief operating officer, or COO (who can also be the president); the chief financial officer, or CFO; and the chief information officer, or CIO. Even though it appears to have been accepted, "chief executive officer" remains redundant.

It's worth noting that in journalistic copy, a board chairperson is not referred to as the "chairman of the board" or even the "board chairman" — simply as chairman or chairwoman. "Of the board" is assumed.

In the continuing effort to eliminate sexist language, many writers refer to a chairman or a chairwoman simply as a "chair." But I can't imagine that too many shareholders would be happy hearing their company is being run by a piece of furniture. If the board's leader is a woman, call her a chairwoman; if a man, stick with chairman. The AP Stylebook says that journalists should not use "chairperson" unless it's the organization's formal title for the position.

Cop and Criminal Lawyer Lingo

Reporters on the police beat and those who cover the courts are notorious for using the bureaucratic jargon of law enforcement. Someone being apprehended is no longer a person, or even a suspect or a defendant. He or she becomes a "subject," an "individual" or even a "citizen." If charged with a violent crime, that person gains the all-purpose tag of "offender." Because the police and the courts want to observe the rules of fairness, both modify their suspect's action with "alleged" or "allegedly," an adjective or adverb that has a particularly sluggish sound to people who like their English crisp and fresh.

Most often, journalists don't need such a modifier at all. All they need to do is quote police or prosecutors, directly or indirectly. Instead of writing "Wilson allegedly stole $500 from an Arlington bank," you can simply write "Prosecutors accuse Wilson of stealing $500 from an Arlington bank." If you must use an adjective or adverb, make it "reported" or "reportedly."

In many police stories, hit-and-run drivers never drive away from the accident site. They "flee the scene" of the accident. But the "scene" of an accident or crime has a catchall quality that makes all such stories sound generic. Generic is easy. It's also unoriginal.

These usages appear in the deliberately bland, presumably unbiased report language of the police officer. They also find their way into the prose of many young police reporters and, regrettably, that of many veteran journalists who started out on the police beat. Suspects or witnesses seem to lose their humanity when they get referred to as "citizens," "subjects" or "individuals." "Residents" seems to work better, but not much.

An "unknown suspect" appears not only guilty but awkward when he or she is referred to as the "offender" or the "shooter." For some unknown reason, it seems better to refer to an unknown perpetrator of a violent crime as an "assailant." (Then again, if English always made sense it would be a science, not a form of expression.)

One common usage is laughable: "The suspect turned himself in to New Jersey police" is quite a feat, especially if the suspect didn't attend the New Jersey police academy first. To avoid this misplaced modifier, try "The suspect surrendered to police" or, to make it clear that the surrender was voluntary, "the suspect surrendered himself to police." It sounds redundant, but it isn't. (See "Your Antecedents Are Showing" in Chapter 5.)

Journalese

As William Zinnser puts it in "On Writing Well," journalese is "the death of freshness in anybody's style." And as columnist Paula LaRocque says, we journalists are in no position to complain about someone else's jargon. LaRocque takes her own digs at what she calls "mediaspeak":

> It's flat and overused and long ago lost any real meaning. We're talking here about verbs such as "spawned," "spurred," "sparked," "fueled" or "targeted." Or adjectives such as "burgeoning" or "skyrocketing." Or words and expressions such as "amid," "worst-case scenario," "level the playing field" and "in the wake of."

At seminars she conducts across the country, LaRocque offers a long list of examples of journalese. Here are a few of the words on her list:

strife-torn
witch hunt
heated exchange
chilling effect
a steep decline
beleaguered
resonate
a whirlwind tour
spiraling inflation

firestorm of criticism
escalated
stunning
rising tide
political football

"No," LaRocque says to these terms. "Nobody talks this way."

Not to be outdone, Paul Harral, editorial page editor of the Star-Telegram of Fort Worth, Texas, jokingly offers what he calls a journalist's toolbox for reporters — especially television reporters, who need a quick, handy phrase and often don't believe they have time to come up with anything original. The journalist's toolbox first appeared in an Internet chat room called the "downhold," populated by former employees of United Press International. Here are some examples, accompanied by Harral's comments:

Iceberg tips, as in, "Investigators say the scandal uncovered today is just the tip of the iceberg." A popular item.

Sighs of relief. "New Yorkers breathed a sigh of relief today as Hillary Clinton finally announced she is running for the Senate." This is a handy phrase. [Please forgive the dated material in this example. The toolbox was written before the 2000 election.]

Wrong place, wrong time. "An innocent bystander was shot to death during a gang battle on the West Side tonight. John Jones was in the wrong place at the wrong time."

Cudabens. "Police report 25 people were killed but it could have been worse." A wonderful all-purpose tool.

The *nightmare* card — often played by the knowing journalist. "A dream vacation turned into a nightmare tonight for the Spinola family."

Brutal murder tags. Very effective in separating brutal murders from sensitive and gentle homicides.

Deadly labels. They modify any event in which there is a death. Deadly accident, deadly shooting.

All-purpose closers.
This one is suitable for deadly accidents, brutal murders, weddings, tornadoes, hurricanes and the return of a life savings — found on the seat of a bus — to a little old lady: "This day is one they'll never forget."

This one is heavily used in Washington stories: "One thing's for sure: nothing is certain here."

Full-blown investigation. Larger than a somewhat-blown investigation but of less intensity than an inquisition.

Other journalists using the site added these items to subsequent chats:

- "Completely destroyed" or, better yet, "almost completely destroyed"
- Mass exodus
- "We don't know anything right now, but here's what we know."
- The drug bust that is inevitably the "biggest" in the history of whatever agency did the busting
- The explosion or tornado that "sounded just like World War II," although that one is obviously going out of style, and somehow "sounded like the Gulf War" hasn't really replaced it.
- Let us not spare those who insist on modifying or qualifying "unique" with "sort of," "nearly," even "very."
- "Conducting an ongoing investigation"
- "Most every." Has "almost" been stricken from the dictionary?
- The victim was shot six times in the back, so "police suspect foul play."
- Fires that "gut" buildings, as if the buildings were fish
- "Perfect 10." We never hear of anyone scoring an "imperfect 10."
- Rescuers are "sifting through rubble."

The Comic Value of Clichés

One way to test if your words or phrases are tired is to determine if they have potential comic value. Often a word or a phrase is funny simply because it's been overused and the expression brings, if not laughter, groans.

In "When Words Collide," Lauren Kessler and Duncan McDonald didn't need to stretch far to develop an example. They end their discussion of clichés this way:

> So, as the sun sinks slowly in the Western Sky, be your own best friend and bid a fond farewell to the tried and true expressions that seem to creep into writing like a thief in the night, robbing it blind of its force.

The following list was e-mailed to dozens, if not thousands, of people. It carried the label "No Traceable Attribution." It's an excellent compilation of the efforts of writers who tried too hard to be original:

> He spoke with the wisdom that can only come from experience, like a guy who went blind because he looked at a solar eclipse without one of those boxes with a pinhole in it and now goes around the country speaking at high schools about the dangers of looking at a solar eclipse without one of those boxes with a pinhole in it.

> She caught your eye like one of those pointy hook latches that used to dangle from screen doors and would fly up whenever you banged the door open again.

> The little boat gently drifted across the pond exactly the way a bowling ball wouldn't.

> McBride fell 12 stories, hitting the pavement like a Hefty bag filled with vegetable soup.

From the attic came an unearthly howl. The whole scene had an eerie, surreal quality, like when you're on vacation in another city and "Jeopardy" comes on at 7 p.m. instead of 7:30 p.m.

Her hair glistened in the rain like nose hairs after a sneeze.

Her eyes were like two brown circles with big black dots in the center.

Her vocabulary was as bad as, like, whatever.

He was as tall as a six-foot, three-inch tree.

The hailstones leaped from the pavement, just like maggots when you fry them in hot grease.

Her date was pleasant enough, but she knew that if her life were a movie, this guy would be buried in the credits as something like "second tall man."

Long separated by cruel fate, the star-crossed lovers race across the grassy field toward each other like two freight trains, one having left Cleveland at 6:36 p.m. traveling at 55 mph, the other from Topeka at 4:19 p.m. at a speed of 35 mph.

The politician was gone but unnoticed, like the period after the Dr. on a Dr. Pepper can.

John and Mary had never met. They were like two hummingbirds who had also never met.

The thunder was ominous-sounding, much like the sound of a thin sheet of metal being shaken backstage during the storm scene in a play.

The red brick wall was the color of a brick-red Crayola crayon.

His thoughts tumbled in his head, making and breaking alliances like socks in a dryer without Cling Free.

The point to be made here is that even journalists with a polished sense of humor find it uncomfortable when it's their own writing that people are laughing at.

Chapter 8 Exercises

Replace the following clichés without altering their meanings:

1. It looks as if inmate Smith *flew the coop.*

2. The company's success appears to be the result of its ability to *stay ahead of the game.*

3. Acme researchers appear to be at *the leading edge* of their field.

4. *There's no stopping him.*

5. After suffering eight losses in a row, the Tigers find themselves in a *meltdown situation.*

6. A corporate spokeswoman said managers are prepared *in the event of* a strike.

7. "Thank you so much." *"No problem."*

8. President Obama said he hopes the talks will provide some relief for *strife-torn* Afghanistan.

9. By the second period, it became obvious that the Mighty Ducks *were history.*

10. The flood's effects continue to *resonate* with residents of the river communities.

11. He admitted a reluctance to cut the budget for a project that was *dear to his heart.*

12. The mayor's staff appears to be dealing with *a rising tide* of criticism.

13. Police say they have been looking for the driver since he *fled the scene* of the accident.

14. "*Stunning* developments in the Springfield fire investigation — details at 10!"

15. "*Brutal murder* in a Boise suburb — details at 10!"

16. A *shocking* display of courtroom fireworks — details at 10!"

17. The spending cuts designed to ease the deficit turned out to be *a drop in the bucket.*

18. It is obvious that the quarterback, selected in the first round of the NFL draft *has it all.*

19. It was *business as usual* today on the floor of the New York Stock Exchange.

20. The loss of the aerospace contract was the apparent result of the inability of the corporate engineers to *think outside the box.*

Red Flags and No-Nos

The Need to Exist Versus the Need for Surgical Removal

Experienced journalists work hard to develop mental files of words and expressions that usually don't belong in their copy. It's useful to think of them as carrying red flags. As soon as these words appear, they wave flags in front of the writer, giving the writer or editor the chance to stop and ask, "Is this word necessary? Is there a better way to say this?" The writer should take advantage of the chance for revision, every time.

Some words and expressions simply do not belong in journalistic copy, and it's likely they don't belong in most other forms of writing. These terms don't need a red flag, they need elimination; these are no-nos. They should never appear in your writing unless in a direct quotation.

More often than not, the red flag words we will cover are simply not needed. They often contribute to wordiness and, sometimes, redundancy. Take the word "located," for instance.

The refreshment stand was located in the lobby.

("Located" plays no useful role in this sentence. Take it out, and the sentence loses none of its meaning.)

If it's used as a verb, "located" performs a legitimate function. That's why it's a red flag word, not a no-no. But even so, the Anglo-Saxon verb "found" does a better job. (Review Chapter 5 for more on this topic.)

Finally, after six attempts during a period of 8 hours and 32 minutes, a helicopter located the shipwreck survivors.

Finally, after six attempts during period of 8 hours and 32 minutes, a helicopter found the shipwreck survivors.

Another red flag word, "extremely," along with its cousin, "very," can kill the impact of the words they are modifying:

He delivered an extremely striking portrayal of Willy Loman in "Death of a Salesman."

Better yet, describe the portrayal in some detail, and let the reader decide if it was striking or even extremely striking.

"Very" is so overused that it has earned its own disease, called the "very disease." Here are some examples:

Standing 25,035 feet, Mount Everest is very lofty.

The war in Iraq is very unique.

Degrees of uniqueness don't exist; something or someone either is unique or isn't. If it is, describe how it's different, and maybe the reader will reward you by concluding that the war is unique. (See "Don't Tell the Reader What to Think" in Chapter 7.)

Using "get" or "got," or "get out" or "got out," usually does nothing more than give the writer an excuse to be wordy.

The Environmental Protection Agency plans to spend $22 million to get the hazardous wastes out of the site.

The Environmental Protection Agency plans to spend $22 million to eliminate the hazardous wastes from the site.

"Hold" or "held" is often misused, and sometimes it is redundant. You hold something in your hands; you hold a degree; a bank holds your savings; but you conduct a meeting or sponsor a cake sale. Here's an example where "held" can be removed:

I attended the meeting that was held at the Moose Lodge.
I attended the meeting at the Moose Lodge.

"Everyone," "everywhere" and "all" are red-flag words because they are usually inaccurate. And they lend themselves to generic or trite statements that lead to gross generalizations. (Review Chapter 7 for more on avoiding generalizations.) Here are some examples of how these terms can be misleading:

Everyone knows that you can't make it in politics without money.

The wreckage was scattered *everywhere.*

All the lawyers ever do is complicate things for their own gain.

Other red-flag words include:

- *never*
- *also* (also worthy of its own disease)
- *both*
- *interesting* (when you can't think of anything complimentary to say)
- *over* (when you use it in place of "about," "around" or "more than")
- *obtain* (For this word, "get" or "got" is an acceptable substitute.)
- *overall*

The Big Red Flag: "That"

"That" might be the most overused word in English. Sometimes it is needed, but usually it represents nothing more than a verbal form of throat clearing.

There is one way "that" should never be used except in a direct quotation: Writers should not use "that" as a pronoun for a human being. Many grammarians spend paragraphs writing about the fine art of determining when "who" or "whom" should be used, but shrug when someone points out that a "that" is not a proper identification of a person. Even humanists, secular or religious, let a "that" slip out when they're describing the representatives of humanity whose cause they espouse.

When it comes to animals, however, journalistic stylebooks recommend using "that."

He spotted some parents and children that were out walking.
He spotted some parents and children who were out walking.

She recently completed a writing class taught by a teacher that the whole student body adored.
She recently completed a writing class taught by a teacher whom the whole student body adored.

The latter example is a case in which a specific fact would have helped. What was the teacher's name? If the teacher was that good, he or she deserves credit. But it's doubtful the whole student body — every student, without exception — adores any teacher.

Special Red Flags: "There is" and Similar Usages

One way to inject Novocain into a sentence is to begin it with a form of "there is" or "there are." Try replacing them with action verbs.

There are many trees that cast their enduring shadows over us.
Many trees cast their shadows over us. (Note that shadows are not known for their endurance.)

There was a mix of people smiling, laughing, frowning and some were nondescript.
People smiled, laughed and frowned. Some wore blank expressions.

There was a cooling winter breeze coming across the courtyard.
A cool winter breeze wafted across the courtyard.

There was a string of popcorn on the tree.
A string of popcorn adorns the tree.

There was the slightest yellow beginning to show on the leaves.
The slightest yellow began to show on the leaves.

There were few smiles, just looks of steely determination.
They displayed few smiles, just looks of steely determination.

There were four or five people jogging along the lake.
Four or five people jogged along the lake.

Another Special Red Flag: "Feel"

Don't get "feel" confused with "think" or "believe." "Feel" refers specifically to emotion or sensory information. If what you're writing about involves thought, then "think" or "believe" is more accurate. To avoid any hint that the writer is making something up or reading the subject's mind, "says" or "said" would be more appropriate.

She feels that this war is not going to end with Afghanistan, Israel and Iraq.
She says this war is not going to end with Afghanistan, Israel and Iraq.

Some people feel athletes who play contact sports must be missing part of their brains.
Some people think athletes who play contact sports must be missing part of their brains.

He feels his youth was interesting and fun.
He says he enjoyed growing up.

She feels that the pursuit of a future either in writing or interior design has equal appeal.
She says she might pursue either writing or interior design.

He feels that the overall atmosphere is both physically hard and abusive.
He says the atmosphere is physically hard and abusive.
    (Or)
He says the atmosphere feels hard and abusive.

Red Flag Tenses: Perfect Doesn't Always Mean Good

Beware of the past-perfect and present-perfect tenses. Both add an auxiliary being verb to a verb that is already doing the work. The "perfect" tenses usually create imperfect sentences that are weak and wordy.

Their ally is seeming to be supporting the other side.
Their ally seems to support the other side.

The soccer ball was eluding the goalie.
The soccer ball eluded the goalie.

He is enjoying a busy life in Cincinnati.
He enjoys a busy life in Cincinnati.

She discontinued her studies because she was traveling across the country.
She ended her studies because she traveled across the country.

She wants to be one of those lawyers who are representing the poor.
She wants to be a lawyer who represents the poor.

The congressman said he is hoping that these corporate accounting scandals will not reflect badly on the administration around election time.
The congressman said he hopes these corporate accounting scandals will not hurt the administration around election time.
        (Or)
"Come election time, I am hoping that these corporate accounting scandals will not reflect badly on the administration," the congressman said. (If that's what the congressman actually said.)

While she is pursuing her academic career, she should be watching out for colleagues who are making catty comments about her.
As she pursues her academic career, she should watch out for colleagues who make catty comments about her.

No-nos: Only Use Them in Direct Quotations

Good writers use red flag terms when they know why they're using them and have given themselves permission. But they also know that some words and usages simply do not belong in journalistic copy or most other forms of writing. Unless these words take the form of a direct quotation, no-nos should never appear in your writing. Usually all they add is extra syllables or words. Often they are redundant.

Here is a list of some no-nos:

- *upon* (*On* means the same thing.)
- *ongoing* (Use *continuing* if you must.)
- *hopefully* ("She *hopes*" may work.)
- *per se*
- *prior to* (*Before* works nicely.)
- *utilize* (*use*)
- *in order to* (Two words too many. A simple *to* works fine.)
- *one* (Used as a personal pronoun in American English, this sounds stiff.)
- *due to* (Usually this means you have a sentence in passive voice that should go active.)
- *a lot* (It's either *a lot*, meaning "a great amount," or *allot*, meaning "to apportion.")
- *etc.*

Special No-nos: Currently and Presently

Currently and *presently* are almost always redundant. The only time *currently* is not redundant is when you're making a distinction in time, such as "She was in high school; currently she's in college." But it's still better to use *now*, which has two fewer syllables and six fewer letters.

Presently is almost always misused. It doesn't mean "now," it means "soon." Since *presently* is often used as a synonym for "currently," it has become an artificial replacement for something that is already artificial.

Rules to Write By

Journalism and communication students get tired of going through the arcane rules of their chosen profession. So do working journalists.

Because journalists often chafe under such rules, they often enjoy reading satire on grammar rules — and what they endured getting through the pages of this book.

In "The News Business," John Chancellor and Walter Mears took a list of special rules from Harold Evans, included in his book "Essential English for Journalists, Editors and Writers." Evans, in turn, got the list from a bulletin board at Denver's Rocky Mountain News.

After all that, here is the notorious list, written by an anonymous copy editor or group of editors:

1. Don't use no double negatives.
2. Make each pronoun agree with their antecedents.
3. Join clauses good, like a conjunction should.
4. About them sentence fragments.
5. When dangling, watch your participles.
6. Verbs has to agree with their subjects.
7. Just between you and I, case is important too.
8. Don't write run-on sentences they are hard to read.
9. Don't use commas, which aren't necessary.
10. Try to not ever split infinitives.
11. It's important to use your apostrophe's correctly.
12. Proofread your writing to see if you any words out.
13. Correct spelling is esential.

Over the years, this list has been expanded by an informal network of donors, including a few of my former students, who send examples to each other on the Internet. Here are some of their additions:

1. Prepositions are not good words to end sentences with.
2. Be sure to use adjectives and adverbs correct.
3. Parenthetical remarks (even when relevant) are distracting.
4. Avoid unnecessary redundancy.
5. Foreign words and phrases are not apropos.
6. Be more or less specific.
7. Watch out for irregular verbs that have creeped into our language.
8. Who needs rhetorical questions?
9. Above all, writing should be sincere, whether you mean it or not.

And the ever-popular "Avoid clichés like the plague."

Chapter 9 Exercises

A. Correct the "no-nos" by eliminating or changing the misused words:

1. Apparently alot of voters disagreed with the issue stands of the politician they rejected.

2. She is currently curator of the museum's postmodern collection.

3. By the time the American scientists had tallied the results, interpreted them, written the journal article, etc., their discovery was no longer exclusively theirs.

4. Hopefully, the economic crisis will have abated by the time his children are in college.

5. The agency requires a letter on the news medium's letterhead in order to issue a press pass.

6. It wasn't the money per se that compelled him to propose marriage.

7. He is presently in charge of operations at the Center for Disease Control.

8. Just prior to walking down the aisle, the bridegroom's shoe fell off.

9. The vehicle came to rest upon a large boulder located in the Martian crater.

10. To utilize the program function, you need to hit "control" first.

B. Edit the sentences to find a more direct tense and to replace red-flag words.

1. Every day while I am gardening, I am chatting with a neighbor that is hanging over the fence.

2. The mayor feels that the members of the legislature do not understand the city's needs.

3. Before the meeting, he is holding a news conference.

4. She feels that her journalistic skills are much better on account of her having taken two classes last summer.

5. Even though this was a playoff game, there were fewer than 10,000 people in the stands.

6. Police said that the ambulance struck an oncoming truck before it burst through the coffee shop.

7. The hearing is scheduled to be held at 10 a.m. Monday.

8. The house appeared to be very broken down.

9. The district attorney feels that the outcome of the trial is a foregone conclusion due to the confession of the suspect.

10. Police said that when they conducted a search of the guest room, there was a 9-millimeter handgun located in the upper left drawer of a dresser.

10

Broadcast Style: Writing for the Ear and Eye

Medium versus Message

Half a century ago, a Canadian pioneer in media studies, Marshall McLuhan, wrote, "The medium is the message." The phrase quickly became a cliché. Not only was it a cliché, it became a glib explanation for a rainbow of communication phenomena to which McLuhan never meant to apply his five little words. But even the quotation's most glib interpretation carries meaning. Even if the medium is not the message, it certainly has the power to alter the message or its importance.

Take our example from Chapter 2: A fire consumes a warehouse, but it injures or kills no one. Look at how two news media treat it. The story might make Page 4 of the second section of the local newspaper. But on an average news day, it will be at the top of the newscast. Why? Because it carries such visual impact, and TV is nothing if not visual.

Using the newsworthiness criterion of "need to know," few stories are more newsworthy than a story about changes in a tax formula, because the great majority of Americans pay taxes. Few subjects could be more significant to the average American.

If we use entertainment as a criterion of newsworthiness, though, a tax story falls to the bottom of the list. An important tax story will usually make the front page of a mainstream newspaper. Its sidebars, or auxiliary stories, might grace the business pages. The story will also attract the deepest thoughts of the editorial and op-ed pages of The New York Times, The Wall Street Journal, The Christian Science Monitor and The Washington Post. Further, it will dominate the appropriate sections of Time, Newsweek and U.S. News & World Report, as well as most business magazines.

If the story does make a broadcast news show, it will be written differently. Here's an example of a state tax story lede as it might appear in a newspaper:

> In an attempt to increase state contributions to local school districts and decrease per-pupil disparities between rich districts and poor districts, Gov. James B. Carlson proposed a plan Thursday that would decrease local property taxes by 10 percent and increase the state income tax by 12 percent, with added state revenues going directly to the school districts.

Here's a broadcast news version of the same lede:

> Governor Carlson says he wants to do something about the big difference between the amount of state money that gets spent on pupils in rich school districts ... and those in poor districts. What Carlson wants to do is raise the state income tax 12 percent. But he also wants to decrease property taxes 10 percent. The governor says he wants the extra money the state gets from taxpayers to go directly to school districts.

No matter how skillfully written, though, chances are that the tax story is going to be relegated to a paragraph in someone's broadcast news summary. A murder, even in a major metropolitan news market where murders occur often, will often nudge ahead of a tax story in a radio newscast. On television, the murder story would be superseded by a fire story. We know a tax story has no entertainment value. With television, it has no visual value either.

Radio news is no more concerned about visual value than a newspaper is (unless a dramatic picture accompanies the newspaper story). But radio does like background noise — an audio "atmosphere" that makes listeners sense that they are in the middle of the story. There isn't much chance that a tax story will generate noise, unless the groans of legislators count. So what you might get on the radio is a 30-second overview of the tax story, simplified enough for the listener to understand it, but providing no real understanding.

Comparing the Media

Perhaps someday the forces that shape the Internet will find a way to unite the immediacy of the broadcast media with the depth that print media can (and sometimes do) provide. Until that union occurs, the journalist is stuck with different ways to write copy for each medium.

Writers for both forms have many things in common. Good journalists subscribe to the tenets of integrity — accuracy, fairness and balance — regardless of medium. Their tone is informal and conversational; in broadcast, it's downright chatty. They like short sentences. Their sentences are shorter in broadcast than in newspapers, and longer in most magazines, but the no-wasted-words dictum remains intact. These writers thrive on active voice and action verbs. They like quotes, but professionals in each medium handle them differently. They all try to describe in detail, but the better writers make use of what fits their medium best.

One element they treat quite differently is the lede. A good, un-fluffy feature might adhere to The Wall Street Journal formula: lead any way you want to as long as the payoff comes in the "nut graf," located three or four reasonably short paragraphs into the story. (Review "The Nut-Graf Approach" in Chapter 3.)

A good magazine article might spend that long just developing the landscape — describing the environment and atmosphere with strong nouns and action verbs.

In contrast, broadcast news stories have no ledes, at least not in the sense that the print media use them. The closest thing to a lede in most broadcast newscasts is the introduction, or "intro," which an anchor reads and then "throws" the story to a street reporter, who carries the story from there. Or sometimes television or radio viewers won't see or hear the street reporter right away; instead they get a "sound bite" — an audio or video quote. Radio listeners might get some natural sound up front. Examples of broadcast "sound clichés" are the clanging of a cable car in a story about San Francisco, the noise of a cash register in a story about the retail industry, or the roaring of jet engines on a runway in a story about an airport.

In television, the taped opening footage should be dramatically or artfully visual. After all, "vision" is the medium's last name. This footage might include the reporter's or interview subject's voice accompanying the video, called a "voice-over." It isn't unusual for a field producer to begin a longer story on, for example, the environment, with 15 seconds of natural sound emerging from some gorgeous outdoor footage before the reporter speaks the first words.

Writing for Broadcast: How to Cater to the Ear and Eye

Writing for broadcast news means always writing for the ear and sometimes for the eye. All general rules of broadcast writing apply to both the audio and video media, but writing for television and other visual media brings a few extra rules. We will come to these, but first let's focus on writing for the eye.

When writing for print media, it's a good idea for the writer to read the copy aloud during the editing process. When writing for broadcast media, the writer absolutely must read the copy aloud. If the writer fails to catch a flub, the anchor might miss it too, to the embarrassment of the newsreader or anchor and the subsequent verbal abuse of the writer. (Take it from someone who's been there.) Reading the copy aloud ensures that the story will retain a conversational rhythm. As with print stories, reading aloud also makes unneeded words and sentence elements immediately obvious.

Reading copy aloud before it's aired also helps eliminate tongue twisters and excessive sibilants such as, "Since she is said to have seen Sasquatch, she has been surreptitiously seen at a San Jose soda stand, superciliously sipping sarsaparilla through a squiggly straw, so say some sightseers who say they saw her." Such a sentence creates microphone noises that sound awful on the air and is guaranteed to put the newsreader in a bad mood.

Broadcast writing is linear. It goes from point A to point B to point C in a straight line, without digression or explanation. For this reason, it doesn't hurt to repeat a fact or two in case the listener or viewer missed it the first time. In other words, be repetitive, even redundant — just as Chapter 5 tells you not to do.

Writers of broadcast copy thrive on delivering short sentences. What would be a numbingly repetitious series of subject-verb-object sentences in print is not unusual in broadcast. This type of writing doesn't create a problem for the newsreader or the person listening or watching.

A rule of thumb dictates that a broadcast sentence should not exceed 20 words. We might be tempted to say the 20-word limit discounts the intelligence of the listening or viewing public. But the KISS principle (Keep It Simple, Stupid) rules in broadcast.

The fact is, when viewers or listeners are engaged in a newscast, they often are not totally engaged. Other things happen in a house or apartment when the TV set is on — things that require viewer attention. Radio listeners usually are doing something else as they listen to the news. Most often, they're driving. By contrast, readers usually absorb themselves in what they read. This explains broadcast's emphasis on short sentences and repetition.

Here's an example of a two-paragraph newspaper lede, followed by how the same lede might be written for radio and television. Note how differently the broadcast lede handles detail. First, the newspaper version:

Responding to an emergency appeal from the U.N., the United States announced Tuesday it will ship $15 million worth of corn to North Korea to assist children affected by severe food shortage.

Nicholas Burns, a State Department spokesman, said the decision was not linked to a North Korean announcement, expected Wednesday, on whether it will accept a U.S.-South Korean proposal to begin peace talks.

Now the broadcast lede:

The United States has responded to a U-N plea to send 15-Million dollars worth of corn to help starving children in North Korea. State Department spokesman Nicholas Burns says the shipment is NOT linked to any expected announcement from the North Koreans. A North Korean announcement would confirm if they will or won't accept a proposal from South Korea and the United States to begin peace talks.

Note a few changes in basic style. U.N. has become "U-N." The amount of $15 million is "15-Million dollars" with a capitalized "M". (If it were $15 billion, the broadcast version would be "15-BILLION" dollars to remind the newsreader to emphasize the "b." That's because "m" and "b" can sound the same, and no anchor wants to get a million confused with a billion.) In addition, the word "not" is capitalized so the on-mike or on-camera reader does NOT inadvertently make a positive out of a negative.

To understand a big difference between print and broadcast news, notice that the two newspaper sentences, each with dependent clauses, have been transformed into three terse, declarative sentences. Note also that the newspaper method of identifying a subject as, "Nicholas Burns, a State Department spokesman," has been replaced with the broadcast style of "State Department spokesman Nicholas Burns."

Here's another newspaper example:

> BOSTON — In his first public court appearance since the clergy sexual abuse scandal surfaced in January, Cardinal Bernard F. Law testified today in defense of the Boston archdiocese's decision to back out of a $30 million dollar settlement with 86 alleged victims of convicted pedophile and ex-priest John F. Geoghan.
>
> Law said under oath that the settlement had not yet gone into effect because it had not been signed by all parties and there was not enough money to pay for it.

Here's the broadcast version:

> In Boston, Cardinal Bernard Law says there was no agreement to back out of. That's because NOT all parties signed a 30-Million-dollar agreement between the archdiocese and several dozen people who say they were sex-abuse victims. The cardinal says the 30-Million dollars was too expensive anyway. That's why he says the Boston archdiocese will NOT pay 86 people who say they were victims of ex-priest John Geoghan (GAY'ghen). Geoghen is the convicted pedophile whose actions opened up a clergy sex abuse scandal last January. Cardinal Law denied the archdiocese reneged on an agreement in testimony in Suffolk Superior Court.

The broadcast lede teases the listener into the story by mentioning an agreement without identifying it in the first sentence. But it is detailed in the second sentence, and "agreement" is repeated. The middle initials of Law and Geoghan are eliminated. Again, the dollar amount is spelled out and the "not" is capitalized. The exact number of plaintiffs isn't clear until the second reference to them. First it was "several dozen," now it's "86." In addition, the ex-priest's name carries a phonetic "pronouncer." The emphasized syllable is capitalized and carries an apostrophe acting as an accent mark, and an "h" is added to the second syllable to make sure the newsreader uses a hard "g," not a "j" sound.

In second and third references to Law, he is referred to as "the cardinal" and "Cardinal Law." This is because repetition and redundancy, so despised by good newspaper and magazine writers, fulfill a needed role in broadcast. A cliché of sorts has developed among broadcast news professionals: "Tell them what you're going to tell them, tell them, and then tell them what you told them. And do it in 30 seconds or less."

Imagine you've fashioned a short, declarative sentence — the essence of direct, clear broadcast journalism. But what if you want to add a clause? Sometimes you must. The general rule is this: Separate the clause from the sentence by placing an ellipsis (three dots) where a comma or a semicolon might be in a print story. This way, the newsreader knows to end the main part of the sentence with the voice up ... then stop for half a beat before reading through the rest of the sentence. But don't overdo it. Short sentences work best.

The broadcast media are the media of immediacy — not deep, but certainly timely. So their preferred tense is the present tense, just as in a print feature when the writer wants readers to feel as though they are right there, watching the story unfold. In broadcast news, the exact time when the story took place is not as important as it is in print. A broadcast story has the most impact when the time is "now." This means the word "today" isn't nearly as important as it is in newspapers. In broadcast copy, if you insert the word "today," you put the sentence into past tense.

However, sometimes present tense sounds funny, like a stilted television attempt to imitate a newspaper headline. Suppose you write, "The governor endorses a news education package," without referring to when the governor made such an endorsement. When writing a story such as this, the broadcast news writer resorts to tenses that print reporters are supposed to shun: past perfect and present perfect.

> The governor has endorsed a new education package.
> (Or)
> The governor is endorsing a new education package.

Some Broadcast Style Pointers

Entire books are written about how to write for broadcast, and this book is not an attempt to compete with them. But here are a few suggestions (see Appendix A for more):

- Numbers one through eleven get spelled out. (In print journalism, it's usually one through nine). The reason "eleven" gets spelled out is that "11" can be misinterpreted as the Roman numeral II (two).

- Avoid using middle initials unless you are referring to someone named James Smith or Robert Johnson who was killed in a neighborhood where there might be a dozen James Smiths or Robert Johnsons. Another exception is when the middle initial is a part of a recognized name, such as George W. Bush, George M. Cohan or Johnny B. Goode.

- Quotation marks cannot be seen in broadcast copy, so what might be good print journalism — quoting accurately, word for word — simply gets lost on viewers and listeners. This is one reason so many broadcast quotes take the form of sound bites. If the on-air reader is quoting, though, make sure he or she uses the attribution first:

  Print example: "Why can't we all just get along?" Rodney King asked.

  Broadcast example: Rodney King asked ... in these words ... "Why can't we just get along?"

- In broadcast copy, "today" is today, not Sunday or Tuesday or Thursday. Likewise, "yesterday" is yesterday and "tomorrow" is tomorrow. Weekday names are used only for dates that occurred up to a week ago ("last Sunday" if today is Sunday) or a week from now ("next Sunday"). Any other day that is more than seven days before or after today is designated by its date. Do not format them as April 12 or the 12th of April, but as April 12th. The first eleven dates of the month are spelled out — September first, August fifth or December eleventh, but it's February 25th.

- Use hyphens (or single dashes) freely to help the announcer, especially with compound words or words with prefixes and suffixes: co-opt, pre-empt, count-down, school-children, re-election, man-slaughter, with-hold and the like.

- Help the anchor as much as you can with pronunciations of strange-sounding words. Do it with simple phonetic pronouncers — anything that can be constructed out of the often-inadequate 26 letters of the English alphabet. For example, Duke University basketball coach Mike Krzeciewski is pronounced (Sheh-SHEHF'skee). Here are some other examples:

former French President Giscard D'Estaing (ZHEE'-kahr Deh-STANG')

Birmingham (BER'ming-um), England (as opposed to BER'ming-ham, Ala.)

Cairo (CARE'-oh), Ill. (as opposed to (KYE'roh, Egypt)

The Anchor and the Reporter

Often a newscast includes not only a newsreader, but a reporter. When this occurs, the newsreader becomes an anchor and sets up every story that involves the reporter. The anchor's setup is called a "lead-in," and it serves somewhat different purposes than a print lede.

Lead-ins serve two main purposes. Just as a lede does in print, the lead-in sets up the story. But unlike the print lede, a lead-in also introduces the reporter — sort of an audio byline.

Often the reporter writes the lead-in and turns it over to a news editor along with audio or video of the reporter reciting the rest of the story, including any sound bites. The editor then incorporates the story into the newscast, complete with a time estimate. The total package rarely exceeds 90 seconds and usually it is under a minute.

National Public Radio (NPR) news professionals take pride in digging into a story more than the average commercial news operation would, so their stories tend to be a little longer. For regular newscasts, NPR reporters write their own scripts and record them, as their commercial competitors do. But in NPR's in-depth news programs — "Morning Edition" and "All Things Considered" — they take a little extra time for an informal dialogue between the anchor (or "host") and the reporter.

Here's a 2002 example from "Morning Edition" in which anchor Renee Montagne (who is subbing for the regular host, Bob Edwards) introduces a story about what became the run-up to the war in Iraq. In retrospect, the story's depth gives us some perspective about the thought processes that resulted in the war.

MONTAGNE: Iraqi opposition leaders are in Washington today for talks with State and Defense Department officials about the future of Iraq. The Bush administration signaled again this week that no invasion is imminent, but the opposition leaders say they believe it will happen. They want to know how they can help and what kind of role they might play afterwards if President Saddam Hussein is overthrown. N-P-R's Mary Louise Kelly is covering the meeting today, and she joins me now.
Good morning.

MARY LOUISE KELLY reporting:
Good morning.

MONTAGNE: Tell us about these opposition leaders. Who are they?

KELLY: Well, the most prominent is Ahmed Chalabi. He's the leader of the Iraqi National Congress. It's an umbrella group that claims to represent a number of exile groups, and this is the group that the U-S government is openly funding. But there are five other groups in Washington today. They include Kurdish groups from the north of Iraq. They include Shiite Muslim groups, and the leadership of those groups is based in Iran. And there's the Iraqi National Accord. So there's six groups total.

These groups, in the past, have not always gotten along, to put it mildly. And so the challenge now is: Can they put their differences behind them? Can they convince the Bush administration that they are really capable of helping to lead some sort of transition to a democratic Iraq? And the other big question is how much support any of them actually command in Iraq. A lot of these people, with the exception of the Kurdish groups, have been outside the country for many years, so how much support they have there, how good are their contacts anymore, it's not clear.

MONTAGNE: So what's expected to come out of the meetings today?

KELLY: Well, this is a chance for the Bush administration and the opposition leaders to look each other over. This is probably the highest-level, the most broad-based group with which the administration has met. The meetings this afternoon are at the undersecretary level, so that's a notch down from Secretary of State Colin Powell. But it would not be a big surprise if more senior people ended up talking with them. There are reports that tomorrow the vice president, Dick Cheney, will talk to them from a video linkup from where he's spending the month of August, at his home in Wyoming.

MONTAGNE: Speaking of Vice President Cheney, both he and the president have been out talking about Iraq this week. But are they toning down the rhetoric?

KELLY: I think it's fair to say that perhaps they are. Both the president and vice president gave speeches in the past couple of days stressing, again, no decision has been made. But there's a tiny shift. Some people are pointing to perhaps a subtle signal. Both talked about listening to other views on Iraq; the president in particular promised to be deliberate, promised to be patient, said he would consult with Congress and with allies. So this is being seen as an effort from the Bush administration to reassure people, "We are not about to go out and do anything rash. We will take other views into account before making a decision."

MONTAGNE: And is this in response to opposition in the rest of the world, which seems to be growing, to a U-S invasion of Iraq?

KELLY: Hard to say. It may be intended just as much for the U-S Congress, to reassure Congress "We will consult with you before deciding what to do." But it's certainly true, as you say, that opposition is hardening. Saudi Arabia this week said the U-S cannot use its territory to launch any operations against Iraq. Jordan's King Abdullah has repeated that, in his view, an attack would have disastrous consequences. And we're hearing this from Europe, too; in particular, this week from Germany, Chancellor Gerhard Schroeder delivered quite a strong speech opposing U-S military action in Iraq.

MONTAGNE: And Saddam Hussein is out giving speeches, not exactly conciliatory.

KELLY: That's right. Saddam yesterday went on Iraqi T-V and warned people that if they attacked his country, they would be "digging their own graves," his words. U-S officials dismissed it. Yesterday the State Department called it "bluster from an isolated dictator." So it does not look like the speech has changed any minds in the Bush administration.

MONTAGNE: Thanks very much, N-P-R's Mary Louise Kelly.

With its unscripted dialogue, this story took three minutes and 46 seconds. In broadcast notation, this would appear as 3:46. In almost any other newsroom, a report that long would be rare. Time is the dictator in the broadcast newsroom, and an understanding of the demands of airtime goes a long way toward explaining the strange rules of broadcast writing.

Variations for the Visual Media

The emphasis on the visual in television is so powerful that sound and words take a distant second or third place. (This applies to a formal newscast, as opposed to a video clip that might appear independently on the Internet.) In a television news script, which is divided vertically, what appears visually occupies its own place. On the left side, taking up about one-third of the page, is space for a few notes. They include visual descriptions, audio notations and directions to the studio director and the technical director.

The right two-thirds of the TV script displays either the copy of a story that involves no outside reporter, or the lead-in of a story that does. Typically, if the reporter's story is on tape, the lead-in will end with a phrase such as, "Here's Mike Morrison with the story." At this point, the notation on the right side might include a "V/O," meaning the reporter's taped narration is a voice-over of the visual story; an "incue," or the first words on the tape; an "outcue," or the last words the reporter spoke on the tape; and a total tape time and "sound under," indicating that natural background sound will accompany the reporter's narration. For example:

V/O RUNS: 45 SOUND UNDER
INCUE: "The car was caught between two trucks. ... "
OUTCUE: "... Morrison, Channel 6 News."

The format varies, depending on network and local station rules.

If the reporter is live, he or she is introduced with a scripted "throw" from the anchor — a phrase such as "Here's Mike Morrison live on the scene." There is also a scripted end to the story, which is usually something such as "Mike Morrison ... reporting from the Farragut Freeway."

To combine the anchor's copy with videotape, the news writer can write the script first and then work with the video technician or tape editor to get the raw footage, selecting segments that will match the script. But usually it works the other way around: The most dramatic video segments are electronically spliced together and then the news writer writes the script to match. Most often, the anchor intro is written first, the video is edited and put together, and only then is the script written. When using the right two-thirds of the script, two lines of 12-point copy equal about five seconds.

For a reporter's voice-over, the news writer crafts the intro and then collaborates with the tape editor to match video with audio. The writer then adds the time, incue and outcue and sends it to the newscast's producer.

An Alphabetical Digest of Broadcast Writing Rules

Because broadcast journalism copy is always meant for the ear and sometimes meant for the eye, it has developed rules that are best explained in contrast to the form of journalism that developed first — the accepted style for print journalism — much of which is displayed throughout this book. A compilation of print rules and practices appears in Appendix A, "Various Points of Style."

Abbreviations
Abbreviations are not frequently used in broadcast journalism copy. First-letter abbreviations are hyphenated unless they are pronounceable acronyms such as U-S, F-B-I, L-S-D (the drug), G-M (for General Motors), P-B-S (Public Broadcasting System) or the E-C (European Community). These titles appear as they do in print: Mr., Mrs., Ms., and Dr. As in newspapers, Dr. applies only to physicians; Ph.D.s in second reference go only by their last names. Nearly everything else in broadcast gets spelled out.

Alliterations and tongue twisters
Read your copy aloud before it goes on the air to make sure there are no abbreviations or tongue twisters. Avoid alliteration, or the repetition of consonants, which adds spice to print copy. In broadcast, alliteration can get a newsreader or anchor into real trouble. Tongue twisters have value only for newsreader training.

Attributions
Instead of ending a quotation with "according to J.P. McDonald, the company's controller," as you might in print, put the title in front and the attribution immediately after the name: "Company Controller J-P McDonald said. ..." (See "Quotations" in this section.)

Days and Dates

It's "yesterday," "today" or "tomorrow." If it's more than seven days before or after "today," it's "the day of the week." For dates, spell out the month, followed by an ordinal number that is spelled out if it's less than twelve. For example: March 23rd, July sixth, October 19th, May ninth.

Ellipses (...)

Sometimes you have no choice but to add a clause to a sentence. When this occurs, put an ellipsis where a comma or semicolon might go in a print story.

Hyphens

Hyphens (as opposed to dashes, which appear as double hyphens) are broadcast workhorses. Use hyphens freely to help the announcer, especially with compound words or words with prefixes and suffixes, or words such as these: co-opt, pre-empt, count-down, school-children, re-election, man-slaughter or with-hold.

Middle initials

Don't bother to use middle initials unless they belong to someone with a common last name, such as Smith, Johnson, Jones, Robinson, Williams, Wilson, Jackson, Martinez or Lee. Sometimes the middle initial is part of a prominent person's recognized name; in this case, you should include it.

Numbers

Spell out numbers one through eleven. Eleven is easily confused with the Roman numeral II (two). This is why it's spelled out in broadcast journalism, even though it's usually not spelled out in print journalism.

Present Tense

Present tense is the preferred tense in broadcast news, because it gives listeners and viewers a feeling of immediacy — of being right there.

Pronouncers

Do the newsreader a favor and provide a phonetic version of a word whose pronunciation might not be clear. Make sure the phonetics are simple and can be constructed from the 26 letters of English.

Former French President Jacques Cirac (Zhahk Shih-ROCK'); gastronomic delicacies tournedos (TOOR'neh-dohz); the Mexican volcano Ixtacihuatl (Ish-tah-SEE'wah-til); Reuters (ROY'-terz) news service; the Chinese city of Chengdu (Chong-DOO'); Louisville (LOO'-his-vil), Colo., as opposed to Louisville (LOO'-uh-vihl), Ky.; the late United Farm Workers leader Cesar Chavez (SAY'-zar CHAH'-vehz, not SEE'-zur Shuh-VEHZ'). If you are not sure of a pronunciation, take the time and effort to find out the correct one before airtime. News sources can get upset if their names are mangled.

Quotations

Direct quotations mean little in written broadcast copy because the viewer or listener can't see the quote marks that set off the direct quotes. All a sound bite needs is an attribution. If you need to make sure the audience knows that it was the subject who said something, and not the announcer, write something such as, "he said ... in these words ..." or "as she put it. ..." (See "Attributions" for more on this topic.)

Read copy aloud before airing

This is something broadcast writers absolutely must do. The practice of reading your copy aloud helps you catch mistakes, maintain conversational rhythm, eliminate unneeded words and sentence elements, and spot tongue twisters, alliteration and unnecessary sibilants.

Repetition and redundancy

These are not the sins that they are in print journalism. Because broadcast is a linear medium, listeners and viewers can't go over a sentence they didn't hear the first time, so it's OK to repeat some of the facts.

Short sentences

Show that you care about your anchor's breath supply. Avoid complex and compound sentences.

Sibilants ("S" Sounds)

Go easy with them. They tend to produce a hissing sound in microphones, and they lend themselves to tongue twisters.

Chapter 10 Exercises

Turn the following newspaper ledes into broadcast copy, 30 seconds for each story. (Coincidentally, "today" is Tuesday in all three of these stories as they might have been covered in today's newspaper and broadcast media.)

1. WASHINGTON — By a unanimous vote, the U.S. Supreme Court Monday upheld the constitutional amendment guaranteeing that women cannot be denied the right to vote simply because they are women. The decision in Leser v. Garrett, written by Justice Louis Brandeis, affirms the 19th Amendment, after Tennessee became the 36th state to ratify it on Aug. 18, 1920.

The decision marked the successful end of the U.S. women's suffrage movement that began in the mid-1800s in upstate New York, led by Susan B. Anthony and Elizabeth Cady Stanton.

The court ruled against Maryland resident Oscar Leser and others who had brought suit saying that Maryland had not ratified what became the 19th Amendment, so Baltimore residents Cecilia Streett Waters and Mary D. Randolph were not qualified to register to vote.

The amendment, which received the endorsement of then-President Wilson in January 1918, stumbled in its first bid to pass the Senate, but finally passed in June 1919 following mid-term elections.

2. BOSTON — The death toll from the March 5 confrontation between British troops and colonial residents reached five Monday. Irish immigrant Patrick Carr died from wounds he suffered during what is becoming known as "the bloody massacre" of two weeks ago.

Three men, ropemaker Samuel Gray, mariner James Caldwell and sailor Crispus Attucks, had been killed instantly. Seventeen-year-old Samuel Maverick, who was struck by a ricocheting musket ball as he stood at the back of the crowd, died a few hours later, early that Tuesday.

The incident began on King Street when a dispute over a wigmaker's bill grew into a confrontation between colonists, who had resented the nearly four-year presence of British troops, and soldiers of the 29th Regiment of Foot. The crowd grew to more than 300 people who were throwing snowballs and objects at soldiers. The soldiers eventually fired into the crowd. Their bullets struck 11 men.

A hearing on the possible indictment of several of the soldiers has been set for March 27.

3. PROMONTORY SUMMIT, Utah Territory — The American dream of bringing the Pacific and Atlantic Oceans much closer together came true Monday as workers — Chinese from the West and Irish, German and Italian from the East — ended seven years of laying railroad tracks across mountains, salt flats and plains from California to Nebraska Territory.

Four spikes cast in silver and gold felt the hammers of railroad men, then were replaced by spikes of steel. The final one connected with a national telegraph line.

Leland Stanford, president of the Central Pacific Railroad, represented the West. Thomas Durant, vice president of the Union Pacific Railroad, represented the East and the old Northwest, met in the dry May heat of this summit northwest of Ogden, Utah Territory. Together, their companies fulfilled the wishes of Congress and the late President Abraham Lincoln, who signed the Pacific Railroad Act in 1862.

Various Points of Style

This appendix makes no pretense of covering the myriad points that comprise newspaper style, but it does attempt to address, in alphabetical order, those that most frequently arise. For a more exhaustive list, go to The Associated Press Stylebook. Many of the word choices below are not included in The AP Stylebook, but they exhibit the preferred choices in good English usage.

How does newspaper style contrast with generally accepted points of good writing as dictated by, say, the Modern Language Association, the American Psychological Association or the University of Chicago style?

Like most good writing, journalistic style emphasizes word economy, active voice and action verbs. Unlike most, however, newspaper style — the format on which all other journalistic styles were built — concentrates on:

Ledes — Getting a lede that legitimately entices the reader to read on or adequately tell the reader what's important about the story, or both, is about half of what good newspaper writing is all about. And, for the writer, it should help organize the story.

Quotes — As much as 90 percent of journalistic research takes the form of interviewing, and that should result in stories festooned with direct quotations.

Brevity — Without sounding like a "Dick and Jane Have Fun" book, newspaper writing emphasizes short sentences and paragraphs. That does not mean that you should not ever use a compound or complex sentence, but you should default to a simple, declarative sentence. Paragraphs are shorter. (See Paragraphs below.)

In examples of word choices below, an asterisk (*) denotes sentences that include incorrect or less-preferred usages. Now, in alphabetical order, are some other pointers:

Abbreviations

"United States" is spelled out as a noun, abbreviated when it is used as an adjective; for example, "U.S. forces remain in Afghanistan while the United States tries to help Afghanistan develop an infrastructure of services for its people."

When you write the name of a state, without a city attached, spell it out: "Oregon." If you include a city or town with it, do not use the postal designation. Instead, use the system that existed before the postal service altered it 30-odd years ago: "Eugene, Ore., is in the Willamette River valley."

Here are the state abbreviations (including Washington, D.C.) used in most U.S. newspapers — note the use of capitals, lowercase letters and punctuation. (Some states continue to be spelled out.)

Alaska	Alaska	Montana	Mont.
Alabama	Ala.	Nebraska	Neb.
Arizona	Ariz.	Nevada	Nev.
Arkansas	Ark.	New Hampshire	N.H.
California	Calif.	New Jersey	N.J.
Colorado	Colo.	New Mexico	N.M.
Connecticut	Conn.	New York	N.Y.
Delaware	Del.	North Carolina	N.C.
District of Columbia	D.C.	North Dakota	N.D.
Florida	Fla.	Ohio	Ohio

Georgia	Ga.	Oklahoma	Okla.
Hawaii	Hawaii	Oregon	Ore.
Idaho	Ida.	Pennsylvania	Pa.
Illinois	Ill.	Rhode Island	R.I.
Indiana	Ind.	South Carolina	S.C.
Iowa	Iowa	South Dakota	S.D.
Kansas	Kans.	Tennessee	Tenn.
Kentucky	Ky.	Texas	Texas
Louisiana	La.	Utah	Utah
Maine	Maine	Vermont	Vt.
Maryland	Md.	Virginia	Va.
Massachusetts	Mass.	Washington (State)	Wash.
Michigan	Mich.	West Virginia	W.Va.
Minnesota	Minn.	Wisconsin	Wis.
Mississippi	Miss.	Wyoming	Wyo.
Missouri	Mo.		

U.S. territories and the names of foreign countries are spelled out.

Access, except

Accept, a verb, means to receive willingly. *Except*, usually a preposition, means "not including." In rare cases, *except* can be a verb meaning to leave out or exclude. But to avoid confusion, it's better to use *leave out* or *exclude*.

I *accept* your criticism, *except* for the statement that I am a waste of carbon.

Access, impact

These are nouns, not verbs. You *gain access*; you *feel impact*. (This is a good example of a losing battle for people serious about using good English. But we try.)

*I can't *access* my games program.

I can't *gain access* to my games program.

*The cheating by corporate executives and audit firms could not have *impacted* Wall Street at a worse time.

The *impact* on Wall Street by corporate executives and audit firms could not have come at a worse time.

Adapt, adopt

Adapt means to adjust to fit new circumstances. *Adopt* means to take as your own, be it a child or idea.

If you're going to *adapt* to the demands of journalism, you're going to have to *adopt* a journalistic style of writing.

Adverse, averse

Adverse circumstances act against something or in its opposite direction. If you're *averse* to something, you don't like it or you're reluctant to pursue it.

I'm *averse* to trying anything that brings with it an *adverse* environment.

Advice, advise

Advice is a noun, the information delivered by an advisor. *Advise* is a verb, what the advisor does.

My *advice* is that you *advise* us the next time you decide that going to Tahiti is more important than showing up for work on a Monday.

Affect, effect

Affect is a verb and *effect* is a noun — usually. In rare instances, *effect* can be a verb. You can, for instance, *effect* change or *effect* a solution. But most often the two words are used like this:

The professor gestures for *effect*, and that *affects* the perceptions of his students.

All, any, most, none, some

In American English, if we're talking about quantities, these words are treated as singular pronouns. But if they refer to individual items, they're plural, so they take plural verbs.

All of the moonshine seized during the raid was sent to the sheriff's office for safekeeping.

All of the troops were safely airlifted to Kabul.

Any breathable air we find in the city belongs in a museum.

Any of the students who are ready to leave class can go now.

The children ate *most* of the ice cream before the picnic began.

Most of the marathoners were dehydrated by the time they reached the finish line.

None of the U.N. countries condemned the Middle East action, but some voiced their reservations.

Almost *none* of the oil designated as "light, sweet, crude" comes from domestic sources, but *some* of it comes from Saudi Arabia.

All, everybody, everyone
Imagine a red flag going up when you find yourself using such words and ask, "Is this accurate?" Usually, it isn't.

Alliterate, illiterate
Alliterate is a verb, meaning to combine words with the same consonant sounds, especially the beginnings of words. *Illiterate* is an adjective, describing someone who cannot read.

To describe *alliteration* to him, she e-mailed "Peter Piper picked a peck of pickled peppers," but it was a wasted effort. He was *illiterate*.

All together, altogether
All together means everything in one place; *altogether* means entirely.

Now the choir members were *all together*, but the choir director said she wasn't *altogether* sure they could all sing on key.

Allude, elude, refer

If you *allude* to something, you're referring indirectly to it or hinting at it. If you're directly referring to it, use *refer*. *Elude* means to escape or avoid someone or something.

"That embarrassing moment you *alluded* to occurred as I was trying to *elude* my ex-wife, who has *referred* me to the authorities," he said.

Allusion, illusion

An *allusion* is an indirect reference or a hint. An *illusion* is a mistaken idea or visual image.

You are obviously under the *illusion* that I didn't understand your *allusion* to my bad habits.

A lot, allot

The expression *a lot* borders on the colloquial and can usually be replaced with *much, many, a great many* or *a great deal*. But if you do use it or quote someone using it, it is two words. *Alot* is not a word, and *allot* means to mete out or distribute.

"We've *allotted a lot* of foodstuffs on this rescue mission," the sergeant said.

Alright, all right, already, all ready

Alright seems to have gained acceptance during the past few decades, but it doesn't really exist as a word. It's two words, *all right* — not to be confused with *already*, which does exist. So does *all ready*, but its meaning is different.

They *already* told you that they are *all ready* for the game to begin.

Already you think it's *all right* to ask me out, and I don't even know your name.

Among, between

It's a matter of numbers. If you are in the midst of more than two trees or people, you're *among* them. If, however, they number only two, you're *between* them.

Even though I'm *among* the people in the unemployment line, I prefer to believe I am *between* jobs.

Amongst seems to be a word in virtually every English-speaking country except most of the United States. Here, it should be *among*. *Amongst* does get used widely east of the Appalachians, but not in journalistic style.

Amoral, immoral

The test seems to be just how sinful the subject is. If she is *immoral*, she is morally wrong. If he is *amoral*, he simply doesn't concern himself with morals, morality or immorality.

Amount, number

Amount refers to quantities that can be counted by pointing at them, but get measured by gallons, liters, pounds or grams. *Number* refers to things that can be counted separately from one another.

Use whatever *amount* of oil it takes. You're going to be cooking a huge *number* of pancakes.

(You might simply say, "Use as much oil as it takes.")

And/or

Awkward constructions like this tend to stop the reader cold. Write the concept out. Instead of "The Mighty Ducks expect to beat *and/or* tie the Red Wings," try "The Mighty Ducks expect to at least tie the Red Wings. They could win." (You could eliminate the last sentence. Technically, it's redundant.)

Anxious, eager

It depends on how much the subject is looking forward to the event. If yes, he is *eager*. If not, she is *anxious*.

The president said she is *eager* for the election to be concluded but *anxious* to learn the results.

Anybody, anyone

Make sure you write *anybody* as one word unless you're describing a choice in a group. *Anyone* is usually one word unless you mean any single person or thing.

"Ask *anyone*," he said. "*Any body* like the U.S. Senate can kill *anybody*'s pet project at any one time."

Area, nature, -oriented

Generally speaking, these terms are too general and are often awkward when they are used as adjectives. And they are usually redundant.

*She taught in the *area* of physics.
She taught physics.

*He was of a pleasant *nature*.
He was pleasant.

*Judging from her rhetoric, she appears to be *conservative-oriented* in her politics.
Judging from her rhetoric, she appears to be politically conservative.

As, like

If you're describing something similar to a noun or pronoun, use *like*. If it's an action you're describing, go with *as* or *as if*. In casual conversation, most of us are apt to use *like* with verbs, and sometimes *as*, even though correct, can sound awkward. But if you're intent on being grammatically correct, you must use *as* when it's called for.

You are *like* an old English teacher of mine who talked *as if* using "like" when one should use "as" will bring an end to civilization as we know it.

Aspect, factor

As nouns, these words are usually weak because they give the writer an excuse to be wordy and less specific. (As a verb, *factor*, as in "factor in," can be useful, but it tends to be overused.)

*Inadequate communication between intelligence agencies was one *aspect* of the failure to recognize potential terrorists.

One reason intelligence agencies failed to recognize potential terrorists was that they didn't communicate with each other.

*Her high school record of extracurricular activities was the biggest *factor* in her successful bid to get into college.

The college accepted her mainly because of her many high school extracurricular activities.

As yet

A simple "yet" will do.

*We don't see the country pulling out of its economic doldrums *as yet*.

We don't *yet* see the country pulling out of its economic doldrums.

Average, median, mean

Many reporters use them interchangeably, but they're not the same thing. *Average* is the group total divided by the number of people or things in the group. A *median* figure has an equal number of figures above and below it. If five people have incomes of $110,000, $50,000, $40,000, $30,000 and $20,000, the *average* income is $50,000, but the *median* income is $40,000.

Mean is a mathematical synonym of average. Technically they differ, but as practical terms, they are interchangeable.

Attribution verbs (See *Quotes, attribution*, below.)

Usually, in a direct quotation, stick with *said*. You can use *says* with an indirect quote or in the rare present-tense story. Repetition of *said* might seem monotonous to the writer, but the reader usually doesn't notice, and it beats reaching for verbs like *states, exclaimed, remarked, averred, declaimed, noted, contended* or *indicated*. Be especially careful using *claimed*. It usually implies that the reporter doesn't believe what the subject said. And *feel* should refer only to the sense of touch or emotion; *believes* or *thinks* is better, but the reader still might wonder if the reporter is making it up. *Said* puts the onus where it should belong, on the person who made the assertion. Exception: If the verb is more specific or more accurate, then verbs like *conceded, replied, explained, recalled, warned* or *admitted* might be more apt. If that is indeed what the subject did, then *said* would be less precise.

Averse, adverse — See *Adverse, averse.*

Awesome
It used to mean "to inspire awe," but it has been so overused that it now means no more than, "Gee, that's nice," or "Cool." For many young men and women, *awesome* apparently has become the only adjective they know to modify anything that isn't merely "cool" or "sweet."

Awhile, a while
Awhile is an adverb, modifying a verb describing roughly how long an action might take. *A while* is a noun, an imprecise measurement of time. The key is whether or not it is preceded by a preposition. If it is, then it's *a while.*

I studied these obtuse journalistic rules for *a while*, and it took me *awhile* longer to understand them.

Bad, badly
Bad is an adjective modifying a noun or pronoun, and *badly* is an adverb usually modifying a verb.

Phydeau is a bad dog. (Modifies the noun dog.)
Phydeau acts *badly*. (Modifies the verb acts.)

This does not mean, however, that you can't feel *bad*; *bad* then becomes an adjective modifying you.

Because, since
Don't use *since* when you mean *because*. *Since* refers to the passage of time. When it's used to explain why something happened, it can be mistaken for when it happened.

Because they won the lottery, they have been traveling around world, and they've been traveling ever *since.*

Because of, due to

Because of links a cause with an effect. *Due to* is an adjective and a preposition that combine with a linking verb to bring cause and effect together. But if you see either *because of* or *due to* in a sentence, you usually have the opportunity to tighten that sentence by getting rid of either one of them and using active voice and an action verb.

*Because of excess spending and inadequate taxation, a balanced budget was not achieved.

Excess spending and inadequate taxation killed any chance for a balanced budget.

*The explosion was *due to* the accidental detonation of a land mine.

A land mine accidentally caused the explosion.

Being that

Usually redundant and always awkward.

*Being that he was the oldest of 12 children, he learned early to take responsibility.

As the oldest of 12 children, he learned early to take responsibility.

Beside, besides

Beside means "next to." *Besides* means "as well as or in addition to."

Besides Georgia, only Alabama is *beside* Florida on the map.

(Although correct, that sounds awkward. You'd be better off writing, "Only Georgia and Alabama border Florida.")

Between, among — See *Among, between.*

Bi-, semi-

Many people say biweekly when they mean it happens twice

a week, but *bi-* means every other time. *Semi-* means half, or twice during the same period, so semiweekly means twice a week; biweekly means once every two weeks. Semimonthly means twice a month; bimonthly means once every two months. Semiannual means twice yearly; biennial (note different spelling) means once every two years.

Bring, take

You *bring* something in; you *take* something out.

Once she *takes* the cashier's check to the dealer, she can get the car and *bring* it home.

Burst, bursted, bust

As a verb, *burst* means to fly apart in pieces. It's the same word regardless of whether it's in past, present or future tense, so *bursted* doesn't exist. The word can also be a noun, as in "a *burst* of machine gunfire." *Bust* does have a separate past tense, *busted*, but unless it's in a quotation, don't use it. It also has a legitimate noun form — a *bust* of Beethoven — and one not so legitimate. "The venture was a bust" is rapidly becoming a cliché.

Can, may

Can implies ability; *may* implies permission. *May* can also imply possibility, but *might* usually works better.

As far as the editor is concerned, the reporter *may* cover any story he wants to, but *can* he?

Capital, capitol

Unless you're writing about finances — "capital expenditures" — *capital* usually refers to a city in which a state, province or national government resides. The *capitol* is the building or complex where lawmakers meet.

Because it is circular and flat on top, the *capitol* in Santa Fe, the *capital* of New Mexico, is unofficially called "the roundhouse."

Capitalization

Journalistic style generally follows the style of capitalization we learned in middle school. In a college or university, though, subtleties in capitalization do exist. A college course, for example, is lower case unless it begins a sentence or it would be capitalized anyway, as would Shakespeare or Japanese. If it is the formal title of a department or school, however, it is capitalized: the Psychology Department, the School of Engineering.

Case

An overused word that is often redundant.

*It is rarely the *case* that, in today's baseball, most batters try to do anything but hit home runs.

In baseball today, most batters try to do nothing but hit home runs.

Censor, censure

To *censor* means to suppress the transmission or publication of written or visual matter. To *censure* is to lay blame, usually in a public forum like the Senate.

"Any Senator who *censors* a report before it is published or aired should be *censured*," the governor said.

Chair, chairman, chairperson, chairwoman

For understandable reasons, many object to the assumption that anyone who chairs a meeting or an organization must be male. The use of *chair*, however, sounds as if a piece of furniture is in charge, and *chairperson* suggests a hybrid that sounds at least as strange. (The AP Stylebook says, "Do not use *chairperson* ... unless it is an organization's formal title for an office.") Most newspapers simply use *chairman* if he is male and *chairwoman* if she is female. The same applies to *congressman* and *congresswoman*.

Character, reputation

Character is often unnecessary and redundant.

*It isn't often that actions of a mild *character* attract much attention.

It isn't often that mild actions attract much attention.

In another sense, according to The AP Stylebook, "*Character* refers to moral qualities. *Reputation* refers to the way one person is regarded by others."

Cite, site

You can *cite* a source in a research paper or news story, or get *cited* for speeding. But a *site* is a location, even on the World Wide Web.

The reporter refused to *cite* her sources or tell police whom she met at the *site* of the crime.

Climactic, climatic

Climactic, a derivation of climax, describes the peak of a process. *Climatic* refers to the weather.

No *climatic* cycle exists at sea level on the equator, so unless sea-level Ecuadorians go north or south, they don't experience the *climactic* cold of winter.

Coarse, course

Coarse means "roughly ground or vulgar." *Course* is an offering at school or from a kitchen, a direction or a part of a transitional phrase between sentences.

Of *course*, some gourmets like to sprinkle *coarse* red pepper or oregano on their pizzas.

Collide, crash

If two moving vehicles come into contact, they *collided*. If only one was moving before it hit a telephone pole, it *crashed*.

The SUV *crashed* into a tree after it *collided* with a truck.

Commas — See *Punctuation, notes on.*

Complement, compliment

Complement suggests yin and yang — that opposites attract. *Compliment* is an expression of approval or courtesy, sometimes of flattery.

You should be *complimented* on how you have used your creative personality to *complement* your partner's rigid mentality.

Comprise, compose, constitute

If you *comprise* something, you include all of it. Together, components *constitute* what is being *comprised*. Something can be *composed* of several things, but one thing *comprises* all the others.

Water *comprises* hydrogen and oxygen, that is, water is *composed* of its constituent parts, hydrogen and oxygen. Hydrogen and oxygen *constitute* water.

Congressman, congresswoman, congressperson — See *Chair, chairman, chairperson, chairwoman.* ("Congress" is capitalized, but *congressman* and *congresswoman* are not.)

Conscience, conscious

If you have a *conscience*, you have a sense of what's right and wrong and favor the former. If you are *conscious*, you might be aware of the difference, or not, but at least you're aware of something.

"The only time that politician has a *conscience* is when she is *unconscious*," she said.

Continual, continuous, ongoing

Continual means steadily recurring, like the chiming of a clock. *Continuous* means without interruption, like the flow of Niagara Falls. Many people write *ongoing* when they mean *continuous*, but *ongoing* is a business cliché.

The space station orbits Earth *continuously*. It gets *continual* additions and improvements.

Could have, could of — See *Of used as have.*

Counsel, council. A *counsel* is an adviser, often a lawyer. To *counsel* means "to advise." A *council* is an assembly or meeting.

Crash, collide — See *Crash, collide.*

Criteria, data, media

Technically, *data* and *criteria* are plural, but almost no one outside academic and scientific circles says, "the data are" or "the criteria are." *Media* is not so easy to shrug off. Not many people use it correctly as a plural either, but they should. The fact that we say "the media is" perpetuates the myth that the news media all come from the same pot, that they are a monolith or a conspiracy. The news media are as competitive as they ever were, and we should view them as plural in the extreme.

Currently, presently

Unless it is used to contrast "then" and "now," *currently* is always redundant. If you do need to contrast times, use the stronger, punchier word *now*. *Presently* is one of the most misused words in English. It does not mean "now," but "soon."

*A former standup comedian, he is *currently* a politician.

A former standup comedian, he is *now* a politician.

Dangling modifiers, misplaced modifiers

If you have a modifier — an adjective or adverb — that doesn't modify anything in the sentence, then it dangles or modifies the wrong word.

*Out of fuel, the rest of the cars passed Jeff Gordon's.

The rest of the cars passed Jeff Gordon's, which ran out of fuel.

Dashes

Known as a journalism "disease," a dash (written as two *hyphens*) tends to overdramatize copy or imply irony where it might not exist. Use dashes only when the drama or irony is clear or if you're defining a word or concept that most readers could not be expected to know.

Samuel Wilkeson Jr. — chief of Civil War correspondents for Horace Greeley's New York Tribune — left because he said he didn't agree with Greeley that the Confederacy should be appeased. Wilkeson went to work for Henry Raymond's New York Times, but then returned to the Tribune — for more money.

Hyphens bring together compound modifiers or take the place of omitted prepositions. (If the first of the pair of modifiers ends in -*ly*, though, it takes no hyphen.)

Good editors are not satisfied with pretty-good copy.

Pro basketball players — and their fans — now endure an October-June season. (Here, the hyphen replaces the understood preposition "through.")

It isn't that I'm a poor reader, it's that this story is poorly written. (No hyphen.)

Data, criteria, media — See *Criteria, data, media.*

Dates

It is either May 20 or the 20th of May. In newspaper copy, it is never May 20th. ("May 20th" is the accepted form, however, in broadcast copy.) And when you add a year, set it off with commas: "Sept. 11, 2001 will always be remembered."

This century, in newspaper style, is the 21st century. It is not spelled out unless the number itself begins a sentence:

"Twenty-first century technological devices will have to wait at least 50 years before they become antiques."

Weekdays are spelled out.

Months are spelled out when they stand alone — but most are abbreviated in dates: Jan. 1 begins the New Year. Here are the abbreviations as well as the ones that continue to be spelled out:

January	Jan.	July	July
February	Feb.	August	Aug.
March	March	September	Sept.
April	April	October	Oct.
May	May	November	Nov.
June	June	December	Dec.

Desert, dessert

A *desert* is an arid plain. A *dessert* is usually something sweet that follows a lunch or dinner.

He said the cake he ate for *dessert* was so moist he could even eat it in a *desert* and it would slake his thirst.

Disburse, disperse

To *disburse* is to pay out, distribute funds in some way. To *disperse* is to scatter, to distribute widely. Disperse can also mean to cause to disappear. To avoid confusion, you might use simpler words.

The company *disbursed* the bonuses at a corporate retreat in Las Vegas. Then the executives *dispersed* to the casinos.

(Or)

The company paid out the bonuses at a corporate retreat in Las Vegas. Then the executives vanished into the casinos.

Discreet, discrete

They look and sound alike, but they are not related. If you're *discreet*, you're letting out no more information than you must; you're not doing anything to attract attention to yourself. *Discrete* means "distinct."

I know you're trying to be *discreet* about your feelings, but whether or not you love me is a *discrete* topic for us to talk about.

Disinterested, uninterested

Disinterested means "impartial"; you have no personal interest in an outcome. *Uninterested* means you don't care.

Reporters are often called on to be *disinterested* spectators, even if they might be *uninterested* in the subject.

Due to, because of — See *Because of, due to.*

Each and every
Two words too many; *every* will suffice.
*Each and every American should remember Sept. 11, 2001.
Every American should remember Sept. 11, 2001.
Each family that lost someone in the air attacks will remember Sept. 11, 2001.

Eager, anxious — See *Anxious, eager.*

Effect, affect — See *Affect, effect.*

Elude, allude, refer — See *Allude, elude, refer.*

Emigrate, immigrate
It depends on whether you're going or coming. If you *immigrate,* you are entering a country that is not your native residence. If you *emigrate*, you're moving out, to another country.

Eminent, imminent, immanent
Eminent means distinguished; it usually refers to a person. *Imminent* means impending and implies threatening, something that could happen soon. *Immanent* means "inherent" or "indwelling," the opposite of transcendent.
My *immanent* belief is that a long, boring lecture from our *eminent* professor is *imminent.*

Enthuse
A misbegotten form of the noun enthusiasm, it tries to replace verbs like "encourage," "motivate," "rhapsodize" or "gush."
She *enthused* about the prospect of attending a prestigious graduate school.

She talked about how eager she is to attend a prestigious graduate school.

Etc.

A sure way to convince readers that you want to con them into believing you know many things, but you can't think of any. A great way to lose reader respect.

The alphabet includes a, b, c, d, *etc.*

Everybody, everyone

"Each" is treated as a single word, even though nearly everyone seems to ignore the rule when writing a complex or compound sentence. The use of *every* would seem to imply "several" or "many," but for some reason ending it with "body" or "one" makes it revert to the singular.

*If *everyone* passes the final exam, they will pass the course.

If *everyone* passes the final exam, he or she will pass the course.

(Or, to eliminate awkwardness:)

Everyone who passes the final exam will pass the course.

Except, accept — See *Accept, except.*

Exclamation points

Save them for quotations from the subjects who are shouting or talking emphatically. Otherwise, they emphasize when no emphasis is needed or lend themselves to editorialization. Either way, they detract from the strength of your words.

*Here is your change, sir!

Here is your change, sir.

Factor, aspect — See *Aspect, factor.*

Farther, further

Farther implies distance; *further* implies degree.

The *farther* I drive this gas hog, the *further* it cuts into my money supply.

Feel

A special word that means emotion or sensory reaction. It should not be used to replace "think" or "believe." In journalistic writing, *feel* can often be replaced with the more neutral *said* or *says*. (See *Attribution, verbs*.)

*The foreign minister *feels* that some countries are not ready for a system as sophisticated as democracy.

The foreign minister *said* some countries are not ready for a system as sophisticated as democracy.

Fewer, less

Fewer refers to items that can be counted. *Less* refers to quantities that can't be divided into items.

Unless we have *fewer* cooks in the kitchen, we're going to end up with *less* broth.

Figuratively, literally

They are direct opposites, but many reporters get them confused. If you're writing about something *figuratively*, you're referring to it symbolically or metaphorically. But if you're treating the subject *literally*, you're telling the reader, viewer or listener that you're referring to it as the word-for-word truth.

When she said she was "*literally* dead with fatigue," she meant it *figuratively*. If she were literally dead with fatigue, she wouldn't be able to talk about it.

Finalize

A piece of business-ese that has found its way into pompous people's mouths and memos. Try *end, add up, finish, polish* or *summarize*.

Good, well

Good is an adjective modifying a noun or pronoun. *Well* is an adverb modifying a verb.

Balzac is a *good* cat. (Modifies "cat.")

Balzac sleeps *well*. (Modifies "sleeps.")

Hanged, hung

A distinction usually ignored. People suspended by the neck from a rope are *hanged*. Anything else suspended is *hung*.

U.S. flags *hung* at half-staff after we learned that the terrorists had *hanged* their prisoners.

Have, possess

Unless you're writing about some supernatural force taking over a body or soul, or someone working for a bank has re*possessed* a car, stick with a form of *have*. It sounds less pretentious. It's also an example of why a short word usually works better than a longer one.

"You'd think if he were *possessed* by the devil, he'd *have* some wealth to show for it," she said.

Historic, historical

An event is *historic* if it has earned a place in history. Research is *historical* if it analyzes the past.

Diana Gabaldon based her *historical* novel on the *historic* Battle of Culloden.

Hopefully

If you go with its original meaning, "with hope" or "full of hope," this word usually makes no sense. For instance, if you say, "*Hopefully*, the truck will start," you're actually saying, "The truck hopes it will start."

But even when you're writing about a human being, *hopefully* doesn't usually work. For example, if you say, "*Hopefully*, he'll never have to go through that again," who's doing the hoping? As the sentence reads, "he hopes," but that's not what you meant. If you mean, "I hope," then write, "I hope."

Horrific

A recent fad word that could fade away, unlamented, as most fad words do. An apparent hybrid between "horrible" and "terrific," it is artificial and unnecessary; we already have "horrible" and "horrifying." And the *-ic* at the end makes *horrific* sound as if it's not really horrible, it's only "like" horrible.

If, whether

They sound interchangeable, but *if* means "in the event that," and *whether* offers a choice. When you do use *whether*, you can often eliminate "or not." It's implied.

He wants to know *if* he will receive the same health benefits *whether* he retires now or in three years.

If it was, if it were

In correct English, it's always *if it were*. The "if" means the statement is conditional or hypothetical, and that automatically sends the phrase into the subjunctive mood, which always takes a "were."

*If she *was* a certified angel, I still wouldn't vote for her.

If she *were* a certified angel, I still wouldn't vote for her.

Illusion, allusion — See *Allusion, illusion.*

Immigrate, emigrate — See *Emigrate, immigrate.*

Imminent, immanent, eminent — See *Eminent, imminent, immanent.*

Immoral, amoral — See *Amoral, immoral.*

Impact, access — See *Access, impact.*

Implement

A clumsy attempt to turn a noun into a verb so the writer can sound impressive. An *implement* is a tool; *to implement* is to carry out, put into practice, make happen, accomplish or simply do. Use plain English.

*We need to *implement* a new procedure so the system doesn't crash again.

We need to carry out a new procedure so the system doesn't crash again.

(Or)

We need a new procedure so the system doesn't crash again.

Imply, infer

Not the same. If you *infer* something, you draw conclusions from a set of facts or premises. If you *imply* something, you suggest something or hint at it.

Because you *imply* something you obviously know nothing about, I'm going to *infer* that you didn't do your homework.

Initiate, instigate

When you *initiate* something, you start it up. When you *instigate* something, you push it forward. Instigate has a negative feel to it.

How can we *initiate* a reform plan if you *instigate* our removal?

Informal writing

Newspaper copy should be tightly edited, but sound conversational. The two are not mutually exclusive, and the best journalistic writing does both. Some forbidding grammar rules are not forbidden in journalism. You may:

Begin a sentence with a conjunction.

End a sentence with a preposition.

Use contractions.

Irregardless

Not a word; the word is *regardless*. But don't confuse it with "irrespective," "irregular" or "irresponsible," which are words. In the case of *irregardless,* the *-less* already implies a negative, so the *ir-* is redundant.

Its, it's

The word *it's* looks as if it should be a possessive, but it isn't. It's a contraction. The possessive is *its*, which looks like a plural, but isn't. Think of *its* the way you would think of *his, ours* or *theirs*.

Now *it's* time for the train to wind *its* way through the Sierra Nevada.

-ize

A disease bordering on an epidemic. Although many legitimate words end in *-ize*, the suffix has been tacked onto a vast number of nouns to create clumsy verbs that usually try to provide a substitute for *make*.

You want to *prosperize* your financial situation; I just want my income to exceed my expenses.

You want to *sermonize*; I merely want to make a point.

You want to *architize* an edifice; I simply want to construct a building.

Kind of, sort of

Unless you mean it literally, as in, "Licorice is a *kind of* candy," use these to mean "somewhat" or "something like" only in the most informal writing. Even then, they're not the same: *kind of* refers to type, *sort of* refers to degree.

*I left the exam *sort of* tired.

I left the exam *somewhat* tired.

Lay, lie

In present and future tenses, use *lay* when you require a direct object and *lie* when you don't. Simple enough until you write it in past tense. Then *lay* becomes *laid*, and *lie* becomes *lay*. Nobody said English always makes sense.

When she is ready to *lie* on the couch, she'll *lay* her TV section on the table. At least, that's what she did the last time she *lay* there, except that then she *laid* the TV section on a chair.

Lend, loan
Although *loan* as a verb has become accepted, it is more precise to stick with *lend* as a verb and *loan* as a noun.

I know I still owe you for the last *loan*, but can you *lend* me an extra 50 bucks?

Less, fewer — See *Fewer, less.*

Less than, under, more than, over
Less than and *more than* are quantities; *under* and *over* are directions.

More than 100,000 people watched the U.S. Navy's Blue Angels fly over the stadium.

It takes *less than* 10 seconds to check to see if there's dirt under the rug.

Likable, Likeable
In AP style, it's *likable.*

"Like" is a refuge for people who cannot express themselves clearly. Granted, it's usually spoken, not written, but the overuse of *like* is a symptom of malignant, muddled thinking. *Like* is not a punctuation mark, so it does not belong between every other word or phrase. When people use it that way, they're saying the point they're making isn't really a point — it's only "like" a point. If you say the guy or chic you're dating is "like, so cool," you're actually saying he or she isn't really cool, only similar to cool.

*And I *like* told him *like* that's the last time he'll ever *like* stand me up, *like*, you know?

In this example, we can infer that she really didn't tell him, and it really isn't the last time, he never really stood her up and you don't really know.

Like, as — See *As, like.*

Literally, figuratively — See *Figuratively, literally.*

Located, location.

Often redundant.

Hollywood is *located* in Southern California and Florida.
Hollywood is in Southern California and Florida.

Loose, lose

In common usage, *loose* (pronounced "looss") is an adjective meaning "not well-fastened or free from restraint or obligation." *Lose* (pronounced "looz") is a verb meaning mislay.

If you wear your cap *loose*, you're going to *lose* it in the wind.

Note: You might feel the urge to change *loose* to *loosely*, but if you do, you're saying something different. In the example, the object *loose* modifies the noun "cap." The adverb *loosely* would define the verb "wear."

Lot, lots

Use as an adjective only in the most informal writing. Otherwise, go with *many* or *much* or *a great deal.*

*A *lot* of the children said they want *lots* more candy with their meals.

Many of the children said they want *much* more candy with their meals.

Majority, plurality

A *majority* of the vote means at least one vote more than 50 percent. A *plurality* means the most votes cast for three or more candidates, but not most of the total votes.

By attracting a *plurality* of 34 percent of the votes, the new governor did not win by a *majority*, but he did manage to beat the other two, each of whom registered 33 percent of the vote.

Mankind

Carries a connotation of sexism. Try "humans," "humankind" or "humanity."

May, can, might — See *Can, may, might.*

May have, may of — See *Of used as have.*

Mean, median, average — See *Average, mean, median.*

Meaningful

A word that is less *meaningful* the more it is used. During the 1960s and 1970s, you could not be blamed if you believed that every college student was in search of a *meaningful* relationship or a *meaningful* course of study. Now, decades later, the word is still overused. Find another way to write it.

*I do not believe you have contributed to any *meaningful* way to what we have done here.

I do not believe you have contributed much to what we have done.

(Or)

I don't believe you've made much of a contribution here.

Media, criteria, data — See *Criteria, media, data.*

Might have, might of — See *Of used as have.*

Misplaced modifiers, dangling modifiers — See *Dangling modifiers, misplaced modifiers.*

More than, over — See *Less than, under, more than, over.*

Names

In first reference, use the first and last name, sometimes a middle initial. Do not use a title in first reference unless it is widely known, for example, President Obama. If the subject is charged with a crime, use the full middle name. In second reference and beyond, most newspapers use the last name only. A few, including prestigious ones like The Christian Science Monitor, The New York Times and The Wall Street Journal, use Mr. or

Ms., but not in first reference. Use Dr. only if the subject is a physician (not a Ph.D.).

Nature, area — See *Area, nature.*

Nauseated, nauseous

A distinction that often gets missed. If you feel queasy, you are *nauseated.*If you make someone else queasy, you are *nauseous.*

On our first date, the woman who is now my wife was *nauseated.* I'm surprised she decided to go out with me again, because she now tells me I was *nauseous* back then.

None

Whether this pronoun reflects a singular or plural noun and takes a singular or plural verb is a question of amount. If *none* reflects a conglomeration, it reflects a singular noun and takes a single verb. If *none* reflects more than one item, it reflects a plural noun and takes a plural verb.

None of the soup is left.

None of the persons who said they supported her campaign were at the campaign kickoff.

Number, amount — See *Amount, number.*

Numbers

Generally, numbers from one to nine are spelled out; all above nine are written in Arabic numerals. Exceptions:

If a number starts a sentence, it is always spelled out: *Twenty-five* years ago, my father graduated from college.

Unless they begin a sentence, percentages are always expressed in Arabic numerals, followed by the word percent spelled out: Mormons make up 2 percent of the U.S. population.

Age usually follows the subject's name and is in Arabic numerals: Tracy Smith, 9, won the third-grade spelling bee.

If a number is less than a million and it does not begin a sentence, Arabic numerals will do, with commas and periods in the appropriate places (114 or 12,343 or 100,000 or 233,421.43). If it's more than a million, use an Arabic numeral followed by million, billion or trillion, but any fractions are converted to decimals and are usually rounded off (3.7 million or 979.2 million or 1.1 billion or 1.673 trillion — not 1,672,886,000,000). In normal print copy, large dollar figures are rounded off too, so the cents almost never appear: $2.034 million instead of $2,033,540.56.

Off of

One preposition too many. A simple *off* will do.

*"Kindly get *off of* your soapbox and listen to reason," he said.

"Kindly get *off* your soapbox and listen to reason," he said.

Of used as have

A sloppy adoption from people who speak with poor diction. It exists only in the most colloquial use of English, and then it's usually spelled with an *a* at the end. For example, when *might have* gets mangled, it becomes *might of*, which translates to *mighta*. From this, we get the popular definition of the subjunctive mood: "coulda', woulda', shoulda'."

OK, O.K., okay

In informal usage, all are *okay*, but in print journalism, *OK*, without periods, is preferred. Use it sparingly, though, and never as a verb unless it's in a direct quotation.

Ongoing — See *Continual, continuous, ongoing.*

Oriented, area, nature — See *Area, nature, oriented.*

Paragraphs

Newspaper paragraphs are usually short. Two reasons: Newspaper columns are narrow, about half the width of a typewritten page, so long paragraphs tend to make a story look vast and gray. And short paragraphs lend themselves to energetic, punchy writing. They often are one sentence; sometimes one word. In addition, direct quotes are usually separated from the paragraphs that precede them and form their own paragraphs.

Parameters

A burglary of the scientific vocabulary by those who practice a business vocabulary. Webster calls it "an arbitrary constant whose value characterizes a member of the system." Not what a corporate business person means. Instead, he or she should have used "boundaries," "requirements" or "guidelines."

*Accountants who get too creative usually work outside the *parameters* of their profession.

Accountants who get too creative usually work outside the *guidelines* and rules of their profession.

Personally

Usually not needed.

*_Personally_, I don't care if I never see another rerun of that sitcom.

I don't care if I never see another rerun of that sitcom.

Possess, have — See *Have, possess.*

Presently, currently — See *Currently, presently.*

Principal, principle

A *principal* is a chief executive of school, a designated leader of a professional firm, a lead in a play or the part of an investment that is not accrued interest. A *principle* is a rule of law or behavior.

She was a *principal* in her law firm, and then her *principles* deserted her.

Prove, proved, proven

Prove and *proved* are verbs; *proven* is an adjective.

The photographic evidence seemed to *prove* that it was the defendant who fled with the cash, but the defense wondered if the pictures had been altered by a *proven* computer-graphics software package.

Punctuation, notes on

Print journalism style follows accepted forms of most punctuation, but it diverges in some small ways. When you write a series of three or more items, the final comma is not needed, because the *and* takes its place.

The Spanish crew sailed in the Pinta, the Nina and the Santa Maria. (No comma after "Nina.")

Semicolons don't get much of a workout in journalistic print style (and no workout in broadcast style), so some of the subtleties of tone that semicolons imply don't often come across. Instead of dividing clauses with a semicolon, the reporter is more likely to transform the sentence into two or add emphasis, sometimes unneeded, with a dash (two hyphens).

At the end of a quotation, the quote mark follows the comma: "That was one fine tractor that hit that deer," Myers said.

Quotations (attributions)

Usually in newspaper copy, unless you have a good reason not to, make sure the attribution is at the end of the first sentence of a quote. If you're introducing the person you're quoting to the reader, give the full title after the name, in lowercase:

"Fourscore and seven years ago, our father brought forth on this continent a new nation," said Abraham Lincoln, president of the United States.

If the paragraph extends to a second sentence, simply continue the quote.

If you're quoting the same person later in the story, after he or she has been introduced, attribute with the last name only, followed usually by "said."

Now we are met on a battlefield of that war," Lincoln said. "We have come to dedicate a portion of that field as a resting place for those who here gave their lives that the nation might live."

Refer, allude, elude — See *Allude, elude, refer.*

Semi-, bi- — See *Bi-, semi-.*

Sensual, sensuous
If something like art or music pleases the reporter, it's *sensuous.* If something like food or sex gratifies the senses, it's *sensual.*

Should have, should of — See *Of used as have.*

Since, because — See *Because, since.*

Site, cite — See *Cite, site.*

Sort of, kind of — See *Kind of, sort of.*

Take, bring — See *Bring, take.*

Than, then
Than is used to compare; *then* refers to time.
Back *then*, most Europeans and Americans of European descent thought they were more intelligent *than* people of other races.

That, which, who
The short answer: *which* is preceded by a comma; *that* isn't. The distinction is important because it changes meaning. It's impossible to contrast them without referring to what grammarians call restrictive clauses and what The AP Stylebook calls essential clauses. (Either can use *who* — see *Who, whom* below.)
Restrictive or essential: Ships that have holes below their waterlines are likely to sink. (Only those ships with holes are likely to sink.)

Nonrestrictive or nonessential: Ships, which have holes below their waterline, are likely to sink. (All ships have holes and all are likely to sink.)

Restrictive or essential: Americans who do not register to vote won't be able to vote. (Only those who are registered will be allowed to vote.)

Nonrestrictive or nonessential: Americans, who do not register to vote, won't be able to vote. (No one in the entire country will be allowed to vote because nobody registered.)

Their, there, they're

The differences should be obvious to a middle school dropout, but even professional writers can confuse them. *Their* is a possessive pronoun. *There* is an adverb that determines location. *They're* is a contraction for they are.

They're going *there* to get *their* assignments.

There is, there are, there was, there were

Starting a sentence with any of these phrases should cause a red flag to pop up and force the writer to ask, "Is this necessary?" Usually, all the phrases do is clutter a sentence and sap it of the strength of its action verbs.

*There was a surgeon who was working intently on a prone figure.

A surgeon was working intently on a prone figure.

They say

A sloppy way to back up an argument that apparently can't be supported any other way. Unacceptable in journalism, it should be unacceptable in any form of writing. Who are *they*, anyway?

*They say the provocative markings were left by aliens.

Eric von Doniken says the provocative markings were left by aliens.

Titles

When the title comes after the subject's name, which it usually does in newspaper copy, it is written in lowercase: "The crowd waited for Bill Gates, the president of Microsoft." If it comes before the name, which it usually does in broadcast copy and occasionally in newspaper copy, its first letters are capitalized: "The crowd waited for Microsoft President Bill Gates."

Time of day

Unless it begins a sentence, a reference to time of day starts with an Arabic numeral followed by a space and "a.m." or "p.m.:" 4 a.m. or 11 p.m. Notice that you simply have the hour, without colon or zeroes, unless they include minutes: 4:27 a.m. or 11:45 p.m. Arabic numerals are omitted only at noon and midnight, when they are simply called "noon" and "midnight."

To, too, two

Getting them confused is embarrassing, but it happens — often.
   *Our *too* dates were *to* crazy *two* be forgotten.
   Our *two* dates were *too* crazy *to* be forgotten.

Toward, towards

Towards is acceptable in places like England and Canada, and its usage is common on the Eastern Seaboard of the United States, but officially, the U.S. word is *toward.*

Uninterested, disinterested — See *Disinterested, uninterested.*

Unique carries no degrees of uniqueness; something is either *unique* or it isn't. (The word is overused anyway.) So to say something is "most unique" or "very unique" is to say it's *uniquer* than any other unique thing, which makes no sense.

Upon

Unless you're being poetic or quoting someone, stick with *on.*

Utilize
Use works better.

Well, good — See *Good, well.*

Whether, if — See *If, whether.*

Who, that, which — See *That, which, who.*

Who, whom
In grammatical terms, *who* is subjective and *whom* is objective. If the pronoun refers to someone doing the action or in a state of being, that person is a *who*. If someone is receiving the action, he or she is a *whom*.

In American English, however, *whom* can sound awkward or stuffy. Consider how this announcement sounds: "These are our customer service associates *whom* have been trained to meet your needs." Or how a book about prominent people would sound if it were entitled "Who's Whom." Sometimes you can simply eliminate the pronoun.

*It isn't just us, it's the children *who* we need to think about.

It isn't just us; it's the children *whom* we need to think about.

(Better yet:)
It isn't just us; it's the children we need to think about.

Note: Many people, even advocates of children's rights, resort to children *that*. Let's remind ourselves that these are people we're talking about.

Whose, who's. *Whose* is a possessive pronoun. *Who's* is a contraction.

If we don't tell *whose* work we plagiarized, *who's* going to know?

Would have, would of — See *Of used as have.*

Your, You're

Your is a possessive pronoun. *You're* is a contraction.
   You're going to get *your* just desserts.

The Beautiful Mongrel: Where English Came from

Learning the History of English: the Point

Developing the skills of any craft becomes more effective and much more enjoyable if you love the material you're working with and know something about it. If you're an aspiring writer, journalistic or otherwise, that material is the English language. The task of learning to understand the quirks and appreciate the beauty of this great, unruly language becomes much easier if you know something of its history.

In a sense, that history began with the Celts. Sure, their direct contributions to the English have been small. But their indirect influences, geographic and stylistic, have helped make the beautiful mongrel, English, the rich language it has become.

The Celts came to what we now call the British Isles in several waves from the mainland of Europe, mainly from France and Spain. Most came not because they wanted to, but because

289

the Germanic Teutons and the Romans, who invaded Celtic turf, forced them to leave. (Celtic, by the way, is pronounced as if it begins with a "k," not at all like a Boston basketball team.)

The Celts and their language originated in continental Europe, apparently in the Alpine neighborhood of northern Italy, Austria or Switzerland. (One theory has them spreading west and south from Ukraine.) They had once stretched all the way from Western Europe to the middle of Asia Minor. (Among the Turkish Celts were the "foolish Galatians" in the New Testament.)

By 600 B.C., the Celts had taken their language as far as the northeast coast of Scotland. Later generations of the Celts were known collectively as Britons, and several generations of Romans would fight them before finally conquering them. Twice, in 55 B.C. and 54 B.C., Britons would prevent Julius Caesar from creating a permanent presence on their side.

It took the Romans nearly 90 more years to establish the province of Britannia. Eventually Britons south of Scotland would fall to troops led by Emperors Hadrian and Claudius. Many upper-class Britons would blend in with their conquerors, become citizens of Rome and adopt Latin as a second language. But some Britons would flee to the Scottish North, to the Welsh West and to Cornwall in the Southwest of England, where they kept Celtic variants alive for nearly two millennia.

It wasn't until about 450 A.D., after the Romans had abandoned their British subjects to try to stop Gothic incursions into Rome, that the Britons again found themselves forced to move. This time, the invaders were Germanic tribes, most of them descendants of the Teutons. Foremost among them were the Angles and Saxons from what is now northern Germany, and the Jutes, from what is now southern Denmark.

Within a matter of a few years, England ("Angle-land") became the realm of a people who spoke only Germanic dialects. They picked up almost no Celtic. Instead of mingling and intermarrying with the Celts, as the Romans had, the Anglo-Saxons pushed the Britons into Wales and Scotland. Some joined other Celts, called Gaels, in Ireland. (Some Gaels went on to dominate Scotland.) The gulf between the Anglo-Saxons and the Welsh

Britons eventually became a physical one. In 767, the English king, Offa, ordered a ditch dug along the entire border between England and Wales. Where "there had been no ethnic blending" now "there was deep and permanent division," writes Norman Davies in "The Isles: A History."

Offa's Dyke ensured that British Celts would have almost no direct influence on the direction or content of English. And the isolation of Gaelic tribes in Ireland and the Scottish Highlands further minimized the effect of Celtic dialects on English. (Lowland Scots, whose forebears dwelt in what is now southern and eastern Scotland, exhibit linguistic roots similar to those of England's North — more on those roots in a moment.)

Today, any direct influence of the British or Gaelic idioms is reflected by family names, place names and a handful of words for physical features like "crag," "tor," "glen" and "loch." Celtic roots also can be found in words that found their way into English through the French, words like "car," "carriage," "chariot," "carpenter" and "lance."

English Language; Celtic Expression

Why begin a short history of English with a people who had so little direct influence on the language? Because the Celts have had what amounts to the last word. It has been said to the point of cliché that "The English invented the language, but it took the Irish to show them how to use it." Some of the pithiest and most poetic writing in English has resulted from taking a Germanic language and twisting it into Celtic structures.

It was the likes of James Joyce who gave English prose much of its poetic expression. In "Finnegan's Wake," Joyce mixes Celtic rhythm, alliteration and puns: "Hootch is for the husbandman handling his hoe. Hohohoho, Mister Finn, you're going to become Mister Finnagain."

Padraic Colum, in his "Anthology of Irish Verse," points to a poem translated from the Irish Gaelic by Samuel Ferguson, "Dear Dark Head." It begins this way:

Put your head darling, darling, darling,
Your darling black head my heart above;
Oh, mouth of honey, with the thyme for fragrance,
Who with heart in breast could deny you love?

The drumbeat of "darling, darling, darling" in Ferguson's
first line sets the whole verse to a music that would not be found
in a more anglicized form of poetry. And where in normal English would a poet even write, "Put your head my heart above?"

James Myers, of Gettysburg College, says another reason
Celtic rhythms sound poetic to proper English ears is that the
Celtic idioms display no true past tense. "I went to the store"
becomes "I am after going to the store."

Nor does the idiom have a true word for "yes." To a speaker
of the Celtic, "yes" merely is an acknowledgement, "Yes, I understand what you're saying." If people from Scotland or Wales
or Ireland want to express affirmation, they are likely to say
"indeed" or "sure" or a Celtic equivalent like *maise* (pronounced
"moo'shuh").

A Question of Pedigree, or Lack thereof

Celtic rhythms have contributed mightily to the mongrel quality of English. That quality has led to three important ways
that English differs from other Indo-European languages: its
simplicity of structure, its disposal of the need to match nouns
and verbs by gender, and its huge vocabulary, which is three or
four times the size of any other Western language.

Celts aside, the history of English rightfully begins in the
mid-5th century, when those Angles, Saxons and Jutes raided
British coasts and took over what is now England. Old English
— old to us, not to them — began as a mixture of the three
Germanic dialects. The first known usage of the word *Englisc*
came from Alfred the Great, who consolidated the three tribes
into one nation. Some words were contributed by the Frisians,
a Germanic tribe that occupied a corner of what is now the

Netherlands. (Many of the profanities we now call "Anglo-Saxon" came from the Frisians.)

The second great influence on Anglo-Saxon, Latin, came from a Benedictine monk, Augustine of Canterbury. In 597, Augustine brought Roman Catholicism and its language to the South of England. That was just about the time that monks from Ireland, who had been cut off from Rome for centuries, were introducing Christianity and Latin to England's North.

Seventy-five years later, Anglo-Saxons were calling themselves Christians. Virtually all were illiterate; literacy scarcely existed outside the church, so the clergy filled a need, and Latin began a strong, if not entirely comfortable, coexistence with English.

The Germanic roots of English were strengthened and broadened in the 800s when the Vikings invaded, forcing newer Danish words and usages on the language. Their influence was felt mostly in the northeastern half of England, which became known as the Danelaw. In "The Story of English," Robert McCrum, William Cran and Robert MacNeil, "nine hundred words — for example, *get, hit, leg, low, root, skin, same, want* and *wrong* — are certainly of Scandinavian origin and typically plain-syllabled ... and in the old territory of the Danelaw in Northern England literally thousands of Old Norse borrowings, words like *beck* (stream) *laithe* (barn) and *garth* (yard) survive in regional use." In addition, place names that end in -by and -wick are of Danish origin.

Although Latin continued to nip at the edges of English, it wasn't until 1066 that English was presented with its greatest Latin influence. The Normans, a group from what is now Norway and Denmark that had settled in northwestern France a century earlier, won the Battle of Hastings. Over the course of three centuries, that event would render English incomprehensible to someone who had spoken it in 1065.

Under William the Conqueror, the Normans took over everything in what is now England: the administration, the courts, the economy, the military — and the official language — but not the language of the people they conquered. The Normans brought with them the language they had begun to learn a century earlier, a French hybrid with Latin roots. But once across the English Channel, Norman French blended with, and finally succumbed to, English. After the Conquest, three languages lived together in not much harmony. The Normans, now the nobility of England, spoke French. The high clergy spoke Latin. The commoners spoke Old English.

Geoffrey, Will and the Boys

Eventually, the three castes did begin to talk with one another so, by the time Geoffrey Chaucer (1343-1400) was ready to write in what we today call Middle English, the singular language of English was ready for Chaucer. He was among the first to write with the mixture of English, French and Latin. And that is the main reason his "Canterbury Tales" take up so much space in high school English literature texts today.

This fusion of three languages can be seen today — most words have at least two synonyms:

Anglo-Saxon	French	Latin
ask	question	interrogate
dead	deceased	defunct
end	finish	conclude
fear	terror	trepidation
frightful	hideous	horrible
go	continue	proceed
gathering	society	community
happy	content	satisfied
help	aid	assist
hereafter	future	posterity
lovely	beautiful	pulchritudinous
lying	unverifiable	mendacious
mill	plant	factory
show	present	demonstrate
small	spare	emaciated

A quick look through a thesaurus indicates that most of these words carry more than two synonyms, none of them exact. In virtually every case, shades of meaning separate them. For this reason, English provides more word precision than any other Indo-European language. English writers need not worry about context or where a word enters a sentence. They can find the precise word to relay a fact, opinion, concept or idea, with exactly the nuance they want. (It's worth noting that of the above synonyms, randomly selected, the Anglo-Saxon-influenced words average 1.5 syllables; the French, 2.3 syllables and the Latin, 3.1 syllables.)

Less than a century after Chaucer, the next great influence on English came in 1476, when William Caxton (1422-1491) brought the first printing press to England from Holland and set it up in Westminster, now part of Greater London. He did so at a time when the language was still sorting itself out and no spelling guidelines existed. Many of Caxton's spellings were Dutch-influenced and, while they made sense in Dutch, they did not in English. Instead, they played havoc with English spelling, and they still do today; take the word "ghost" as an example; the "h" came from Caxton. Or the fact that two U.S. presidents of Dutch descent, the Roosevelts, pronounced their first syllables with a long "o." It wasn't so much that Caxton imported Dutch spellings as it was that English spelling was in a great state of flux at the time. Some monks had been in the process of standardizing some of its spelling conventions when he interrupted the process.

Since the days of Chaucer and Caxton, English has been heir to many additions, modifications and codifications. In 1531, Sir Thomas Elyot incorporated some new usages. He introduced words like "education," "dedicate" and "maturity." He apologized for "maturity," calling it "strange and dark." But he added that soon these words would be as easy to understand as "other wordes late commen out of Italy and Fraunce," and said such borrowings from Latin contributed to "the necessary augmentation of our language." Latinizations have proved to be great auxiliaries to basic English and essential to word precision, but in no way have they taken the place of the language's Anglo-Saxon core.

According to McCrum, Cran and MacNeil, a couple of hundred words were imported from ancient Greek by a group of scholars known as the Oxford humanists: William Grocyn, Thomas Linacre, John Colet, William Lyly and Thomas More (he who lost his head in a religious dispute with Henry VIII). Among the Greek borrowings: "agile," "capsule" and "habitual." Francis Bacon strengthened the Latin influence on English by adding words like "catastrophe," "lexicon" and "thermometer."

It wasn't long before King James I ordered six committees, comprising a total of about 50 scholars, to write an English version of the Bible that both the Church of England and the Puritans could agree on. Although the committees were to consult Latin and Greek sources for accuracy, they were to translate from half a dozen English Bibles that had been published in the 16th century. In 1611, after seven years of work, the leading scholars accomplished what committees almost never do: They made the Bible clearer and more poetic.

When the King James Version was published, the man who more than any other individual altered English was still alive. In addition to his other contributions, William Shakespeare (1564-1616) added dozens of words and phrases to the language — many now clichés. (Well, maybe not all by himself. A fringe of scholars insist that many of Shakespeare's works were written by others, including Francis Bacon.) British journalist Bernard Levin has catalogued some of them:

Greek to me, salad days, vanished into thin air, won't budge an inch, green-eyed jealousy, play fast and loose, tongue-tied, tower of strength, hoodwinked, in a pickle, knitted brows, virtue of necessity, sleep not a wink, stand on ceremony, short shrift, cold comfort, too much of a good thing, seen better days, fool's paradise, as luck would have it, clear out bag and baggage, the game is up, high time, the long and the short of it, the truth will out, your own flesh and blood, lie low, crack of doom, foul play, teeth set on edge, one fell swoop, without rhyme or reason, give the devil his due, good riddance, an eyesore, dead as doornail.

To the possible detriment of the language, we can't get away with some of the inventiveness that allowed Shakespeare's word-play. For the serious writer of English, Shakespeare's freewheeling is no longer an option. We might accept his transformation of a conjunction into a verb and a noun — "but me no buts" — but we turn our collective noses up at business bureaucrats who turn verbs into nouns — "impact" or "access." We do so in the name of communication — clarity, craft and crispness. I believe we're usually right, but there's no question that our communication rules have killed much of the creativity a writer might display. Inventive and imaginative writing still exists, but it requires some skill to write that way and still stay within the rules.

The language continues to change through contact with people as diverse as African-Americans — who profoundly influenced the Southern accent— rap artists, pidgin speakers in the Pacific, London cockneys and Liverpool rock stars. They provide nuggets of inventiveness that make their way into English slang. If a nugget is particularly imaginative or particularly apt, it survives a decade or two and becomes part of the conversational style used by most English speakers. If it stops being apt, it might die like an old cliché, but if it hangs on, it might make it into the dictionary. And the dictionary began the infringement on inventiveness in English.

Dr. Johnson and the Beginnings of Modern English

More than anyone else, Samuel Johnson (1709-1784) began the process of formalizing the language, its usages and spellings. He did it with the 1755 publication of his Dictionary of the English Language. It is worth noting that even 250 years ago, Johnson was aware that the language does not stand still; that even then the acceptance or rejection of a word or phrase depended on a living process. In his preface to the dictionary, he put it this

way, "No dictionary of a living tongue ever can be perfect,
since, while it is hastening to publication, some words are bud-
ding and some fallen away."

This sentiment was echoed by the American wordsmith H.L.
Mencken, who wrote in "The American Language,"

> A living language is like a man suffering incessantly from
> small hemorrhages, and what it needs above all else is
> constant transfusions of new blood from other tongues.
> The day the gates go up, that day it begins to die.

By that measure, English isn't about to die anytime soon.

The codification of English that began with Johnson continued in the United States with Noah Webster (1748-1853), who
published his dictionary in 1828. Exactly 100 years later, the first
edition of The Oxford English Dictionary, the OED, was published in twelve volumes.

English, the Equal-Opportunity Borrower

Certainly, none of these efforts have stanched the flow of new
words into the language. The United States and Canada, especially, have benefited from a slew of words from Native Americans and the Spanish. And the French, who settled Quebec and
parts of New Brunswick, have enriched the vocabularies of Ca-
nadians and New Englanders. But this process had begun long
before either became independent of the British.

The Oxford Companion to the English Language lists dozens
of words that came directly from Native American tribes. Most
provided names for things not found in the Old World: chip-
munk, hickory, moose, parka, pecan, raccoon, squash and toma-
hawk. Many terms arrived by way of the Spanish, who dominated most of the New World by the time the English founded
its first permanent colony, Jamestown, Virginia, in 1607. These
terms include: avocado, barbecue, cannibal, chili, chocolate, co-
coa, coyote, guano, hammock, hurricane, jerky, potato, tobacco,
tomato and savanna. The Oxford Companion also lists several

words that began with Native Americans or Caribbeans. They were filtered through French, then Spanish and finally made it to English, among them: buccaneer, cashew, cayenne pepper, cougar, jaguar, petunia and tapioca.

By the end of the 1900s, an entirely new set of Spanish words had entered the language, mainly from Mexico, through the Western U.S. territories and states. Cowboys adopted many from their Mexican counterparts, the "vaqueros." They include: bronco, desperado, lariat, maverick, mustang, poncho, ranch, rodeo, stampede and vamoose. Take for example the hot pepper known as a "chile" in the Southwest or a "chili" in most of the rest of the country. Both came from a Spanish spelling of a *nahuatl* (Aztec) word. Generally speaking, "chile" came up from Mexico through New Mexico, Texas and Arizona, and "chili" migrated through the Caribbean.

The United States isn't alone in its ability to absorb words from other cultures. The British borrowed many words from Hindi, which is spoken mainly in northern India, and passed them on to us. They include: "bungalow," "dinghy," "dungaree," and "shampoo." We can thank the Malays and the British for "amok," "bamboo," "caddy," "camphor," "gong," "kapok" and "sarong." And we can thank Tamil-speakers, from southern India and Sri Lanka, and again the British, for "cheroot," "curry," "mango" and "pariah." Australians have adopted many words from that continent's Aborigines, and New Zealanders have taken some of their vocabulary from the Maoris, the Polynesians who occupied New Zealand before the British showed up.

Since the middle of the 19th century, English has been bombarded by new scientific, medical and technical terms, a process that has only accelerated as we have entered the 21st century. Just think of some of the computer and communications terms we use in ordinary conversation that would have baffled most people in 1975. If you were to tell me then that you were going to "e-mail," "Google" or "text" me, I would wonder which part of my body was being threatened. Today, we "fax" people, if we have a "modem." Back then, we wouldn't have dreamed of doing such a thing. Nor would we have discussed it on our "cell phone" — if we'd had one. In 1975, "software" was in its infancy. Now it is carried on a "disk" or "diskette," neither of which has anything to do with a spinal disc or an Olympic discus.

Computing has taken a number of existing terms and redefined them. "Monitor" was a verb or an ironclad vessel. "Enter" was a command to open the door and walk in. A "laptop" was where a sweetheart or a grandchild sat, and a "mouse" was an unwelcome houseguest. Computer people are responsible for introducing technical terms like "scalable," "turnkey" and "access" (as a verb), and then making them part of the language of business and commerce.

On rare occasions, a word from old technology enters the modern vocabulary. "Chad" has been a man's name or, pronounced with a French accent ("shahd"), an African country. But since the 2000 election, nearly all Americans know that chads are pieces of cardboard that dangle from a punch-card system, especially a voting system.

Regardless of how many new words enter the language, however, and how many we lose through cliché and decay, the language at its base has not changed since the time of Chaucer. It bears repeating that the base remains the most influenced by Germanic words and usages. And the power of the language continues to come from the humble idiom of Anglo-Saxon peasants.

Sure it does, but with some wee help from Celtic cousins.

Bibliography

Bennett, Martyn. "Illustrated History of Britain." North Pomfret, Vermont: Trafalgar Square Publishing, 1992.

Black, Jay; Steele, Bob; and Barney, Ralph. "Doing Ethics in Journalism." Greencastle, Ind.: Society of Professional Journalists, 1993.

Bliss, Edward Jr., and Patterson, John M. "Writing News for Broadcast." 2nd ed. New York: Columbia University Press, 1978.

Block, Mervin. "Writing Broadcast News — Shorter, Sharper, Sronger: A Professional Handbook." Chicago: Bonus Books, 1987.

Born, Roscoe. "The Suspended Sentence: A Guide for Writers." Ames, Iowa: Iowa State Press, 1986.

Cabrera, Luis. "Earthquake Rocks Northwest. Seattle Panics, but Escapes Catastrophic Damage." The Patriot-News [Harrisburg, Pa.] 1 March 2001: 1.

Cahill, Thomas. "How the Irish Saved Civilization." New York: Doubleday, 1995.

Chancellor, John, and Mears, Walter R. "The News Business." New York: Harper and Row, 1983.

Colum, Padraig. "Anthology of Irish Verse." New York: Liverwright Publishing Corporation, 1948.

Davies, Norman. "The Isles: A History." New York: Oxford University Press, 1999.

Dunn, Marcia. "Spacewalkers pull off toughest Hubble repairs yet." The Associated Press 16 May 2009.

Fox, Ben. Story on high school shooting in El Cajon, Calif.: The Associated Press 19 April 2002.

Fox, Walter. "Writing the News: A Guide for Print Journalists." 2nd ed. Ames, Iowa: Iowa State University Press, 1993.

Goldstein, ed. The Associated Press Stylebook. New York: Basic Books, Perseus Books Group, 2004.

Graham, Betsy P. "Magazine Article Writing." 2nd ed. New York: Harcourt Brace, Jovanovich, 1993.

Hanson, Christopher. "The Dark Side of Online Scoops." Columbia Journalism Review May/June 1997: 17.

Hayakawa, S.I. "Language in Thought and Action." 4th ed. San Diego: Harcourt, Brace, Jovanovich, 1978.

Johnson, Gene. "Quake Damage Estimates Rise to $2 Billion." The Patriot-News [Harrisburg, Pa.] 2 March 2001: A5.

Kessler, Lauren, and McDonald, Duncan. "When Words Collide." 4th ed. Belmont, Calif.: Wadsworth Publishing Company, 1996.

Kiberd, Declan. "Synge and the Irish Language." Totawa, New Jersey: Rowan and Littlefield, 1979.

Kilpatrick, James J. "It's All Very Relative When Dealing with These Two Words." Chicago Sun-Times, Universal Press Syndicate 13 April 1997.

Kilpatrick, James J. "Nouns, Adjectives and Verbs that Go Clunk in the Night" Chicago Sun-Times, Universal Press Syndicate 1 June 1997.

Klaus, Mary. "W. Hanover Twp. Feline Hospice overrun with Rabbits." The Patriot-News 24 March 2001: B1.

Knight, Robert M. "A Journalistic Approach to Good Writing: The Craft of Clarity." 2nd ed. Ames, Iowa: Iowa State Press, a Blackwell Publishing Company, 2003.

LaRocque, Paula. "Journalese: Annoying Practice Falls Short of Clarity, Communication." Quill 83.6 (February 1996): 31.

LaRocque, Paula. "Quest for Perfect Lead May Turn into Disaster for Writer." Quill 83.2 (July/August 1996): 51.

Layden, Tim. "Faster than Fast." Sports Illustrated 25 Aug. 2008: 61-63.

Lederer, Richard. "Can't Find the Right Word? Keep Looking." Writer's Digest May 2001: 36.

MacNeil, Robert. "Wordstruck." New York: Penguin Books, 1990.

McArthur, Tom, ed. The New Oxford Companion to the English Language. New York: Oxford University Press, 1992.

McAdam, E.L. Jr., and Milne, George. Johnson's Dictionary: A Modern Selection. New York, Random House, 1963.

McCrum, Robert; Cran, William; and MacNeil, Robert. "The Story of English." 1st American ed. New York: Viking Penguin, Inc., 1986.

McDonald, Daniel, and Burton, Larry W. "The Language of Argument." 9th ed. New York: Longman, 1999.

McMahon, Patrick. "Quake Shocks Seattle: 6.8-magnitude Temblor 'Hits You in the Stomach.'" USA Today 1 March 2001: 1.

McMahon, Patrick. "Northwest Takes Quake in Stride: Natural Disaster Comes with the Territory, Many Unfazed Residents Say." USA Today 2 March 2001: 1.

Mencken, H.L. "The American Language," 4th ed. New York: Alfred A. Knopf, 1995.

"Latest on Possible War Against Iraq." Montagne, Renee and Kelly, Mary Louise. "Morning Edition." Natl. Public Radio. Washington. 9 Aug. 2002.

Myers, James P. "Writing Irish: Selected Interviews with Irish Writers from the Irish Literary Supplement." Syracuse, New York: Syracuse University Press, 1999.

Ousby, Ian, ed. "The Cambridge Guide to Literature in English." Cambridge, England, and London: Cambridge University Press and the Hamlyn Publishing Group, Ltd., 1988.

Perry. Tony. "Ancient Greek plays resonate with Marines." Los Angeles Times 15 Aug. 2008, California/Local section.

Roberts, David. "Romancing the Stone." Smithsonian July 2002: 86-96.

Rooney, Edmund J., and Witte, Oliver R. "Copy Editing for Professionals." Champaign, Ill.: Stipes Publishing, 2000.

Rubenstein, Steve. "Plain Speaking Also Falls Victim to Cisco's Ax." San Francisco Chronicle 10 March 2001: D2.

Ryan, Beth. "Feature Writing." www.snn-rdr.ca/snn/nr_reporterstoolbox/featurewriting.html.

Spalding, Rachel Fischer. "The Tom Tom Club. Cruise and Cruz appear in public together. EW.com catches up with America's new power couple at the premier of her 'Captain Corelli's Mandolin.'" Entertainment Weekly's EW.com 14 Aug. 2001.

Strunk, William, and White, E.B. The Elements of Style. 3rd ed. New York: Macmillan & Company, 1979.

Sullivan, Kevin. "Africa's Last and Least: Cultural Expectations Ensure Women Are Hit Hardest by Burgeoning Food Crisis." The Washington Post 20 July 2008: 1.

Synge, John Millington. "Collected Works." 1. Buckinghamshire, England: Colin Smythe, Ltd., 1982.

Thomas, Dylan. Quite Early One Morning. New York: New Directions Publishing Corporation, 1968.

"Transplant Network to Share Resources." USA Today 24 July 2000.

Weingarten, Gene. Sept. 7, 2008. "Brevity ... is the soul of twit." The Washington Post Magazine 7 Sept. 2008: 35.

Zinsser, William. "On Writing Well." 5th ed. New York: HarperCollins, 1995.

Index

About the Author

Robert M. Knight has been an adjunct professor of journalism at Gettysburg College and Northwestern University. He has written for the Chicago Tribune, The Christian Science Monitor, Reuters, and The Washington Post. He is a former senior editor and broadcast editor of the City News Bureau of Chicago and a past president of the Chicago Headline Club chapter of the Society of Professional Journalists. He is the author of "A Journalistic Approach to Good Writing: The Craft of Clarity." He lives in Gettysburg, Pennsylvania.